KINGDOM'S
Unveiled

AUTHOR:

CO-AUTHOR

TERRI MEIDINGER

WESTBOW
PRESS
A DIVISION OF THOMAS NELSON

Special thanks to Materialized Vision for managing production and creating the Kingdoms Unveiled web page.

WestBow Press books may be ordered through booksellers or by contacting:

WestBow Press
A Division of Thomas Nelson
1663 Liberty Drive
Bloomington, IN 47403
www.westbowpress.com
1-(866) 928-1240

ISBN: 978-1-4497-4526-4 (sc)
ISBN: 978-1-4497-4527-1 (e)

Library of Congress Control Number: 2012905908

Printed in the United States of America

WestBow Press rev. date: 05/22/2012

Special Thanks!

I appreciate Materialized Vision for working with West Bow Press to ensure the publishing of this book. The time and effort to do it in a fashion that was honorable before the Lord, put my mind at ease as I continued to travel; an ambassador for the King. May God continue to bless you beyond your materialized vision!

I would like to thank all those who helped make this book possible. With appreciation, researchers brought light to the things of darkness as I encountered which the world wanted to stay hidden. May God bless all those who divulged pertinent information knowing they were helping expose a dangerous web of deceit! Thank you for the courage. Special thanks to my family and extended family as they endured the hours of listening to the twisted tales. Opening the doors of your homes there is no way to express my gratitude; it was wonderful meeting the Family of God. This book could not contain all the amazing Royal family.

Those who blessed financially and with gifts of donated items, I want to say thank you! People's lives were changed as God met their needs. From clothing and bathrooms to books, hearts were changed because of your donations of love to the Kingdom. Thank you again!

A special appreciation is sent to all those who donate gifts of love to Spirit FM and K-LOVE. Through the encouragement and praise throughout the territories of 9 different States, it kept my heart in tune with the constant feeding of victories in Jesus' amazing love in your lives.

A special appreciation goes to my dear friend Tiffany Wright for using her God given talent on a beautiful cover design. It expresses the heart of the True Believers in the Way.

Contents

Resources

Holy Bible-New International Version, Zondervan Publishing House, copyright—1973

Holy Bible-King James Version, Thomas Nelson &Sons, no copyright date-Bible 1882

The System Study Bible, The System Bible Company, copyright-1933

The Georgia Guidestones, Elberton Georgia

Forward

The author of two other books, I learned from other people the need to express myself differently. Book one, ONE FROST-BITTEN APPLE HOLDS ITS FLAVOR, was written from a rejoicing point of view. A book declaring that the God of yesterday was still performing miracles in my today was written for my children and grandchildren. As they went through the different battles, the book would remind them God is a Miracle Worker. All they needed was the faith of a mustard seed. I realized when a woman said, "It was good, BUT I can tell, you haven't went through anything." I fell short of the mark. Assuming all people would understand every miracle, the believer is broken and crying out for help.

Book two, TEARS OF THE FATHER, was my testimony of God's Amazing Love in spite of the situations that were going on with my family after my husband's death. With dreams and visions revealed to me, God reaffirmed the lessons through the inspired Word of God. A preacher told me it was Biblically unsound. If the Bible is the inspired Word of God, then the" RHEMA Word" should BREATHE LIFE, out of the passages, in the believer's SEARCHING AND LISTENING to hear promises, guidance and direction. Wanting only to show people the lessons of hope and encouragement to those struggling with death, sorrow and problem teenagers, it was written from a prayer journal. I realized the next book needed Biblical references so they might see where I was being taught.

This masterpiece was written after working on the boardwalk in Ocean City, Maryland. I met powerful family members of the kingdom. Some received Christ, when God used me as a vessel of witness, others through their moments of struggle. With victories proclaiming this Awesome God that we serve, a group of Jews were listening and learning about Jesus. Not even living by the law, the group watched God work as miracles were done before their eyes. God's face shown down on me and they were curious about the God I serve. The cruelty of one of the Jews left me wondering what God saw about these people. Why were they His chosen people? Rejoicing, I am chosen to be a part of His chosen Bride.

It was after attending a church service in Virginia, that I realized the need for people to know about the keys to the Kingdom of Heaven. The man from the pulpit said, "There are keys to the kingdom. The only way you get them is to go through me. I will give you my blessing after you have sat on the front row every Sunday and Wednesday night for a year. Then I will give you my blessing. Just because you work in the nursery doesn't mean you receive my blessing. You have to listen to my teachings for a year". I was sick, to think the family of God was receiving anything but a blessing. The preacher was pronouncing a blessing contingent on church attendance and listening to his wisdom and direction. He was unable to teach undeserved kindness for he spoke of conditional blessing. He wore the garment of curses like a cloak that was tied around him with a belt. The one in leadership hadn't exchanged his garments, therefore was unable to help others with accepting their garments of praise. The man was teaching his blessings, He was unable to speak forth the blessings of the LORD, which should flow continuously from the Believer's mouth. When sharing God's amazing love, that is a blessing. Revealing how the Grace works, one must understand Grace is not a subject. It is a person with power, honor and glory, JESUS.

Does it not say, bitter water and sweet water cannot flow from the same fountain? The blessings that matter are the blessings that ABBA, Father has already given through faith in His gift of His Son. JESUS' blood is for more than salvation. The power of Jesus' blood is the LORD's love activating power. When one is born again salvation, healing and redemption is in the blood; crowning you the BELIEVER with loving kindness and tender mercy.

With a passion instilled in my heart, I became an ambassador for Christ. Sharing The EL SHADDAI's Amazing Grace that man could not offer, for man's goodness was always Jesus' salvation and their works. The LORD's creatively designed and ordained plan, before the beginning of time, stemmed on one condition, God taking care of His creation in Love. Through Adam's sin it broke the promise God made on man's side. God can't look on sin. God didn't reject us even then. Through FAITH on their part, the forefathers saw the Amazing love and goodness on them. The favor of the LORD was on those who BELIEVED God's love for them. Man asked God to let us live by works. Man still chooses to live by works. The LORD still shows His favor on those who choose to Rest in His Working in their lives according to His promises.

Experiencing the 'Rhema Word', the dreams and visions are real and the scripture will be able to reveal the truth shown to me. The experiences are unique but organized by the Mighty Hand of God. Christians are to beware for there are wolves in sheep clothing. Ignorance can be the Believer's downfall.

The journey I was taken on opened doors with 32nd degree Masons and people in the occult. Even though the secrets divulged could get them killed, converting to the faith they stood on Jesus. Deliverance, which was able to break the blood oath given up to the 10th generation, was done. The Pagans are the same way about blood oaths if divulging information. One faced his death 4 weeks after sharing. I was advised to leave Ocean City for my life was in danger. The interesting twists and turns laid out a picture of the Bride of Christ. We need to be made aware of the sinister plan for any that refuse to move over and 'coexist' with those who are against Jesus. The definite separation of two different brides are laid out; one excepting all religions and the other "peculiar"; standing, lifting up the risen Lord, Jesus. May the Redeemed of the Lord say so!

Jesus is My Tower of Strength. Standing in the tower is my Protection. Jesus is fighting my battles while I feast, rest and praise. While I listen to the needs of the weak and lost coming to my castle, I take them to the King of my Castle. With hands of mercy and compassion, King Jesus ministers to their needs. The one entering and I, stand in awe at the generosity and love shown to those willing to receive. Hopefully, they too will choose to let King Jesus rule and reign in their lives. The King tells them softly, "I AM willing to protect, preserve and bless your life out of the storehouses in the Kingdom of Heaven. Just recognize My Righteousness over you and you will experience Life in Abundance. The position you are in is not servant, but my precious Bride". I saw healing when they stood on His promise of restoring them from the bed of sickness. I find strength and comfort to know My King Jesus will not surrender me to the desires of my foe.

Chapter 1

Faithfulness Recognized

My journey started with a fast. Wanting God's direction, he led me to Ocean City. Savoring the brisk walk on the boardwalk I began looking for work. I wasn't in an extreme hurry but knew it could take time finding a job. Not yet spring, the town was pretty much dead. Majority of the stores on the boardwalk were still shut down. Over and over I heard, come back in a month. Although the task of looking for a job was in my thoughts, I was in utter amazement soaking in the beauty around me. The sun sat on top of the water shimmering like diamonds dancing. The rays jumping off the great body of water rose up into the air. The sunrise looked like a throne room on a glassy sea. The exquisite gift from the King showed his royal subjects a demonstration of His love for them. Each morning the Artist of the heavens created something new and breathtaking for those who desired to see the rising of the sun, realizing God used his artwork to express His love.

As His masterpiece unfolded with definition and passion the separation of the water from the clouds came alive. The deep darkness was brought to humbleness as the powerful radiant sunlight began to conquer. Watching the sun do all the work of removing the darkness I realized that was what really happened in my life. Darkness had surrounded me, but Jesus' faithfulness gracefully brought forth a beauty of artistry by the Master Designer of my life. Jesus' luminous perfection of radiance trickled through me destroying the darkness in his timing. The royal bloodline I belonged to was filled with the crimson colors just like the crimson in the sky. The golden ribbons in my heart and mind were sashes of victory from the King of Kings. My life radiated an irreversible confidence in my loving friend, Jesus.

The moment of perfection was broken by an overwhelming putrid odor. Trying to block out the fishy scent, I continued watching the water. Something jumped unexpectedly. Dolphins! Were they jumping in exaltation of the glorious day? As they headed toward the glistening sun, I wondered if the animal kingdom was praising God or just savoring the companionship with one another. I would have to get past the fishy smell. The exquisite beauty in my new surroundings was to be savored.

Watching the waves crashing onto the shore brought a sense of respect to all those watching the great body of water which welcomed everyone. Encouraging even those who held fear to enjoy what it had to offer. The realization of the dangers involved kept me sitting on the shore. I hoped given time I would conquer my fear of what was in the water that couldn't be seen. Could I face with courage something that held so much power? Surfers were out to master the powerful wave. With the enormous size and massive strength the surfers were seen tossed up in the air like a rag doll only to be swallowed alive by the wave. After showing off its torrential power, the ocean continued to drop as it went rippling down the shoreline leaving only white foam on the beach. Power was challenging man to experience the ultimate act of bravery. The surfer's identification with the demand, waited for the perfect wave hoping to be able to ride it out.

Once again, my mind wandered to the spiritual realm. How many people were scared to go in the Sea of Grace? Learning to trust my own instincts, fear controlled my actions and thoughts of staying out of the water. (Not knowing or understanding grace, undeserved kindness leaves man in disbelief and fear, running on human emotions and thoughts, their unwillingness to venture out to the unknown.) Scared, some people never leave the security of the religious shore where "enlightened" men are able to explain the deep hidden secrets. The gazers unaware, the All-knowing God understands He must meet each individual at their own level. He meets some on the shore while others are wading in the sea. Others try to ride the waves hoping to stand with strength and courage. When wiping out, the Sea of Grace receives the fallen one totally swallowing up the challenger. Total submersion in grace brings on an excitement causing the graced believer to look forward to the next wave.

Considering the large ocean, what stopped the ocean from going right over top of this resort town? Was it the hand of the Almighty or just His spoken word? [2] There was no logical reason the ocean held back the remainder of its great body of water. God had already taken care of the intricate details of protection on those that he loved even if no one considered the length, width and the depth of His almighty powerful hand.[3] Just as the oceans had to be held back so was the massiveness of God's grace. Grace was to be experienced through eternity, although the life in abundance began in the believer of Christ's righteousness today.

With a special joy in my heart I continued walking. With a God given peace and confidence I started leaving resumes in the different businesses. I finally encountered a man hiring. He had six stores, five on the boardwalk. Wanting to work on the boardwalk the request was made to the Lord, now I was seeking favor and goodness. Instead of filling out an application, I was to tell him about myself. With a life full of interesting and eventful situations, what was needed to acquire the job? My children always say I give out to much information. I stood for a moment trying to decide what was pertinent. Summarizing my life into a nutshell, "I'm an energetic salesperson. Explaining how I had met my husband while doing sales, there was a glimmer in the man's face. Teaching women cardio-self-defense showed the energy I needed to be able to endure a strenuous run throughout the day. Raising three teenagers after my husband passed away hopefully exhibited the ability to work without being told what needed to be done.

The interested business owner said, "You can quit looking, you're hired." After describing himself, I was interested and intrigued in the man who was to be my boss. My heart leapt inside, Israeli! The passion I have in my heart for the Jew was no longer just a flicker.

The fire for God's chosen people had been ignited. I wanted the secret of God's love for these people. Working with a financially blessed Israeli man, God was going to show this man his anointed grafted in daughter. Jacob was surprised at the passion for his people. I stopped asking questions after hearing his answer to one question "What tribe do you belong to?" He was a Jew of the tribe of Judah. The Holy Spirit shut my mouth. His answer left me whirling. Telling him goodbye and thanking him for the job I left. Everything inside me was ready to burst. Did Jacob acknowledge Jesus in his bloodline?

Did he know the difference of the victory wall over the Wailing Wall? Silenced by the Spirit, I couldn't say anything, left me a little bewildered?

As I headed back to my apartment I was walking on air. I skipped steps darting up the stairs. Living on the fifth floor had been a treat. Enjoying the view from the patio, I could see a motel designed as a castle. Daily I could remember God's Kingdom come. The lightness in my spirit reaffirmed His will be done.[1] Friends and family questioned the sanity of moving to where I knew no one but my son. Terrance and I love life and enjoy adventure. A change for the better was about to be experienced. Running into the apartment out of breath, I shared with Terrance the awesome news. "I got a job! I got a job!" Terrance jumped off the chair and grabbed me. He hugged me tight and blurted out, "I knew you would."

"You won't believe it, Terrance. I'm working on the boardwalk. The icing on the cake, my boss is a Jew!" I exclaimed with sheer excitement. Terrance now understood. He had always saw me as a bible thumper, it wasn't till recently that he realized the real passion in my heart; anything and everything to do with God and his chosen people. Terrance knew this adventure was definitely God directed for me. He was curious what was in God's plans for him. He was just learning to walk trusting God's faithfulness in his journey of faith. A year ago he saw me as an enemy and now we were friends. How much of my life had he really missed because of his own self-centered ambitions? How much had I missed out on his life because he wouldn't open up and share with me? He wanted to take advantage of the time we had been given. He too was looking forward to seeing

God bless his life. Terrance had encountered a moment with God that I found interesting, changing his heart toward God. Experiencing his hand of mercy was what he craved. With his spiritual eyes open and tenderness in his spirit, Terrance was going to watch for God's goodness on him.

Pearl Drops of Wisdom

1. Your kingdom come, your will be done on earth as it is in heaven.

   Matthew 6:10 NIV

2. For He spoke and stirred up a tempest that lifted high the waves.

   Psalm 107:25 NIV

3. Your arm is endued with power; your hand is strong, your right hand exalted.

   Psalm 89:13 NIV

Chapter 2

Introduction to Love

After an exhausting day at work, I sat waiting for Terrance. With only one vehicle, schedules were coordinated so neither Terrance or I had to walk home from work. He was cleaning disasters left in condos by vacationers which required little thought but a lot of hard work. Speed was critical in this job which Terrance seemed to enjoy. I watched him carry scrub buckets and cleaners although he didn't notice his ride was there. He was in a conversation with someone at the van he was emptying out. Laughing as he worked combined with his body language, I was sure it was a female. His looks combined with an outgoing personality drew women to his side. With an air of confidence Terrance's bubbly personality encouraged those he met. His smile radiated on the ruggedly handsome man, with wavy dark hair underneath a baseball cap. His lean muscular physique had been chiseled due to his last job of candle making.

Qualities had been learned leaving an everlasting impression in his actions. Accuracy and precision were critical to create the perfect color and scent. Due to carelessness, acid had been spilt several times, so cautious deliberate decisions had developed in this young man. Having to work quickly so the wax wouldn't set before the candle maker was ready, he learned to move quickly and do the job correct first time around.

As I watched Terrance's behavior, I couldn't help but smile for he reminded me of his father. I had fallen in love with the shell of the man not really knowing or understanding the depth of character which made the man. Terrance walked with the confidence of his father, both having situations that had built character. Through life experiences made up from his own choices, Terrance had been brought to the foot of the cross. The resurrected Lord was about His business of redeeming Terrance's life from destruction.[1] Radiance from above penetrated through the darkness in his life so that the physical which had a lot of his earthly fathers' features was enhanced by his spiritual Fathers' attributes. The impressive handiwork of the gentle hand of the "Father" was undeniably evident. I dried the tears that had begun to well up in my eyes. Terrance had already experienced more life in his twenty years, because of choices, than most men his age. God was building a man of strong character using the foolish mans mistakes and submission to Christ delivered victories.[2] He was being groomed by his Father as his earthly father watched in the heavens. Through the wooing of the Holy Spirit the rebellious son was learning to submit to the heavenly Father of his own free will.

I was brought back to reality when I caught a glimpse Terrance. Who was this mystery driver that made him not even think to inform me he didn't need a ride. Feeling somewhat like a spy, I followed a short distance behind tickled he had met a friend to chill with. When Terrance entered the apartment later, the information that was needed to appease the curiosity was willingly talked about. He wasn't just infatuated.

As he talked about the girl there was a twinkle in his eye and a spark of life had been lit in his heart. "Mom, she is different. Her son is the most important thing to her. She has two jobs so she can spoil her son with good things. She is beautiful. Her eyes", I didn't really hear the rest. My son had fallen for the exquisite beauty. Having put her son as first priority, Terrance had found someone who desired to love and be loved. This girl with no name, wanted to pour her love out on one which all he had to give was love.

The importance of love had been rekindled after many years of not wanting to give love or receive love after the death of his father. God's gentle lessons were obvious when Terrance had been blessed with his son little Atreyu. With love for his father, the little ones eyes were closed when he was received in the heavens at two months old. The Father wanted the father to realize he loved him as much as the little one Terrance had loved. He was to be as a child and trust in all things, the love and faithfulness of the Father.[3]

I was brought back to attention. "I don't even have her number. We were going to meet after she got off work somehow I lost it." I could see the frustration at his carelessness. I asked Terrance, "Wow! What's this girl's name that has you so infatuated?" Terrance threw himself down on the couch in disgust. "I can't remember." I started laughing which just made things worse for the love stricken man. His brain had turned to putty. I had never seen Terrance so flustered. Usually, his mind was like a sponge retaining everything. Even though he had tried to hide his brilliance going through school, teachers could see past the charade. This was different. This woman had not only won his heart but held his thoughts in her hand, restricting the ability to concentrate.

Striving to act normal, Terrance turned into a nervous wreck. Would she call when he didn't? Had he blown his chance to be with this exceptionally beautiful woman? Had he found the woman he wanted to share his life with? Terrance sat texting friends while chatting with me on commercials. With frustration at his apparent crisis he tried to stay busy taking his mind off his dilemma. Like a shot of morphine giving instant relief, Terrance felt an instantaneous joy when to his surprise she called him. He was determined to impress this girl who was on her way over to pick him up. Waiting for the girl of his dreams seemed like an eternity to the young man. Striking up a conversation with me, you could tell he was trying to kill time. "So, what is her name?" I asked? Terrance stood there with his mouth hanging open. He wanted to take a sledge hammer to his brain. He had done it again. His girl had no name. He pulled his phone out of his pocket and typed in Beach Girl. Yes, that definitely suited her. Embarrassment kicked in, he couldn't just ask her name. He felt like an idiot trying to justify his inability to answer. Terrance laughed, "I'll listen for her name to be called at work."

I had to smile as my son went out the door. Entering unfamiliar territory, real love made my heart began to ache. Embracing the memories of my first and only love brought a joyful sorrow to my heart and mind. I went to bed with a non-relenting agony in the spirit. The Spirit of Loneliness had a deep hold.

PEARL DROPS OF WISDOM

1. Who redeemeth thy life from destruction; who crowneth thee with loving-kindness and tender mercies.

   Psalm 103:4 KJV

2. God resisteth the proud, but giveth grace to the humble. Submit yourselves therefore to God. Resist the devil, and he will flee from you.

   James 4:6a-7 KJV

3. But Jesus called unto him, and said, "Suffer little children to come unto me, and forbid them not: for such is the kingdom of God. Verily I say unto you, whosoever shall not receive the kingdom of God as a little child shall in no wise enter therein.

   Luke 18:16-17 KJV

Chapter 3

꧁

Freedom in the Display of Crimson

Watching the waves rolling in on the shore, I savored my time with the Lord. Peace was brought to my heart as I sat in awe even though the darkness seemed so great. The unique opportunity of working on the boardwalk was allowing me to experience other cultures without leaving my own homeland. I hadn't even considered this experience till I had started working with a girl from Russia that worked here the year before.

Sasha articulated perfect English with a definite accent. The petit framed girl was proud of her family as she explained pertinent details to me. Due to dedicated service to the military, her father was provided for when he retired from the military. It wasn't really enough for them to survive, yet was better off than the majority of the Russian people. She was in America on a foreign student exchange program, hoping to make enough money for another year of college. Sasha believed America was where she would be able to escape the poverty in her own country, especially if she could marry an American. She could stay and never have to go back to the things she despised. I realized as she shared her deep rooted feelings for the people of her country, I knew nothing about Russia. Sharing the pain and suffering of her country, tears welled up her eyes. She was one of the lucky ones. The poverty within her country was extreme. While she always had food on her table other children would get up in the morning to go beg for food. Beggars were not just children. Even the elderly were amongst the crowd willing to work or scavenge for food just to survive. The depth of sorrow was in her voice as she shared the burden of her sister left in Russia. In fear of a grim future she was not only working for herself but hoped she could somehow make life better for the one she loved so dear. Sasha worked the grueling hours not only for college but to make her families' life a little easier.

Staring at the waves bringing things up out of the deep waters onto the shores, I realized the things that were buried deep in the heart and mind of this woman were being brought up and surfacing for a reason. One statement continued to haunt me, "Americans have no idea what they have, freedom and wealth. Your poor are all richer than the majority of the Russian people. The American people are just lazy." I was offended by the statement of laziness. There were many going to bed hungry because of the loss of jobs or health. The opinion, Americans were lazy, had been taught to her. She knew no better than to judge all by a few. I realized this girl had no clue the poverty hitting those living in the country that Sasha saw as rich.

The Russian grapevine had not explained to this young, wealth craving dreamer the true picture of suffering within the United States. Did she need to know children were going to bed hungry here? With severe job loss, people were now losing their homes and filling shelters across the nation. The loss was not due to laziness but due to the decline in the economy and jobs being given to those from other countries, legal or illegal. Did she need to know the crumbling economy was doing the same thing in the United States as in Russia? Americans couldn't work yet foreign exchange students could. Where were the rights for the American workers? I was overwhelmed, for many Americans had been turned away daily from our store. There were positions open but the Israeli manger would only hire those from another country. I was told after interviewing different qualified people, they were either not cute enough or they were lazy even though they hadn't worked with them at all. Minutes later a girl would come in to the store, unable to understand and speak English fluently, walking away with a job. Resentment began to take root in my heart as well as jealousy and anger for Americans turned away. The strings of control lay in the hands of someone who wasn't even American. Was laziness the issue or Americans couldn't be controlled? Liberty was given to those from other countries as the chains of control tighten around the lives of those who lived here.

Sasha was thrilled to have real freedom. The freedom she talked about seemed so much different than the way I saw it. The liberties that Americans had become accustom to, were slowly being taken away. With the government being able to see the movement and activities of people and the right to listen to their conversations left me with the feeling that Big Brother was watching. I felt like it was an infringement on the rights as a U.S. citizen. People were being controlled in many areas. Yet to Sasha, it was freedom to enjoy life in a way she had not experienced. Was she wrong in her feelings or was this foreigner unaware of the tradition of freedom? Had she not come from a country where their every action was scrutinized? Questions followed by confusion surfaced from the depths of my thoughts. The American government was directed toward monetary substance therefore the issues of control were led by an elite group. My anger issues were directed towards privacy, speech, and values. Due to cold hearts very little compassion was seen. I considered carefully Sasha's freedom speech. It had been directed toward the freedom to buy what she wanted and when she chose to, without the restrictions and limitations that had been placed on her. The many different choices of clothing options with the prices that she could afford left her in a reality that was not the same as those who lived here and had responsibilities of having house payments, car payments, insurances and EST. The benefits that she had were not the same as the regular American.

As I looked out to the deep Blue Ocean, I knew the critical need was to share Jesus. She told me she went to church a couple of times and had felt peace while there. She knew nothing of Jesus and his help in her situations of need surrounding her "today". The situations here were only temporary yet eternity was soon to come. Did she know where she would be when the trumpet call was given for the banquet being held in honor of the King? Was she going to be attending the great feast or would she have greater sorrow to come than what she already knew?

I considered Aviel, the Israeli that had a room in the same apartment. He shared his life in Israel with me as we shared a kosher meal together. The love he proclaimed for his God made me stop to consider. He said the name of his God was so holy he couldn't even say it. He didn't know the blessed Messiah Jesus but the adoration he held for JEHOVAH was seen on his face. Sharing miracles he had witnessed, I wondered at God's amazing love. He answered the Jews prayers sent to JEHOVAH without the understanding of the ultimate sacrifice that he made. Aviel would be powerful when his eyes were opened. Trusting in his God, believing in his power he waits for the Messiah. With anticipation he waits for the new temple to be built. Listening to Aviel, a deeper reverence for my God was placed in my heart.

I had to smile for the love of the Jew was strong. Was it Aviel or Natali that left such a great impression of God's goodness on me? Natali a young pretty Jewish girl, reminded me of what Mary the mother of Jesus might have looked like. She held a beauty that stemmed from the inside out. I saw her walking on the boardwalk early in the morning. As she came toward me, there was a golden hue surrounding her. The Spirit told me to take care of her for she was chosen. I have no clue for what, but the girl had a tender and compassionate spirit about her.

Fighting the battle of the judging the different nationalities by the ones chosen to represent the different countries, the Jews were still my favorite. Three different people from Israel, with three different personalities revealed the attitudes of what they thought about the country that held a melting pot of mixed races called Americans. The homeland that held my heart, I would defend. Due to one from Israel that expressed openly what he felt about Christians and freedom, he let me understand the Gentile was still a Gentile. He daily left me with the impression of servant-master. I was to learn my place. Once again the judgmental thoughts rose from deep within.

*   *   *

Satan sat on his throne rubbing his chin. Watching the battles within Terri's thoughts he knew this would be an intriguing battle field for this blood bought believer. She had to have known the reputation of this beach resort town. With determination he would find her weak spot. Her love for her country was a good place to start. He called the Spirit of Prejudice to the front line. "I want you to place those with the attitude of resentment toward the Americans in Terri's store. Make sure they say hidden secrets of the heart. Spirit of Anger, I want you to manipulate Terri's thoughts with a field of coals so that the anger begins to seethe through her heart and mind," said the Master of Evil. "She wants to see the world so we will bring the things of the world to her. I will set the traps personally so that she will not realize the snare we have caught her in. We must destroy this strong and courageous soldier of the Army of God."

* * *

In the heavens, Jesus sat with the great crowd of witnesses. The crowd was quiet as they watched their King. With angelic voices singing in the background the rhapsody of song left a gentle peace in the air as the King was working on a masterpiece for those in the heavens and the earth. With a gentle guiding of his finger, the heavens came alive with a crimson shade that left the crowd in awe. The sun that had been shining was covered when he put a dollop of crimson on top, then with his finger he covered the canvas with the shade that had softened the hearts of those that he loved. While the family of God watched in the Heavens they wondered if any on earth was observing the new design for the start of their day. The darkness was being drenched with the power of the crimson leaving awe to all watching the sun rise.

* * *

I sat watching the wave's crash into the shore. Then I caught sight of the crimson hue on the water. I glanced up and noticed the crimson sky. Instead of a yellow sun, it had a crimson color surrounded by dark clouds. Looking back at the water, it was a sea of burgundy because of the color of the sun. I was reminded the crimson sea was the only thing to submerse myself in. Immediately, I realized my thoughts must be captured and cast into the sea or I would be consumed with anger and bitterness instead of joy. I began worshipping and praising God for the glorious day. I began to sing from the depths of my soul. The waves of God's Amazing Grace washed my thoughts of confusion, sorrow, and pain. My heart was filled with joy as I worshipped the King of Righteousness not only in the spirit but with my mouth. Jesus would reveal what he wanted to the Jew, the Russians, the Hindu and the Buddhist. I was to let myself be poured out.

*   *   *

A melody of praise was being sent up to the heavens. The redeemed saints in heaven joined in the sing along. Terri's voice led the group in the praise and worship hour.[2] The heavens and earth were once again singing songs of jubilee together for the one on earth was in agreement that His will be done on earth as it is in heaven. God's great display of love in his masterpiece for the brand new day had left a fresh new and deeper understanding what must be done in order to stay at peace.

King Jesus adjusted the helmet of salvation that had tilted to the side a little bit. He knew Terri needed the whole armor on.[3] He tightened the breast plate with His righteousness. He handed the shield of faith and placed the sword in Terri's hand, touching the tongue. He spoke gently, "Guard your every word. May each thing you say be seasoned with grace!" With the belt of truth about the waist Jesus knew His daughter was ready to go out into the battle field where the enemy held control. Then he bent down and touched the feet. "My peace goes with you so you may walk in peace," He said.[4]

*   *   *

The job of the Kingdom was for each person entering the store to feel welcome and special. The needs became transparent as I began to socialize with the customer. Hearing and seeing their physical needs anything from boogie boards to clothing, turned around so I heard their burdens and their joys. As the customer shared their life stories the needs began to emerge. I was on a mission and the mission field was Ocean City. The prayer of the warrior was, "Lord speak through me and may your healing hand be seen. May, the "Son" shine on me as the sun shines on the water!" [5]

Pearl Drops of Wisdom

1. Casting down imaginations and every high thing that exalteth itself against the knowledge of God, and bringing into captivity every thought to the obedience of Christ.

    II Corinthians 10:5 KJV

2. Thou art my hiding place; thou shalt preserve me from trouble; thou shalt compass me about with songs of deliverance.

    Psalm 32:7 KJV

3. Finally my brethren, be strong in the Lord and the power of His might. Put on the whole armor of God that ye may be able to stand against the wiles of the devil
    Ephesians 6:10-11 KJV

4. Stand therefore, having your loins gird up with truth, and having on the breastplate of righteousness and your feet shod with the preparation of the gospel of peace. Above all taking the shield of faith, wherewith ye shall be able to quench all the fiery darts of the wicked. Take the helmet of salvation and the sword of the Spirit, which is the word of God.
    Ephesians 6:14-17 KJV

6. Make thy face shine upon thy servant; save me for thy mercies' sake.
    Psalm 31:16 KJV

Chapter 4

───────── ⋘⋙ ─────────

Treasure Seekers

Continually, the Lord gave me lessons through his creation. The tide had washed out while I observed the seagulls which were diving and circling around me. The group was in their own way treasure seekers. After a grand announcement from a noisy seagull many hungry scavengers had arrived to feast from man's handout. The fight for the tiny morsel was on. The younger inexperienced seagulls would often nip the ground around the actual delicacy. The coveted morsel would be swooped up by a trained scavenger bird. Some ate the tiny rock thinking they were receiving what had been offered. The treasure was unknown because of ignorance. Unable to smell the treasured morsel they only followed the direction the object was thrown unsure, where it landed.

Jesus said, "Babes in Christ are like the young seagulls. Tidbits of Grace are thrown out but the young believer misses it for they are ignorant of what they should be ingesting. The bread of heaven can be snatched up, leaving the stones to be eaten. They are hungry so will accept whatever is offered even if it brings bitterness to their soul. I want to give babes the feeding of Grace. So, they might grow only in Grace.[1] Out of ignorance they eat the rocks of the law.

I fed the Israelite's daily with fresh bread of heaven. They were ignorant of the Grace poured out upon them. The craving of the flesh over the manna was desired. Fear and dissatisfaction with my daily provision brought the lust of what they thought was greater to surface, quail. Those who continue to consume the law instead of my daily provision of Grace are plagued daily with leanness to the soul.

I noticed a group of seagulls that were willing to soar and dive for the treasured tidbit of food. The competition between the expert flyers was obvious as some became aggressive toward another. Deliberately flying into each other often made both seagulls lose the coveted trophy. The intimidation by the aggressive fighters was forced on all the surrounding scavenger hunters. The pecking order was definitely seen. Jesus whispered softly, "There are many willing to do the projects set out before them assigned by the church. The different stunts are not necessarily what I want them to do. Taking the tidbits from those in leadership gets the believer busy working in what they deem important. Often time's service becomes a competition depriving them of what is important; receiving the manna from heaven by listening to Me. The believer needs to stop and learn to listen. If they desire to hear My voice, I will speak for they need Me to teach them. My message is different than what is being taught.

Jesus said, "I desire faithfully emptied servants. I want to do the work through them. Most strive to impress man or himself. They become tired and weary, feeling they are doing all the work."[2] I, myself longed to hear well done thou good and faithful servant.[3] I thought it was strange that He wanted me to rest while He worked through me. As I listened to the teaching, I felt foolish. Was there anything I could say that I have done good or faithfully? Sitting beside the one who is faithful and good, I realized the work I did was nothing,[4] there was only one that was good and was able to make changes that last.[5]

My attention was drawn to some sea gulls standing back. They were larger than those performing the amazing air show of diving in for their food. I wondered if they were the oldest sea gulls out there. Were they too worn out to run for food? Were they lazy and just willing to wait for the tiny tidbit that would be thrown to them directly? Jesus said, "Notice the older, wiser treasure seekers waited patiently. I still gave the desired morsels to the seagulls that hungered for the food. Not one of them had to impress the other with their learned abilities. They waited for the morsel to be given. Many people are in such a hurry they won't wait for My word to be swallowed. The feasting given is on an individual basis. Having tried the way of diving and stunts in religious appearance, some wise believers found it was all in vain. Remember Mary? She is elderly and having to be taken care of. Yet, she daily asks Me to use her to further the kingdom. Her witness of My love is stronger than many others proclaiming to work in my name.[6] As she went through the fire, My faithfulness was seen. Like the wise seagull the treasure seeker will wait patiently for the morsel of grace. Those watching will see the feeding from heaven."

Jesus stopped and looked out toward the beach. I followed his gaze. There was a family walking the shore picking up seashells. The mother was trying to teach the little girl what to look for. The bouncy little one ran in circles trying not to get wet as the wave washed on shore. She would run pick up a shell that had washed up from the deep. A squeal of delight was heard as the little girl was waving something. A wallet containing money and no identification washed up on the shore. Someone else's loss had been this tiny little girl's treasure. A treasure, the little girl and her parents didn't expect but were delighted to find. The little one became more earnest in watching evermore carefully. The taste of the hidden treasure from the sea was understood a little better. The excitement for an adventure, with the sea in control, left the little girl with an attitude of what else could be found if she looked for it. Unaware of the monetary value involved with her find, the little girl continued to run the seashore picking up all the treasures from the sea.

My attention was caught by two men using metal detectors. The sounds would go off as hidden treasure was detected. The men would dig for the mysterious treasure. Disappointment was seen by their actions when it was a useless object. The disappointed treasure hunter would throw out the garbage that had been detected. The disappointment would turn to elation when an old coin or a piece of jewelry was found. The ocean had once again impressed the treasure hunters. Perseverance and patience kept the treasure seekers searching for the hidden mysteries in the sea. Once again someone else's loss had been another man's treasure.

Jesus whispered softly, "Seek the hidden mysteries in the Sea of Grace.[7] The treasures washing up to you are not always monetary value. Some may be hidden secrets that I have to tell you.[8] The little child saw all the gifts as special. With no clue what could be done with the seashell or the wallet, she was willing to accept all that was brought to her. Be as this child and trust I am good.[8] You may not understand why I offer a gift to you, but accept it for what it is a gift. It may be needed now or given to another down the road. As the men were with the metal detectors, you have to throw out what is not good. Satan will want you to stumble. If words are given, search the pearl drops of wisdom out of My love letters to you. I will show you the truth. You also know My voice, so listen. The depth of the truth is urging you on. My words of wisdom, I want to share with you." As the Spirit taught me, I understood the wisdom would be embedded by the Shepherd, just as the nails that nailed my Savior on Calvary's tree.[9] Endurance and patience is critical while searching for the treasures of the Sea of Grace. Jesus said, "Seek Me first and I will reveal the rest of my hidden treasure that is for you." [10]

Pearl Drops of Wisdom

1. At that time, Jesus said, I praise you, Father, Lord of heaven and earth, because you have hidden these things from the wise and learned and revealed them to little children.

   Matthew 11:25 NIV

2. Come to me, all you who are weary and burdened, and I will give rest . . . learn from me . . . you will find rest for your souls.

   Matthew 11:28-29NIV

3. His master replied, "Well done, good and faithful servant!

   Matthew 25:21 NIV

4. There is none good but one that is God.

   Matthew 19:17 KJV

5. I count all things but loss; for the Excellency of the knowledge of Christ Jesus my Lord . . . I count them as dung that I may win Christ.

   Philippians 3:8 KJV

6. Why is light given to those in misery . . . who search for it more than a hidden treasure.

   Job 3:20, 21b NIV

7. So that they may have the full riches of complete understanding, in order that they may know the mystery of God, namely Christ, in whom are hidden all the treasures of wisdom and knowledge

Colossians 2:2-3 NIV

8. O taste and see that the LORD is good; blessed is the man that trusteth in him.

Psalms 34:8 KJV

9. The words of the wise are as goads, and as nails fastened by the masters of assemblies, which are given from one shepherd.

Ecclesiastes 12:11 KJV

10. Seek ye first the kingdom of God, and His Righteousness; and all these things shall be added unto you.

Matthew 6:33 KVJ

Chapter 5

Tradition of Slavery

Striving not to judge others, I learned to swallow the harshness displayed from the Jewish manager, Esau. Having an uncircumcised heart unto Jehovah, the door to witnessing started by exposing his disobedience to the law. Esau did not see Jesus as a prophet, but as a heretic. He fired a woman after she tried converting him to Christ. With ears closed to hearing about Jesus the Messiah and eyes that were only for wealth offered by the world, he was left only with the tradition of cruelty. Proud of his heritage, he carried himself with an air of arrogance. The generational curse deeply rooted by the Egyptians, he would master others. [1] No one would be his master. He demanded servant-hood from those who were lower in race and position of life. Desiring to humiliate those underneath him, he would grab, push and even do choke holds on some of the women till they were bowed with their face to the ground before him. He pushed me from behind a couple of times. I warned him; you don't mess with an anointed child of God. When confronted by the owner, he justified his actions saying he was just playing with them. Hearing the girls cry out due to cruelty, I begin to pray for God to become more powerful over the one causing so much pain to others. With abusive intimidation he would break down the spirits of women, bringing them to submission. They were possessions to control as he saw fit.

Sharing a house with nine Russian women and three of Jewish descendent, the animosity of bloodline heritage was definitely seen. Neither group trusted the other. Being American and a grandmother, there was a respect shown from both the Russians and the Israeli toward me. With interest in their countries language, lifestyles and music, I opened my heart to all that were in the building. I could see those professing religious faiths living what they believed surrounded by those who believed in nothing.

Natalie, a Jewish manager of one of Jacob's stores exemplified a tenderness and compassion toward the Russian girls. In the position of leadership she modeled respect for the women working beside her with an air of dignity to her God, Jehovah. She never spoke her faith to the women but displayed genuine concern for her girls. Natalie had earned their friendship and respect. The atmosphere of her store was different than the stores that Esau ran. As the one was spoken with kindness, the other held their contempt. The attitudes of the different managers reflected on the conversations held by the workers. I sat listening to the young Russians complaints and tried to comprehend through the language barrier. Rubbing their swollen leg muscles with tears in their eyes, the message was loud and clear, we all ached. Each one of the beauties that had been sent from overseas now had phlebitis or varicose veins causing so much pain. Had the yearning for the desired wealth really been worth the humiliation and agony that was being so dramatically dealt? My vision was what was more critical. By ten o'clock every evening, my eyes would not see clearly. The pain behind the eyes was so extreme; headaches were a daily event that had to be prayed over. The 16 hour days were affecting all of us, as we worked six or seven days a week. Lunch breaks were given when and if Esau chose to give it. The girls would be allowed between thirty minutes to an hour depending on the generosity of the manager's mood for a sixteen hour day. There were times where I would only get twenty minutes. No breaks were allowed. Never imagined I would choose to be treated as a slave.

I was there for a different reason. I was there to share the good news.[2] Jesus prayer became a passion of mine. Thy Kingdom come, Thy will be done, on earth as it is in heaven. The abundance of grace and Jesus' righteousness could be obtained now on earth; joy, peace, healing, deliverance and solid victory. The stain in the heavens stayed in the heavens and he had more to offer his children if they knew how to use the keys to the Kingdom. We didn't have to wait till the destruction of this world or our deaths to have His kingdom reign on earth. I wanted to encourage each one to trust His love for them. I wanted to be a vessel that Christ reigned in.

Some coming to Ocean City needed salvation others needed something else offered out of the basket full of grace. Sowing seeds of life changing grace to the different people was the mission that I had accepted from the Almighty. My life was not my own. I wasn't a slave to earthly man but a servant of the Kingdom of Heaven. The inexpressible joy was seen radiating, for it was an honor to be able to serve the people that Jesus loved. Co-workers saw the strength of His vitality on me even though they didn't comprehend the ability to keep on running. As people would make comments, I would let them know this fifty year old woman had found the fountain of youth. Psalm 103 made promises and one was that he would renew the youth.[3] I was standing on the promises. I drank continuously from the spring of Living Water feasting on the basket of fruit only the Holy Spirit could give. The Spirit was bearing the fruit in and out of season. I learned to trust his faithfulness moment by moment, watching Him work continually in and through me.

The territory was so dark and evil. Many craving sexual freedom indulged in the baskets of lust. Unconcerned about the residual effects that could stem from indulging, they left with more shame and guilt. The thought what happens in Ocean City stays in Ocean City, allowed the diseases of the soul to run rampant. Lacking wisdom and discernment they became prey to the snares set to entrap them. There was a yearning in the hearts of the confused and lost to confess to me their deep dark secrets. I watched the Lord open doors of hearts and so did Esau. He watched daily the odd behavior of the customers. He wondered why people would divulge needs, prayer requests and testimonies to a total stranger. People commented on the peace and joy when they entered the store.[4] The presence of the King was felt. I knew it was the servant's job to demonstrate the values and principles of the royal kingship. The oneness with the King of Heaven left a definite display of uniqueness that drew the spiritual needs out.

Yet with all the goodness, slavery in the sexual lust basket was evident and alive. Esau's hand of control was extended out toward prostitution. Sexual favors were set up for men desiring to enjoy the women of beauty. One Russian girl was let go for refusing to cooperate. Esau told the owner she was lazy. Truth was she knew the Hebrew language and understood the conversation. She warned me to watch out! Both Israeli men ran stores; the one man in New Jersey and Esau, who was in charge of 4 stores in Ocean City. The cloak of seduction and enticement was to lure men of every nationality to the hidden lucrative market.

I had heard of the white slave trade but didn't really understand the ability for entrapment till I met a captain of a ship running drugs, guns and women to other countries. The man delivered girls of all ages for the wealth offered. The captain, unaware he had found interest in a child of a king began to tempt her with traveling the world. Very cautious how much information was divulged to me, the secrets were slowly revealed. He ran up and down the eastern seaboard picking up the precious cargo. The captain wanted to share his boat of wealth so I might experience different freedoms on the seas. Offering travel and love, he described places of interest he wanted to share. The Holy Spirit unraveled the web of deception. Recognizing the evil, I could see how young girls could be enticed. The naïve would fall victim because of the poisonous venom coming forth out of the sea captain's mouth. Her freedom would be traded for a greater bondage; prostitution for those in other countries willing to enslave.

Realizing the control of one evil aspect just led to another criminal activity kept me cautious. I became angry when men were told they could have the evening with me. After declining, I would confront Esau. There was a sadistic humor when he spurted out, "You should be glad men even want you at your age." I had to admit to myself I did appreciate the compliments and interest shown but I didn't desire to be offered up to the world by someone desiring to make a profit at the expense of my soul. I did hope there would be another man in my life, but I desired a powerfully anointed man of God.

The day arrived when I walked in on a conversation where the product for sale was me. The 2 men desiring to spend the evening tried enticing with wining and dining. I politely refused. At that point Esau laid out the details of where I lived and which apartment. The building was owned by Jacob so all pertinent details were known and divulged. In fear of my own safety, I called Terrance. The element arriving daily in Ocean City was like a continual meat market. His fear for me had already been expressed. Several times, he helped me do projects. Hearing the details, chain locks were installed on my apartment door. Terrance desired to confront Esau and do damage in a chivalrous way. I reminded him, who defends me in a lasting way. Prayers for God's protection were over the girls and me. God heard and would answer my prayer.[5] Anger stirred in my heart at the man. I went to the owner to expose the business. He point blank said, "If it is about my nephew I don't want to hear it. This angered me more. He didn't want to hear anything derogatory? Did Jacob know the criminal and cruel activities behind the scenes? Others had went and complained. They received the same response.

On a blessed day off, my spiritual eyes were opened wide. Two girls were sleeping in the room of the building I was responsible for. A man broke in and began to take advantage of one young Russian girl. Hearing screams and yelling in Russian, I tore into the room. Escaping out of my grip, the man took off running. Following the perpetrator down the steps of the apartment I hollered at an American man to call the police. "Whip" stayed with the girls as I raced down the street. Cornered after a long chase, fear raced when the man saw all the police cars pulling up. He tore out in a run again only to be captured. I wondered had it been a set up like what was planned for me? The urgency to protect the girls became more essential. My talking was done! I wanted the power of the Almighty to be seen.

*   *   *

There was terrible wailing coming from the earth into the heavens. Unable to control her bodily functions a woman had left a disaster all over herself and the floor. Embarrassed and ashamed, the agony from the sick woman was heard. The crowd of witnesses watched for they knew something she didn't know. Her situation was a major intricate part of a bigger scheme of things. She was being used to force a challenge in a holy war. The witnesses wondered would Terri standup for righteousness before a man who was against God or would she crumble under pressure to save her job.

Demonic forces, led by Satan were gathering at Esau's store. The heavenly host equipped with weapons of defense was also in the store. When Jesus heard the wailing from the child in need he sent Terri on an errand for the battle of control was about to begin . . . Unaware of the situation down the hall, one of Terri's customers needed merchandise available in the other store. Jesus showed the need at the door, without hesitation Terri led the two women to the bathroom across the hall. Jesus spoke through his servant comforting the woman who was embarrassed and ashamed. Everything would be taken care of. The crowd continued cheering the servant on even though she was unaware of the showdown. Terri ran into the store and picked out a dress. After paying Sumon, the gift was delivered to the woman. Jesus noticed his servant wondered what had happened to the other woman but went back into the store for the merchandise needed for her customer. Sumon gave back the money paid for the dress and told her Esau wanted it purchased from his store. Jesus watched as his confused servant hustled back.

Walking into the store, the heaviness could be felt immediately. Taking the product to the customer, Jesus watched his servant walk up to the counter to pay for the dress that had been purchased for the stranger. In front of the customers, Esau displayed the intense military training in his stance and voice as he began the interrogation. Yelling," What are you doing helping that lady? Did you know her?" He became explosive, "You are not to help people. You don't buy clothes for strangers. They are to buy from us." Jesus watched his warrior no longer stay calm. He brought to her memory the passage of the Good Samaritan.[6] With a righteous anger Terri wondered, how many people had seen the woman and walked by? Had Esau? He wasn't in the store when she left. Had he witnessed the scene of compassion? Jesus watched as the peacemaker tried to explain the need of compassion to the man but the more she tried the angrier he became. He hollered out again, "you are not to help people. Let them help themselves. You don't buy other people clothes and you only buy from this store." Jesus watched as Terri no longer stayed calm, "You have no right to tell me I can't help people. At all times, if God shows me a need, I must do His bidding. Our store showing compassion could possibly bring in others just because we care."

Jesus smiled for he saw the thoughts of the servant; she wasn't sure but wondered if one of those women were an angel standing by God's loved child. She wasn't about to divulge that information. Jesus knew Terri thought it was a divine appointment testing her heart to see if she saw others needs more important than money?

In the heavens the crowd watched, for after the servant's bold stand the battle between good and evil was at full force. The angels were taking control over the evil that had ruled within. The courage taken by the warrior on earth broke all the chains that were trying to take Terri captive. The slavery being enforced by the cruel vindictive master of evil was being brought to a halt. As the battling forces in the spiritual realm continued to rampage, the battle in the earthly realm continued the fight verbally. Jesus stood in between Esau and his servant, Terri.

With eyes open to the fighting stance that Esau had taken, Terri stood in a defensive stance. If Esau literally jumped over the counter she would be ready to fight. The crowd in the heavens knew it wouldn't be a fair fight, even though Terri knew the martial arts. Not considering, he was specially trained in the Israeli military. There would be no contest. Terri didn't stop to consider, the fighting ability of one in the Mossad. Fighting for righteousness and truth in the store was a spiritual battle that needed to take place. She was just being asked to take a stand. Angered by her response of defiance to his control, he displayed his authority to dismiss her. Holding up his hand as if he was a great Pharaoh, he screamed, "Leave me!"

He expected her to go back to work in the humble position in life, groveling before his Excellency and her job.

The battle wasn't over in the warrior of righteousness' eyes. The battle had just begun. Jesus took his servant to the time clock. Esau's face dropped as he watched her clock out. Righteous anger was seething. Walking out the door, her hands raised to the heavens she was heard proclaiming, "Lord show him your power, might, and love for those who have been calling out. The girls working here need deliverance from the tyranny and cruelty. We're tired of this man trying to prostitute us out. Let him see your hand rise against him. Move him out of this store." As she walked away, the man was heard yelling, "You know what will happen if you leave?" She never looked back. This man was put in the capable hands of the Almighty.

*   *   *

In the deep caverns below, Satan grimaced. The soul of this man was at stake. This blood bought believer dared to put one belonging to him in the clutches of the Almighty. She treated him like he was an enemy. "What happened to the passion of God's chosen people," jeered Satan. This mere mortal was nothing going up against one of the powerful anointed ones looking to Jesus for deliverance. The Spirit of Doubt hated to remind Satan, seeds of grace had been planted for months now. The genuine fear was seen on Esau's face when Terri proclaimed, "Lord show your power." He has seen her God work all summer. We cannot let him understand Jesus is Jehovah.

"Don't let up on this man," Satan said. We can't afford to lose this one. He brings much to our kingdom. The sorrow from the disloyalty in the marriages and cruelty from his hand sows seeds of discontentment for these Russian girls. The hatred of the Russians for the Jew will become stronger through their suffering people. Money was their weakness but soon their way will be what I choose for them. Their hearts will become numb to what is right. The Spirit of Doubt cut him off, "Not if you don't stop Terri. You saw what happened the other day. It left a powerful impression in all their lives including the managers. They were $500.00 short of what they wanted to hit. It was late and very few on the boardwalk. The manager was saying the goal couldn't be obtained. You remember what happened? Terri told him it was possible, just call out to Jesus. She looked up raising her hand to the heavens; asked the King to bring in the customers so they could reach their goal." The Spirit of Greed said discouragingly, "The amazement on the faces of the workers left a haunting imprint on my thoughts. They didn't do any hard work yet the store was blessed in minutes. Immediately both doors had people flocking into the store. They went $1000.00 over what they had wanted. Jesus impressed them. The women went straight back and just started grabbing clothes off the rack." "It was impressive," chimed in the Spirit of Jealousy. "Terri is trying to show them the God of the Old Testament is still the God of "today." She must be stopped." Satan listened to the demons discuss the miracle on 22nd street. He wasn't impressed in the least. Was she aware of the distinct difference of the three categories of the Jewish faith she had ran into; the Messianic Jew, the Jews that loved Jehovah and the Jews that belonged to Kabala? If she isn't aware of the separation, maybe he could plant seeds in filthy compost. She would have distaste for the entire race. What was Almighty going to do to Esau? He managed 4 stores and his influence of stirring up strife and the sexual bondage was working. It would cripple his business that he had worked so hard to build.

*   *   *

In the heavens, the crowd stood in awe as they looked upon the One who sat on the throne. "Finally, she asked for my power and deliverance to be seen by others," said Jesus. "With love for the four Israeli's, she has been praying they would receive the spirit of grace and salvation through her blessed Jeshua. She wanted only my gentleness and goodness for them. She prayed for the blessing to be obvious, that she carries the truth.

Using the Levitical laws and exposing the disobedience of not sacrificing, she watched the Jews come under derision. Unable to sacrifice, for the temple was torn down, left the question which was more important; the altar or the gift on the altar. Jesus continued talking to the redeemed, "Carefully seeds have been planted. She wants them to recognize I was pierced for their transgressions by their people for their people. Zechariah proclaimed once again now in the heavens, "may they mourn and grieve for what they did to their Messiah! [7]

I heard her request. As she has spoken so be it! He will remain out of the store for the agony of the afflicted girls has been heard. Compassion will be shown to those working in the store. Business will flourish in his absence so that he and the Israeli owners will know I AM the great I AM. I desire mercy and compassion instead of fasting. As he is bed ridden for 2 months, he will see my face is looking on my servant, Terri. When his day of fasting comes, he will lay pondering all that I have done.

Pearl Drops of Wisdom

1. And the Lord said, "I have surely seen the affliction of my people which are in Egypt and have heard their cry by reason of their taskmasters; for I know their sorrows."

    Exodus 3:7 KJV

2. And he said unto them, Go ye into all the world, and preach the gospel to every creature.

    Mark 16:15 KJV

3. Bless the Lord, oh my soul and all that is within me, bless his holy name. Bless the Lord O my soul and forget not all his benefits: Who forgiveth all thine iniquities; who healeth all thy diseases; who redeemeth thy life from destruction; who crowneth thee with loving-kindness and tender mercies; who satisfieth thy mouth with good things; so that thy youth is renewed like the eagles.

    Psalm 103:1-5 KJV

4. But the fruit of the Spirit is love, joy, peace, longsuffering, gentleness, goodness, faith, meekness, temperance: against such there is no law.

    Galatians 5:22-23 KJV

5. Faithful is he that calleth you, who also will do it.

    I Thessalonians 5:24 KJV

6. But a certain Samaritan, as he journeyed, came where he was. And when he saw him he had compassion.

    Luke 10:33 KJV

7. And I will pour upon the house of David, and upon the inhabitants of Jerusalem, the spirit of grace and of supplications: and they shall look upon me whom they have pierced, and they shall mourn for him . . .

    Zechariah 12:10 KJV

Chapter 6

Victories in Many Disguises

In the heavens, the bride of Christ rejoiced for the chosen on earth were coming into agreement with them. The redeemed stepping out from the norm of religion, were accepting the gifts offered from the "Anointed One". With power and authority believers were seeing the Holy Spirit moving through their confused and desperate lives. The great crowd stood in awe, as glory to glory came out of disaster to disaster. Singing loudly from the well spring of the heart, the songs of the redeemed were joined by the saints in the heavens. The bride recognized Christ the warrior, now saw their groom showing his passion for the bride as he continued to perfect them for the Father. There was an enthusiasm to adorn his bride with every precious gift. Those in the heavens saw sorrow on Jesus' face, when his bride at the footstool was not ready to receive the gifts he offered.

As battles raged forth, the valor of the faith-walkers realized their victories were won. The powerful warriors saw though actions, the faithfulness of the commander as spoken in his Word. The more the soldier of Christ trusted the Commanders decisions, the easier the battle for the blood bought believers. Word of the impossible was changed when Spirit of the Great I AM, worked in the supernatural. Jesus loved watching the bride in the heavens and the earth. Rejoicing with the Father, over the ones that he had been given, Jesus joined in the celebration of praise. The unadulterated worship in the heavens combined with the praise offerings sent up from His anointed ones on earth ushered a sweet smelling aroma into the beautiful city. The hint of frankincense and myrrh left a calming peace in the air as the radiant beams extended from the throne. Jesus enjoyed his family in both dimensions; the heavens and his footstool. Vessels that are not able to contain all that I AM, must surrender each battle till our hearts are one in thought and ways.

"Watch the excitement on the boardwalk," Jesus said. "The different exhibits portray what is in the heart. Some find the piano keyboard and the fries enough to enjoy, while others look for the extreme entertainment. Some look to the beauty from nature, while others enjoy seeing masterpieces from a skillful artist. As you watch, you can see what is important to the buyers, sellers, and entertainers. There is a definite separation of those that believe in Me. The love is evident by the praise offerings that they display to others. The crowd in the heavens saw the activities on the boardwalk. They watched an artist create a painting using spray paint and different objects. He was not a usual artist but his designs were unique and creative. He tuned out all the hoopla and crowds that were standing there watching his abilities. The artist had learned to only hear the music that was in the background. With an image in the artist thoughts, he began to work. The passion from within flowed across the canvas as the creator developed his picture. The connotation when finished was a futuristic masterpiece. The witnesses in the heavens were amazed just as the crowds on the earth. The talent whether the man realized it or not was God given.

The sound of shovels digging in the sand caused those in the heavens to look toward the sand art. The master builder supervised those who were just learning the craft involving the elements of the earth. With a keen eye, the artists put definition and detail for the image that was close to their hearts. The Romans Road was laid out so there would be no excuse.[1+2] Gifted artists showed different aspects of Jesus' life, death and also lifted up His resurrection. The detail that was displayed in the masterpiece made out of sand brought joy to some. The testimony honoring the King encouraged the family of God, yet brought anger to those that were against Him. Those of darkness verbalized maliciously. The heavens rejoiced at the creative masterpiece proclaiming Jesus is King of Kings and Lord of Lords. The praise offering from the hearts on earth sent up a sweet aroma into the heavens. The dynamic boldness of the redeemed ones were not challenging man, but proclaiming to all God's creation in the heavens, the earth, and in the caverns of hell who was to be worshipped. Victory over death and hell was proclaimed.

A terrible clanging broke forth breaking the peaceful harmony of praise in the beautiful city of Zion. Chains could be heard hitting a park bench as a message of hell fire and damnation was preached. The ridicule and judgment spewing forth was not seasoned with grace. Tears welled up in Jesus' eyes. The man didn't show freedom, deliverance, or victory. With the promise of no message would be void, Jesus sent the ones past the Christian in chains that needed to hear the message of rejecting forgiveness.[3] The bondage displayed did not encourage the deliverance Jesus blood had offered, but represented the chains of enslavement because of sin. By his works, it was evident the preacher was concerned for souls, yet the message of grace was not offered up to those in dire need of hope, forgiveness, and love. The man was assuming all on boardwalk was evil, as he pointed his finger at anyone passing by. Believers would shake their head as they passed by, only to make comments when entering the store. Some Christians were angered by the representation, for they were brought to Christ through the message of love and hope. Leaving thoughts of confusion; was it heavy chains of religion instead of freedom through Christ.

Honor and respect was displayed by a man who was a statue painted in gold. The living memorial's garments showed he was a soldier from Vietnam War. The man painted in gold had never been in the military, but showing respect to his father who had been killed in Vietnam. His dedication of silence was in honor of his father and the other soldiers who gave the ultimate sacrifice.

The heavens watched a veteran soldier from the Iraqi war. As he passed the soldier of gold, tears welled up in his eyes. His trophy of remembrance was nothing like what was being portrayed on the boardwalk. He walked with two artificial legs that were not gold or silver, but were made out of titanium. The respect he received was from other veterans those who understood the battles and the loss. The intent stare from the man in gold brought amazement to those watching beside him. They admired his dedication. As the rebuilt soldier watched the man of silence, it pierced to the very core of his being. Silence had become his enemy, for it was a companion that replaced his legs. The silent treatment from the living memorial was taunting him with the event that brought agony to his soul. The golden irony of silence showing respect stirred anger from within.

Titanium legs weren't what bothered him. The man would do it all again. He questioned the fact whether the Iraqi people appreciated the American soldier fighting for freedom and life in their country. The American soldier felt like everyone was staring at him. Instead of asking what happened, people's eyes were mocking him. Their silence was more deafening than the bomb that had exploded taking his legs from him. He left one battle field leaving behind comrades who fought with him and beside him to a battle field where he was all alone. The discouraged broken vessel that once stood as a tower of strength now battled his emotions. This mighty man of valor needed someone to care, what he had given up for the fight for freedom.

* * *

The Lord touched my eyes. Seeing the burden but not knowing details, I asked the Lord to comfort the man. Wisdom, discernment and knowledge, and graced speech were needed for the man's wife began sharing her life situation. I asked her what happened to the man that she loved. With tears in her eyes, she shared how her husband had been blown up by the land mine. Choking back tears she said," it wasn't the loss of the limbs that made him angry; it was the attitude of the people". The staring made the man feel judged by society. The pointing fingers and the whispering to others hurt deeper than the exploding fire. If they would have just asked him what happened, he would be willing to share the price it cost for freedom for others. He was discouraged people didn't see the intense gift that was given.

As the wife tried on the selected garments, I went over to the man who permeated confusion, anger and bitterness. Welcoming him back, I extended a hand of friendship and told him thank you for serving our country. As the man shook my hand, the tension relaxed in his face. We went toward the dressing room where his wife was changing. Answering questions he opened up and shared his thoughts. "My friend, I do understand the cost of freedom somewhat." I explained the price my husband gave was his life. He left behind three teenagers that struggled. I let him know Jesus even understood greater. He had given His life for all mankind's sin. He understood, for the man of war was a brother in the Lord. Finding out we were family, barriers came down. Sharing the passion the two of us had, it was if we had known each other a long time.

The government couldn't deny his service for the country, for the legs were replaced and he was honored with a purple heart. Vietnam veterans, who contracted the Agent Orange in organs that were not on a list, were not even acknowledged with benefits to the surviving family members. The veteran could not understand justice and neither could I. Somehow the conversation went to Jesus once again. He understood what it is like for people to deny the cost of freedom. Some were so consumed in their lives of shallowness that the gift didn't matter. Others chose to not believe in a God of love and mercy. The religious saw his forgiveness but refused to submit. He gave His life at Calvary so that mankind could be set free from the laws that condemned man to the ultimate price, death. Man chose to follow laws; therefore they became slaves to sin, works, and laws. Man still chooses to go on his own merit instead of His." What was the evidence of Jesus' service to mankind? Both of us testified on His amazing life redeeming works in our lives. What was Jesus trophy? Jesus received a bruised heart so that he would, one at a time win a believing heart.

Before he left the store, I tried leaving words of encouragement. "Don't look for praise for bringing freedom or you have your reward.[4] Your "Heavenly Father" who sees in secret, blesses openly. When doing Christ's bidding, service for man is noticed. Jesus has a greater calling for your life. He wants to help those who have suffered as you have mentally and physically. The soldiers witnessing death and sorrow will need to know how to receive help. You can bring others to freedom in Christ, for you experienced the same fears, sorrows and loss.

Don't worry about trying to learn to walk on those titanium legs. Jesus will help you stand and run. Walk courageously in his mercy. Share what he has done for you instead of what you did for another. That is what matters. What you accomplished lasts but a moment as you have found out but what He did is everlasting through eternity."

*   *   *

With kernels of tenderness and love the crowd could see the chains that had held the man in bondage, be released one at a time. The brother in the Lord was receiving a gift from the King personally that changed the man before their very eyes. The burden that was lifted off suddenly made the man stand upright. With courage and boldness, the man made a decision to stand in valor. He had been given back respect and honor. The mighty man of valor was being called to a position that only could have been given by the King of Heaven. He had been called to be a soldier for the cross,[5] the limitations that had been put on him in the physical realm were turned to be used as a weapon of victory in the spiritual realm.

After hugs and tears, the good-byes were said. The husband and wife left the store with garments for their physical needs but were equipped with spiritual armor that was given from the kingdom. The great crowd in the heavens noticed his garment of white and the armor given to him made the man look powerful. The soldier who had fought for freedom in the physical realm was now equipped to be used with power in the spiritual realm. He would once again stand beside others and help fight the demons and the underworld. The victory over his thinking had opened the door to his true purpose in life and that was to help fight for the Kingdom of Heaven. His weakness would become an inspiration to fight the good fight; those were direct orders from the General. Jesus told him, he would expose the traps, snares and land mines that were being set by Satan.[6] There were no words for the difference of appearance in the man walking once again out on boardwalk with his titanium legs except for; he was a man walking in the confidence of the Lord.

The soldier of victory stopped and watched once again the living memorial. While some looked at the statue of gold, others wouldn't even pay any mind. A harassing group of teenagers walked by jeering and taunting him exposing their cold hearted hearts didn't understand. The man painted in gold standing proud and unflinching, received treatment that some veterans coming home from their tour of duty received. The mighty man of valor walked up to the silent man and looked straight into the eyes that had once penetrated to the depths of his soul. No longer did he feel resentment and anger, with pride he stared into the silent gold statue. With no words said, the eyes did all the talking. The living statue moved. The stare down between the two left many wondering what thought had been exchanged. The gold statue took his hand to his head and saluted the soldier in respect of the true hero in the crowd.

PEARL DROPS OF WISDOM

1. For all have sinned and fall short of the glory of God.

   Romans 3:23 NIV

2. For the wages of sin is death, but the gift of God is eternal life through Christ Jesus our Lord.

   Romans 6:23 NIV

3. So is my word that goes out of my mouth: It will not return to me empty, but will accomplish what I desire and achieve the purpose for which I sent it.

   Isaiah 55:11 NIV

4. Be careful not to do your acts of righteousness before men, to be seen by them. If you do, you will have no reward from your Father in heaven.

   Matthew 6:1 NIV

5. Suffer hardship with me, as a good soldier of Christ Jesus. No soldier in active service entangles himself in the affairs of everyday life, so that he may please the one who enlisted himself as a soldier.

   II Timothy 2:3-4 NAS

6. For this reason I endure all things for the elect's sakes, which they also may obtain the salvation which is in Christ Jesus with eternal glory.

II Timothy 2:10 KJV

Chapter 7

Rebels Turned Toward Piracy

With an excitement following them, three boys and a girl came into the store to look for something to take home with them as a souvenir. Their first time in Ocean City, they wanted something that would be bold and yet with taste. The characteristics of two boys were full of life in their actions and speech flowing with energy. The reserved calm of the other two left an era of dignity in the area surrounding the group. Joy entered the store with the vivacious group. Loving the attitude of the vibrant young adults, I was drawn to these kids. Full of life they desired to find a shirt that involved what they felt inside. As I worked with them, they found tee shirts that could promote their piracy tenancies. The one could mimic a pirate to the tilt which added a spirit of joyfulness that made other customers join in their fun.

After the other customers left the store somehow the conversations became more subdued. Two of them began to tell me their backgrounds. They had been problem teens. Their riddled lives had been consumed with courts and juvenile sentences. Consumed with doing what was right in their own eyes, they had looted many people.[1] Leaving destruction in their paths, the boys had become pirates in their thinking; having the right to take what was not their own. The booty ill-gotten was an adrenaline rush each time they had succeeded in pillaging the unsuspected victim. Drugs had also played a part in the boy's choices. As things were taken, they were sold for a price in order to obtain the desired delicacy. Living a life that led them to spiraling out of control, they ended up in the hands of the authorities.

That is when Jesus came into their lives. Salvation was revealed to these rebels of society. Those that had been cast aside with no hope to change were changed by given hope. Man's hand couldn't break the chain of thievery, yet God in his infinite wisdom had chosen these three boys to band together and become soldiers of fortune. Never would their lives be the same. God hadn't just showed them salvation, but had poured out his benefits of being children of the Kingdom of Heaven. They explained how they were receiving from the richness of the Father and giving to the poor and broken hearted. They were pirates for the Kingdom. They were determined to get back the things that Satan had taken from them; their lives, friends and family. Love, joy, peace and wisdom were just a few of the things they were receiving from the King. All had lives redeemed from destruction. The spoil would be divided.[2] Loving the resurrected Lord and trusting Him they were determined to go to Satan's domain and get their friends out of the clutches of Satan's hand. The power he held over their friends was nothing compared to their Captain's mighty hand.

The sound of the pirate voice was strong and powerful and held my interest. No question why I liked these guys the minute they had walked into the store. They were family members recognizing the keys to the kingdom. I could see how these two were being used to draw in the youth, for they had captured the interest of the other workers within the store. The rebels for the kingdom were preaching Grace to the Nepalese and the Israeli in a way they had never heard the message before. With enthusiasm and vigor with the lingo of the pirate gristle the international barriers of religion stood no chance. They were drawn to the group of pirate's who radiated a message of forgiveness, redemption and love. The group of unbelieving co-workers drew closer, just to watch and listen to the two desiring to have others set sail with them on the Seas of Victory.

With voices that went back to their normal speech the two proclaimed their mission that God had put them on. They had just finished working at a special camp for juveniles. The kids they worked with were younger than they were, when they had started their criminal activities. The pirates working for King Jesus understood the power that these other kids felt when they were able to create chaos in other people's lives. It was the thrill to have escaped the authority. The kids were brought to the same place where the youth leaders had landed, the dungeon with shackles and guards watching their every move.

Powerfully redeemed men, God was using, were challengers of the underworld with weapons given by their King.[3] Coming out from prisons into the kingship, they were vigorously sharing the keys to the kingdom.[4] The keys they carried; key of salvation, key of deliverance, key of healing and the key knowledge were often asked for.[5] The key of righteousness over the believers' righteousness very few seemed to know was available. Through the fall and winter, men taught the word at a bible college to the group. Summer was powerful to them. The Spirit taught lessons of grace with hands on experiences, serving on the highways and byways. They were at the footstool of Christ being taught grace in a greater portion so they could teach grace.

* * *

Satan sat in the deep caverns below seething. The smoke coming up from the rivers of fire surrounding his throne was beginning to choke him. Creeks of hot molten lava had widened since believers of God's saving grace began living what they believed in. These boys were no different. They were reaping the benefits of being kings and priests of the royal family. The attitudes of the redeemed ones were causing destruction within his spiritual realm.

Satan made an expression of contempt when he listened to the two boys talk about how they were like pirates now. How could they understand the ways of piracy in the spiritual realm? The gall these two had to think they could challenge him and his authority. Their goal was to take souls out my hand with power and might through Jesus leadership. The cocky boldness these two held caused a trembling to surge through the Spirit of Evil. They were walking in a confidence that was obvious to all in the store. The rushing wind of the Holy Spirit was still like a fire of excitement in the believers of today. He had to stop these believers before there was a revival in the land.

He glanced at the young adults from Israel and Nepal. Why wouldn't people enter the store to cause disruption? If someone would have just entered long enough to take their minds off the blood bought, victory speaking, anointed class of believers. Satan realized it wasn't just Terri he had to worry about. There was victory claiming Christians rising up everywhere. He hollered for the demons to come to his presence. When they stood shaking before him, he smiled thinking he held their fear and respect. He roared, "How could you not send in people to break the concentration level that penetrated through to those I have a choke hold of unbelief on?" The demons still quivering before their master said shakily pointing, "Did you not see?" Satan turned the direction they were pointing. Falling to his knees, Jesus stood at the door. He stopped all business from being done except the business that was important; saving souls.

Terri needed to be stopped before she talked to anyone else. There she was already talking to a fisherman. She was telling the fisherman how Jesus best friends were fishermen. They had followed him, watching the Master Fisher of Men work. Peter listened with ears that were no longer dull. The master fisher of men was about to bring in another fine catch. The man had belonged to the Pagans and was hungry for something new.

Satan was not about to let this man go. The man with pagan beliefs would be taken first before he would come to know the love of the risen Savior. Satan devised a plan to stop the message from sinking in. He would kill the man before he had time to make a decision. He would worry about Terri down the road. First things first, kill Peter.

Pearl Drops of Wisdom

1. . . . But every man did that which was right in his own eyes.

    Judges 17:6 KJV

2. Therefore I will divide him a portion with the great, and he shall divide the spoil with the strong.

    Isaiah 53:12a KJV

3. Who redeemeth thy life from destruction; who crowneth thee with loving-kindness and tender mercies;

    Psalm 103:4 KJV

4. Then I will set the key of the house of David on his shoulder, when he opens no one will shut, when he shuts no one will open.

    Isaiah 22:22 NIV

5. I will give you the keys to the kingdom of heaven; whatever you bind on earth will be bound in heaven, whatever you loose on earth will be loosed in heaven.

    Matthew 16:19 NIV

Chapter 8

Rescue by Captive

Called by the ocean, Peter found the career of his choice to be one involving the powerful uncontrollable body of water. The grueling job of sword fishing was the occupation that Peter had been doing for some time. He went into the job thinking about the money but learned to appreciate the beauty of the sea. With the rugged face one could tell the elements: the sun, wind and salt water had taken its toll on the forty year old man. It wasn't just the weather that had put a beating on him. Peter had been with the pagans. His best friend was his alcohol. He had left the territory filled with secrets. Lives that he had helped destroy. Thinking he had control of his life, Peter found he wasn't in control when he was with the pagans.

The group had been like a family. With similar goals and desires the biker found that they would cover his back. He learned to defend the leaders even if it would have taken his life. He agreed with the code. That is until he found he had to leave the group, his life was spiraling out of control. He took what little he had and went to where he couldn't be found, a job on the water. No one would look for him there. He could travel the sea. Stopping at different ports for women and booze leaving behind no trail, destiny would prevail. He could maintain a life without women but knew he had to have the alcohol. It helped him relax and forget. He wasn't going to let man manipulate him any longer but wasn't aware the substance abuse controlled him more than man ever could. The bottle had brought him to a place where he had to hide from others.

Peter had heard about God, but Jesus was new to him. I encouraged reading the Bible. Every day he would read a Psalm or a Proverb but said he really couldn't understand most of what he read. He knew if he kept trying to follow the Good Book his life would get better. He said he believed in God just wasn't so sure about the Jesus "stuff".[1] One trip back from out at sea, Peter told me "Jesus found me. He showed me, who he is." Even though he didn't have a learned religious background he had experience something beyond words where Jesus had gotten his attention.[2] Peter continued speaking with so much enthusiasm, "I know more about Jesus than most get to know him."

With excitement in his voice, he said he was in a 100 ft. boat catching and gutting out sword fish. It was a dark cloudy day. The weather was cold fishing off the North Carolina coast in the middle of January. The waves were high due to a storm rocking the boat as water crashed on to the deck. Peter said his body was frozen even though he had a heavy coat on. His feet were wet even though he was wearing heavy boots. It was so bitter cold that his hands hurt to move them. The dampness in the air just made it so miserable that he never felt like he could warm up. It was just a terrible day to go fishing, yet the demand for sword fish was high. The fishing hadn't been good this trip so it was critical to try in spite of the weather. It was essential to the group of fishermen, for they were heading back to dock after this one last try. The waves kept washing up on the deck of the boat. It was hard to stand on the wet deck. It was as slippery as snot. He told me, he grabbed on to the rail for the situation was dangerous.

*   *   *

Everyone in the Heavens knew what was going on the spiritual realm that Peter couldn't see. Satan stood on the bow of the ship. He lifted his arms high as the waves reacted to the one commanding the storm to brew. The height of the wave put fear in among the group of fisherman as they watched the waves crashing into the boat. Could the ship maintain the pounding that Satan had demanded? He didn't care if all the men were lost at sea; he just didn't want Peter to receive the victory that Terri had so carefully laid out.

*   *   *

Peter's heart was being softened to the God who loved him the way he was. Peter found himself thinking about God. He had seen Greg a couple of days before. Greg was a born again Christian, with the background of Paganism. He believed in God but battled his thoughts constantly. They had been in quiet a heated conversation. Greg knew God had his hand in things but Peter was sure God didn't control all things. That would interfere with "free will". Where was the fine line of God in control without it messing with man's own choice? Peter took advice from the "Wisest Man, Solomon" daily as he read a proverb a day. Was it right for God to try to dictate his way on man?

Suddenly the bait was received. As the pulley was trying to reel in the sword fish, a wave slammed the boat. Water came rushing onto the deck. Peter was hit and knocked overboard into the water. Swallowing the salt water, Peter sunk into the deep. Over dressed for the swim he found himself being sucked into the abyss. The clothes weighing so much, there was no relief to be found. He began to cry out to the Lord. The desperate flailing in the water as the waves were there to drag him down he knew there was no way to survive without the help of the one he had just questioned about control. Amazingly, how in the darkest hour of Peter's life he wanted God to take control of his situation. No matter how much he willed to survive he knew there was no hope. The temperature of the water alone would bring him before the King. Whether drowning or freezing, Peter needed the hand of the Faithful One. Remembering the conversations that we had, he knew Jesus could save him from the death he was facing. He didn't want control of his life he wanted one that was greater than the sea to rescue him.[3]

*   *   *

Satan smiled a wicked smile; he thinks God is going to save him in these last moments before death? He won't have time. The muscles had already slowed down and the freezing process had already begun. Satan jeered, "The unsuspecting fool did not see my hand that shoved him into the water. Now, the other fishermen must not be able to see him in order to rescue him." The waves continued to ride high rocking the boat leaving the sounds of cracking throughout the boat. The group seemed more concerned about the fish and the boat. Satan started laughing in his sinister laugh knowing the men were not aware that Peter had fallen overboard.

*   *   *

God in the heavens smiled. He knew that this dear young child was challenging Christ Lordship over the power of the sea. Jesus knew this was part of the birth process of this child. Peter realized that his ways brought sorrow as his life was reviewed before his eyes. Jesus also realized the battle wasn't a fair fight for Satan was trying to stop this child from making the greatest decision of his life; choosing to follow Christ with total submission. Jesus looked at Jonah. Jonah laughed. "Oh no don't do it Lord. I stunk downright awful after the whale heaved me on the shore.[4] I stunk for days. I couldn't get the smell out of my nostrils. I was sure everyone could smell me. The people of Nineveh probably changed just because they saw you use a whale as a learning instrument.[5] I was embarrassed to think how many people saw me walking down the street. With all that rotten algae hanging off me, I looked worse than anything they had seen except the leprous maybe. We both fell under the same category: unclean. How many didn't believe my fish tale? Generations of parents have told their children my most embarrassing moment. I don't think anyone has had a greater fish tale." The great crowd of witnesses laughed as Jonah joked with Jesus. The friendship between the two was obvious.

*   *   *

The plight of Peter became one of pleading in the heavens, [6] deep in the water now caught underneath the boat; Peter could feel the strength leaving him. There was no place to grab a hold. As he tried treading the water his legs ached with a numbness that was caused because of the blood beginning to freeze. The storm was so bad there was nothing anyone could do to help for none saw a glimpse of the man fighting for his life. The rocking of the waves caused nausea for the men that were used to the sea. The adrenaline rush to capture the fish in spite of the storm was the determined goal for those who knew nothing of the plight that Peter had found himself in. The sword fish thrashing for its own life was being slowly reeled in.

Jesus opened Peter eyes. The sword fish dove deep into the water than Peter heard, "grab the fish." Peter couldn't do anything for the thrashing sword fish was slippery. Peter tried to grab on again, only to miss once again. Then as if the fish was literally stopped, Peter reached up and grabbed the tail of the fish. Jesus smiled for he knew the man had made a choice. Peter wanted Jesus in control

*   *   *

Satan saw and heard the master of the sea tell the man how to be rescued. Satan wasn't willing to hand over this piece of treasured property without a fight. He added torture to the fish by escalating the spirit of fear more powerfully. Did Satan whisper the song of death to the swordfish? The fish did not want to meet his death at the end of this line. The weight of the tail of the fish beat Paul violently against the boat sides. The group of fisherman spotted Peter hanging on to the tail of their great catch. Unable to throw out the life line they watched as Peter was brought up out of the sea by the swordfish's tail.

At this moment the heavens weren't the only that could testify at the miracle that was being done for the fishermen on board saw the incredible impossibility. Once again God's creation was being used to help open the eyes of a strong willed, self-controlled rebellious man. The sword fish was fighting to be set free from the line that was to bring forth his death. [8] Peter could be heard pleading for the lifeline not to break so that he might be able to continue to live. Both were fighting for life. Peter's frozen hands hung on to the slippery 400 lb. sword fish praying he might be brought up out of what was to be his watery grave. The fish was the vessel God used to transport his child to the safety of the boat. After the hoisting of the fish the jokes began to run rampant on the boat. Shaking from the frozen water, the group tried to bring back the warmth of his body temperature. Peter listened to the group but inwardly began praising the Almighty for the goodness and mercy that had been shown to him. Peter proclaimed the amazing love and protection of Jesus.[9] He realized God was in control the whole time. Peter was convinced Jesus' hand held on to him as the fish was drawn in. He didn't know how he hung on otherwise.

* * *

The crowd in the Heavens watched as Jesus bent down to the swordfish. Did He tell the swordfish about the character on his tail? The fish still did not want to die, but realized his job for the King of the Sea, was to bring the child of the Kingdom to the surface. The swordfish looked into the eyes of his Creator. As the fish was laid out on the deck, the master patted his precious creation that was caught because of obedience.

PEARL DROPS OF WISDOM

1. I rejoice, not that you were made sorrowful, but that you were made sorrowful to the point of repentance; for you were made sorrowful according to the will of God in order that you might not suffer in anything through us. For the sorrow that is according to the will of God produces repentance without regret, leading to salvation; but the sorrow of the world produces death.

    II Corinthians 7:9-10 NAS

2. Let the wicked forsake his way, and the unrighteous man his thoughts: let him return unto the Lord, and he will have mercy upon him; and to our God, for he will abundantly pardon.

    Isaiah 55:7 KJV

3. We know that all things work together for good to them that love God, to them who are called according to his purpose.

    Romans 8:28 KJV

4. Now the LORD had prepared a great fish to swallow up Jonah. And Jonah was in the belly of the fish three days and three nights.

    Jonah 1:17 KJV

5. And the LORD spoke unto the fish, and it vomited out Jonah upon the dry land.

> Jonah 2:10 KJV

6. The waters compassed me about even to the soul; the depth closed me round about

> Jonah 2:5a KJV

7. Yet hast thou brought up my life from corruption, O LORD my God

> Jonah 2:6b KJV

8. I sought the LORD and he heard me and delivered me from all my fears.

> Psalm34:4 KJV

9. And my soul shall be joyful in the LORD: it shall rejoice in his salvation.

> Psalm 35:9 KJV

Chapter 9

Rebellious Choppers

The summer was coming to an end and the last big hoopla was getting ready to roll around once again. The closing of the season was signaled by bike week in Ocean City. Designing shirts to show the store was biker friendly; I became engrossed in the concept of perfection. It wasn't speed these bikers wanted. It was the attitude of freedom. Born, live, and ride free. The Indian, shovelhead, chopper, and the Harley held the true biker attitude set off with the classy sound of the pipes. I began working with the girls from Russia ahead of time, so they would understand the freedom riders. They were petrified of the element and considered them evil. I didn't know if it was engrained in Russia or personal encounter but there was fear of all those riding into town. All bikers were welcome to Ocean City, but no colors were allowed. Assuming all were the same, the Russians and Napoleons were ready to dismiss the gathering as evil to the core.

Satan had deliberately manipulated the biker world. They were like a family, belonging to the dangerous elements of society. Whether an Outlaw, Copperhead or Hells Angels, fear was set in stone. Dangerous were the capabilities of the biker, when riding with the notorious bike gangs. The reputation that had developed through the years left unquestionable fear and mistrust due to the killing and drug involvement. The different gangs demonstrated the rage within their hearts and minds. The biker wanted freedom to live their way. No one having control over their thoughts and actions, the different bikers still ended up being controlled by organizations. The insecurities were hidden by the patch showing to whom they belong to.

There were bikers riding into Ocean City who rode amongst friends not belonging to any group. Husbands and wives sharing time together, found a way to escape with others who just loved the ride bringing them closer to the creation. Freedom came with the wind, blowing in their faces. Laying the bike down low on curves was an adrenaline rush for all those just wanting to ride. Not needing approval from any man to enjoy their freedom. The lone wolf still ran in packs.

The reputation was a stench that the Christian ministry bikers knew and understood. Riding vehicles of grace, many had been bikers their whole lives. Jesus revealed himself in a moment of devastation of some sort. Some from prison and others brought back to life after a debilitating wreck, all receiving a transformation of the heart was sent back to those they knew. The preachers were given the burden for others who were trapped in the snares of the demonic controlled realm of wickedness. They accepted the rebel warrior call.

The attitude of some of the workers of the boardwalk stores dreaded seeing the bikers come into the stores. Voices uttering ridicule, hoped they wouldn't come to their stores. I looked up to the heavens and say audibly, "Lord, please send their customers my way." With extreme judgment being cast out, it caused me to defend the ones that showed the attitude to be free. Not only did I want to see the business succeed but was thrilled I would be able to check out the different bikes. I wished I had never gotten rid of my husband's bike. The sportster was one made in 1976 right before Harley Davidson went bankrupt. When John passed away, I tried to learn to ride without his direction. The Harley ended up being walked home as I began despising the treasured token for bringing into reality my emptiness. It became a constant reminder of my loss. The bike was to be Terrance's when he became old enough to ride it. The seeds of the rebel freedom was in this child and he would be "bad to the bone" on it. I remembered seeing him sitting on the bike more than once, when he thought no one saw him. I had been afraid Terrance would end up dying in the ultimate rush for freedom. The loss could be felt still while listening to the girl who knew nothing of freedom. What right did she have to judge her husband? He was a biker. He was just a "good" biker.

I felt the adrenaline rush as the bikes roared on the street. The sound of the pipes screamed out to me from the depths of my soul. There was no fear just excitement. Counting blessings, I gave God thanks for the experience of enjoying the bike week through His protection plan. Would I meet another couple like Robert and Norma? Married for years, they learned to be one with each other on the bike. Norma loved riding on the back with her husband in control. As I rode with Pork Chop, I was impressed with the two in front of us. They exhibited freedom united as one, on the bike that made other bikers watch in amazement. Driving down the road at a good speed, Norma put her arms out. Seconds later, Robert could be seen letting go of the handle bars. Extending his arms out, the couple's hands were joined together. As they would go around a curve to the right, I saw the two lean at the same time to the right. The bike was being controlled by the two leaning and riding together as one. The same would happen when the curve went to the left. The couple had learned to trust the other and experienced freedom together in a beautiful oneness with the bike.

The loud rumble of bikes brought me back to the task at hand; finish up the t-shirt displaying the 'choices' of the attitude of the biker's heart. I had tried to prep the two Russian girls working. There was no way to explain the attitude and behavior they would confront. Language wasn't the only barrier. Fear and intimidation would walk in soon enough. A biker and his wife had come in earlier that week. The man was insulted when one of the girls compared his Harley to a moped. I wanted to laugh but the attitude of the biker showed he was insulted. He tried explaining the huge difference that had caused so much disgust. He also explained the difference between the biker and any other customer they had worked with. The smile setting on the naïve faces only agitated him. To no avail the language and cultural barrier was too wide spread. It was obvious the girls were virgins to the hard core culture. The biker said, "You better work with them or the bikers will chew 'em up and spit 'em out. This is no place for the naïve!" I knew he was right.

The reality of the dangers involved was not hidden from me but knew they wouldn't understand. Trusting in YAHWEH NISSI, the LORD my banner and protector[1] was in charge of the store so no one would mess with the girls or me. The beauty and innocence of the girls was more for concern. One was studious looking. With the dress style of prim and proper, her air of dignity showed she was determined to succeed. Observing the bikers brought the student 'learning from experience' to step out of her. Somewhat afraid to talk to them but willing to help if they weren't scary looking. She would help the customers that didn't look like bikers to try to sell them. Striving to sell to people that dressed and acted like what she was accustomed to. The other was a complete opposite. Her dress style was definitely what would attract them. Having a cute figure and a skirt length stopping at the buttocks there was not much left to the imagination. Where the language barrier fell short, the message still was received. Entice with sex, watch men buy. With her beauty, I was aware there could be issues that could stir even the meanest biker to crave this beautiful peach. Only I wasn't going to let anyone pick the fruit under my watch. The girl was definitely afraid of the men but welcomed the advances that were made.

Biker after biker came into the store. Some held a presence that was a tad bit scary even to me. All of the rebels for freedom were buying t-shirts to commemorate their bike week adventure. The ability of heat transfer was to carry a message for all to know they had been a part of bike week. The art work displayed on the shirt was chosen by the wearer, reflecting their deep thoughts. From hard core skull and serpents to the simply elegant bike with "Live Free" the outstanding proportions, of the man's thoughts were on exhibit. Some creating an illusion of their dark side, while others were abhorred at just the display of anything so demonically evil. Several people were bold in stating their comments to me, "How can you support this. Casting their judgmental looks at me, I wondered if they knew I was a Christian. Did the light of the Lord show forth, is that why they judged[2] so harshly? Whether I agreed or not, I wasn't to judge the customers' choice.

After the condemnation and guilt settled in, a breath of fresh air entered the store. There were two men and a woman that were looking for the perfect t-shirt. The group wanted something that looked "bad" but needed a hint of humiliation to be brought to the surface. Browsing through the biker decals than looking to the humor and questionable suggestive options, the group did not seem satisfied with the different choices that could be printed. Laughing and jeering at the one man in the group they asked me to create a special shirt just for the friend. The situation was an original. I couldn't help but laugh with the group. Joyfully sharing the dilemma of his biker bud, he wanted to have a constant reminder of Ocean City Bike Week. The embarrassed and humiliated tough guy blushed to have the details aired out for the world to hear.

The two friends, after riding in, went down to the beach. They were going to go boogie boarding. Never experiencing the rush of going up against the magnificent powerful ocean, the thrill for adventure came alive. He no longer wanted to just observe but wanted the personal involvement with the board against the waves. A man in mid-life desired to challenge himself to try the unknown. The thrill for life was alive in him. He saw an expression of freedom that only the strongest of surfers could master. He wanted to experience the exhilaration of riding the wave. As the man took the challenge of adventure, he felt alive. Laughing and gulping the salt water, the adrenaline rush was extreme. Then the great body of water took a piece of the man. The powerful opposition overpowered his mouth. The man's teeth were sucked right out of the man's open mouth. The extreme intent to challenge such a great opponent had left the man with mixed emotions, pride of accomplishment and an embarrassing smile. Most people had no clue the man had false teeth. Now a t-shirt was needed to express the tough biker dude losing a part of himself in Ocean City. Even the embarrassed man smiled, at the thought there would be a remembrance of his adventure. His teeth could be replaced but the memory of his daring spectacular challenge of dominance would last forever. They would go shopping while I worked on it.

When they left the store I made a sign and hung it up so people could hopefully find the lost teeth. The man had stated how expensive they were and hoped someone would find them. After posting the sign within minutes another couple came into the store. They had seen the "choppers" down on the beach. The great body of water had washed up the evidence for all to see. Someone had challenged and lost a piece of him. I sent a co-worker down the beach to look for the teeth. He came back without them. The rebellious choppers didn't want to be found!

Wrapped up in the whole scenario, I began looking at all the different decals hoping to come up with what had been requested. Taking note of all the facts I began writing the words that seemed to automatically flow into my head. Wanted! Rebellious choppers lost in Ocean City. Now it was critical to find the right biker decal to put with the words. I looked up and my mouth dropped. Right in front of me was a decal that said, "Rebellious Choppers". The skull displaying a huge set of chopper teeth had a smile that voiced silently, "I dare you to mess with me." The large empty sockets showed the hollowness of the darkness. With a confederate flag in the background the face screamed with the statement of rebellion and freedom at the same time. Instilling fear and possible anger to those that were against the symbol of the flag, the world would know this man was not to be messed with.

I looked forward to the return of the group. The message was loud and clear to the events that had transpired. Yet, as I looked at the statement, I saw a different message. All the bikers were welcome in my store. I had used the summer to witness and encourage people of all walks of life, faith, and race. Standing in awe, I was there to encourage, witness, and give the message of Grace to the rebellious lost bikers. Judging the attire of man was not to be seen from me. I was only to see men and women needing encouragement and hope. When I was to speak the door would be opened to the one challenging the amazing Sea of Grace.

The rebellious one spewing forth curses against Almighty would finally with curiosity dive into the sea wanting more. Just as the biker no longer wanted to sit and watch from the shore those enjoying the water, so was the spiritual man. The soul searching for truth would no longer want to sit and watch others receive life[3] in abundance surmounted by peace. Struggling with animosity toward God and man finally would courageously test the water of faith. A tongue that used to deny the existence of Jesus would proclaim His living within him. Exchanging curses for praises, the redeemed one would have his mouth touched by the Holy Spirit. The power of the tongue would be like a double-edged sword[6], fighting Satan for the souls riding the highway to hell. The empty eye sockets would become windows to the soul. Vision with depth would see beyond the physical into the spiritual realm. The warrior would see the real enemy and its legions coming against people he cared about. The rebel flag in the background would be draped by a banner of love. The redeemed biker would rebel against the forces of evil. Standing up and raising the hand to conquer the demonic forces winning the destructive souls. The redeemed biker was riding for the kingdom on the highways and byways, one ride at a time. The "Bad to the Bone" would minister to the hard hearted biker world.

The blood commonly seen with the gangs of violence was part of the initiation into the brotherhood showing the one joining was down for the cause. The preachers of Grace were initiated into the kingdom brotherhood by the blood of the Leader himself. The garments of wickedness[4] were rolled in Jesus blood. Sharing the dedication and devotion from the Leader, the greatly redeemed hoped to see only Jesus blood spilt on the bikers ride for freedom. The one that is redeemed from the lifestyle understood a deeper level of Grace. The strong in 'Grace freedom' rider wants to convince those bent on traveling the Highway to Hell there is a better ride. Once experiencing the same pain and shame, the messenger of Grace now, 'lives to ride' and 'rides to live' the King's Highway, which is the Way of Holiness[5]. Jesus didn't make them give up their bike instead wanted to use it as the vehicle of Grace that could take them further than ever imagined. Love would shine brighter than the chrome shining on the bike. Amazing love would take on an enemy that held fear and anger.

*   *   *

In the deep caverns below, Satan was seething. The disaster had once again been turned around and left a solid message in this faith walker's mind. Was this woman willing to challenge his authority over those that he held a solid grip on? The contempt he had for this woman who was constantly causing resistance in his tyranny, had to be contended with. "I will send one that is Pagan up against her. Satan started laughing, "Watch this woman who likes to stand firm, quiver at the presence of one of my Pagan followers. She knows nothing of the Pagan, so she will be afraid of him." The Spirits of Control and Anger brought a legion with them and stood beside the intimidating biker.

*   *   *

The anger in the man's spirit was strong. The demonic world had been an integral part of his life, so he knew how to exercise the power of control and fear over others. With the articulated voice of mastery he faced me with a bold message, "real bikers do not wear those t-shirts. They do not want to advertise who they belong to. You should be afraid of the real biker! You should be terrified of me, I am a Pagan! We have stripped people, homes and businesses leaving nothing but death and destruction behind us. Blood trails of our reigning still hang in the balance. Do not challenge our power and authority for terror will be fall you."

I knew the colors were not to be shown at all in Ocean City or they would be escorted out. Not concerned about what group he belonged to, my God promised protection. I knew he needed to leave the store. My colors, represented by Jesus righteousness of crimson, white and trimmed in gold must have been showing through for the spirits within the man knew to come directly to me not one of the girls. Thankful for that, I stood with courage and spoke. "Real bikers or real demons controlling man, which are you? Real bikers want freedom. Bikers controlled by demons only know slavery, they are told who to kill or destroy. Jesus wants to give the biker real freedom. You have a choice, freedom or choosing to be controlled by Satan. Choosing to do evil keeps one constantly on the run. Freedom eludes the one choosing to follow a life of theft, cruelty and destruction. If you do not receive freedom in this life, neither will you obtain it in the next. The attitude of the man in the store went from angry and controlling to sheer hatred. He hollered, "You know nothing. You will experience the depth of fear you should have toward the real biker." With no fear, I stood dumbfounded as the man stormed out of the store. I wasn't done talking. I wanted to say, "I wouldn't want to wear flames of fire showing my future habitat either." I was curious why he came in the store, belligerent, just to proclaim such arrogance.

*　　*　　*

In the caverns of hell, Satan was seething. The arrogance of that woman! She wasn't afraid of that biker at all. The legions couldn't do anything for the angels with their weapons drawn and ready to attack stood all around Terri. What was going on? Her store was known for being personal and fun. The bikers were telling other bikers clear on the other end of the boardwalk about the girl that customizes whatever you want. Satan looked in on the store. There was a long line waiting for customized shirts. Was it laughter he was hearing? The groups gathered and waiting for their t-shirts to be made were not looking tuff or bothered for having to wait. The groups of different biker groups had left their hostility outside the building. They were talking football? Another avenue took their minds off their waiting. Rival biker groups were pulling together and having fun. Satan couldn't take it anymore. He motioned the demons standing outside the store to follow him. The angels in the store put down their weapons that halted the demons from walking into the store.

*   *   *

The presence of the Lord put joy into the room. It wasn't a religious gathering it was a relationship gathering. Jesus had fun helping me work and talk with the customers. The Russian girls which had started out scared started smiling and just watched the group as the bikers socialized without alcohol, sex or drugs. They were having fun even though some didn't know Jesus was there. They just liked being in the store and said they were going to have the rest of their group shop there. I knew why people were having fun. Jesus was in my store and that made everything better.

PEARL DROPS OF WISDOM

1. And Moses built an altar and called the name of it JEHOVAHNISSI (the LORD my banner)

   Exodus 17:15 NIV

2. But I say unto you, love your enemies and pray for those who persecute you.

   Matthew 5:44 NIV

3. From the lips of children and infants you have ordained praise because of your enemies, to silence the foe and the avenger.

   Psalm 8:2 NIV

4. Every warriors boot used in battle and every garment rolled in blood will be destined for burning, will be fuel for the fire.

   Isaiah 9:5 NIV

5. A highway will be there; it will be called the Way of Holiness. The unclean will not journey on it; wicked fools will not go about on it.

   Isaiah 35:8 NIV

Chapter 10

New Chapter of a Faith-walker

Here it was already fall and the first time I had three days off in a row. The last six months seemed like a whirl wind in my mind as I took a deep breath of fresh air. Enjoying the warmth of the Indian summer, I began to swing on the playground outside the hotel. With a gust of wind, a shiver went down my spine. Feeling the tension drift with the clouds being brought together by the wind, the air slowly drifted apart only to bring life to another spot in the heavens. Just as the natural force of air caused the clouds to move, the spirit had moved powerfully bringing people of every color and race into the store. Just as the cloud was there for a moment so were the people in my life. They drifted in and danced out. As one would try to determine the image in the cloud, was there a distinguishing difference seen in the store as customers drifted in? Was there a genuine sense of being cared about like a person of importance? Whether money was spent or not, did people leave richer?

Being a child of a King, had I left an unmistakable imprint on people's lives where my citizenship[1] belonged to? Would encouragement, love, and joy be the testimony or had they left feeling judged and hated. Was the request for the Lord's face to shine on me as the sun shines on the water, answered? Was there a reflection seen that glistened with evidence of His love and faithfulness?

Watching the clouds multiplying, I began to feel the chill in the air. The fall leaves were dancing around me. The term of servant-hood on the boardwalk was coming to an end. Just as the leaves that were dancing around then blowing away, so were my summer friends and acquaintances. Co-workers from Russia and Israel were heading back to the countries they had come from. Nepalese friends were going back to the colleges that they desired to graduate from. All had intermingled in each others' lives, like the leaves dancing. The sound from the rustling in the wind left a song behind that echoed with a roughness as the leaves would hit the pavement or objects in their way.

What kind of melody was heard in the heavens as the great crowd of witnesses looked on? Was there a rejoicing praise on the lips of any on earth thanking God for a fruitful season? Was there a genuine gentle caring melody heard or was it hard core heavy metal full of harshness and bitterness and cruelty? I realized the opinions of the separated were all one sided as each one looked at the other through their own rose tinted glasses. Each individual with their own unique opinions and thoughts would cause ripple effects that would be felt and passed on to their loved ones in other countries.

Jesus had laid out a three day retreat where He could admonish, encourage, and direct my path once again. I wanted to go camping. Just sit by the fire and write. A hot tub would help me unwind. The Lord laid on my heart, the driving ten hours to Hot Springs and back would be exhausting; rest was needed. Directing me to a hotel in West Ocean City that had trees, I felt surrounded by nature. There was a hot tub right in my room. While checking in the lady said, "I'm going to up-grade your room for the same price. I have a room with a fireplace in the middle of your room and a hot tub." I was dumb founded. "Oh thank you! That would be awesome! In my heart, "Oh thank you Lord. What a marvelous gift." Walking into the room, it was simply elegant with gold hue curtains open and the sun shining into the room. The golden color stitch in the comforter had a shimmer because of the rays shining into the room. I felt like a gift of heaven had been opened up to me.

Suddenly I had mixed emotions, elation and loneliness. There was no one to tell or share it with. This room cried out it was to be shared with someone. I had watched people all summer who were in love and sharing their lives. The room felt very big and lonely. With the sudden realization that the kids were raised and husband gone, I was facing myself for the first time. I tried calling family to share the joy. Terrance and Tiffany couldn't be reached, which made my reality even more depressing.

I no longer carried the title, single parent raising teenagers. Learning and sharing the beach life with Terrance, we became close friends not just mother and son. Shortly after moving, Terrance met the girl of his dreams. Tiffany had a rare exquisite beauty with a kind gentle spirit. Having some spit fire too, the girl was everything Terrance had wanted. He left his mother and clung to his wife[2] like he was supposed to. The empty nest syndrome hadn't snuck upon me; instead it came crashing in like the fifteen foot waves that would crash on shore. Standing in this beautiful room, the realization of no one to share it with left an overwhelming sense of wanting to be needed and longed for. Desperation to be loved and to love someone caused agony from deep within.

Life had changed so radically when John passed away. Three teenagers left at home were constantly battling depression. With hearts no longer believing in the God they were raised with, they found solace in drugs. Fighting for their lives against authority, health issues and the faith, I kept my own feelings locked inside. I asked the Lord to fill the emptiness with more Jesus. Facing the loss at different times but reminding myself; the living needed help not the dead. Standing on the promise of raise up a child in the Lord, when they were old[3] they would come back to the faith. I wanted to help carry them till they were able to stand up and walk again. Arriving on God's time table, they were walking and once again growing in the faith. Not the exact thoughts of mine but each one had experienced a moment where the Almighty revealed himself to them. The Author was about his business directing their lives. What should I do now? What would happen to the characteristics that God had instilled of love and nurturing others?

I stared in the mirror as the reality of no one to share my life with jumped out of the mirror. My reflection staring back at me seemed all distorted. There was no joy, no strength and no hope. It was as if instantly I realized my age and station in life; fifty year old widow with no hope of love again. Was it the love of John that kept me going? Maybe it was the promises of keeping the children together no matter what? Sagging to the floor, I wept.

*   *   *

The raging Demon of Loneliness had been waiting for this moment for a long time. Throughout the summer he had deliberately caused situations to arise so he could have a constant poisonous venom drip running. Satan smiled as the demon continued to slowly penetrate into the deepest levels of Terri's thinking. The climactic moment had arrived. Satan sat on his throne laughing at the broken woman. She hadn't expected this extreme emotion to come alive. Rubbing his hands with glee, he let out a horrendous laugh that rocked clear into the heavens. The demons started dancing around with delight as the anguish poured from the dark well of sorrow. The Spirit of Loneliness was slowly tearing the heart into pieces.

*   *   *

With the wicked sinister laugh echoing through to the heavens the crowd gathered to see what was causing the heavens to rumble. All were mystified as they watched the bent over woman sobbing into folded hands. With the beauty of the surroundings they could not understand why the woman was crying so hard. Missing all the beginning events, they knew the woman was in dire need of healing. They watched as Jesus knelt beside the dear child of his. He wrapped his loving arms around her and let her sob on His shoulder. He had brought her to the place where he had wanted to pour out his love for her. It was time for her to face her fears. The time of healing was to start today in the place that he had chosen for her to receive her victory. He helped her stand up and walked her to the bed where he gently laid her down. Totally exhausted she slept with Jesus sitting beside her. He knew this would be a hard battle to fight for the love that she had shared with one, could not be shared with another till she cut the soul ties. He had shared special moments with her all summer. Different situations in her life had started yearning to experience greater love again. The next three days would be wonderful as they shared the retreat together. The divine touch created plans that would forever change the heart and life.

He was tickled to see she loved the room. Jesus smiled as he remembered the expression when she was told there would be a fireplace in the room. Her soft excited, "thank you" made his heart leap. Jesus loved her beyond words and desired to see the enthusiasm light up her face again. He whispered, "You have sown seeds of Grace with many tears but you will have songs of joy as we carry the sheaves together. I will never leave you.[4] I have much more to pour out on you. I want to impress you with my goodness, my precious bride.

Pearl Drops of Wisdom

1. But our citizenship is in heaven. We eagerly await a savior from there, the Lord Jesus Christ.

    Philippians 3:20 NIV

2. For this reason a man will leave his father and mother and be united to his wife, and they will become one flesh.

    Genesis 2:24 NIV

3. Train up a child in the way he should go and when he is old, he will not depart from it.

    Proverbs22:6 KJV

4. For he hath said, I will never leave thee nor forsake thee.

    Hebrews 13:5 KJV

Chapter 11

Love Story

Awakened by hunger pains, I laid on the bed gazing at the now darkened room. Looking around, the giddiness of my surroundings kicked in once again. With the logs burning in the fireplace I savored the goodies brought, as the hot tub filled. Gazing at the fire, peace came over me. The warmth from the fire was as if the flames were jumping, extending long arms that wrapped a loving embrace around me. Submerged in the warm water, the world seemed no longer to exist with its cares and burdens. The feelings of sorrow and loneliness that had surfaced and bubbled up just hours before were drifting off with the rising steam, leaving total satisfaction. Drifting in thought to the last time I had been in a hot tub.

Once again thoughts automatically went to the love that had been shared with John. Tears welled up at the thought of intimacy shared as if it was yesterday. The private moment had been deliberately initiated by my lover in order to show his affection for his bride without the children. As the lovers snuck away in the middle of the night, the passion was shown. I was still the most important thing to him. I blurted out, "Why did you have to take him from me! With all the children needing two parents, we wanted the best. I know you could have touched him with your healing hand. Why didn't you? If you hadn't taken him, my kids wouldn't have messed up their lives so radically. Taking him left anger, resentment, and a longing in each one of them. The battles would not have been the same, if you would have let them have both parents. They would have turned out better. I tried my best but my best wasn't good enough. There is not enough good in the world and you took what was good out of our lives."

The heated bubbling water held no comparison to the bubbling heated battle going on in the depths of my soul. Self-pity was directed toward the loss my children suffered. As I poured out my anger, resentment, and pain the heavens could see the anger directed toward God. All the feelings buried deep in the depths of my soul were now coming to light. Fighting battle after battle for the children I had not dealt with the loss of my husband at all. Everyone could see the depth of the love that had been locked inside the heart and mind. I would only share the little tokens when it was deemed necessary to friends, family, and acquaintances in order to minister to them. I never let people see the intimate feelings felt for the man I saw as perfect.

* * *

In the heavens, the crowd of witnesses watched as this powerful woman of faith deliberately judged this righteous holy God. With all the bitterness in her soul the crowd stood aghast to think someone would come so boldly before the throne and tell him how things could have been better for her and her family. As they watched the challenging attitude toward someone who cared so desperately, the crowd all turned toward John. In his humbleness, his eyes dropped to the marble floor that he was standing on. Tears welled up in his eyes as he watched his bride of seventeen years pour out the agony she felt. The loss of her friend and lover had definitely been festering within her mind and spirit for a long time. After turning the table of the disadvantage of no father through the critical teenage years, to the ultimate loss of her best friend, Bible partner, and lover the woman seemed so confused. John had no idea how The Redeemer could resolve her issues. John watched as the Lord received the tongue lashing, Jesus touched Terri's forehead. John watched Terri fall asleep.

* * *

As I slept, Jesus gently took me by the hand and led us on walk through time. Showing the past in a way I had never seen before. Walking in the desert, I came up on a house that looked empty and worn out from the outside. It had many different rooms unique in its own way. I noticed the Lord waited for me to open the door. The first room was nothing spectacular. The wood floor was worn by time. There was a trail engraved in the floor showing wear and tear from walking. There were two rocking chairs placed in front of a fireplace. The old wooden table had a Bible sitting open. A towel hung over the chair that showed it had been used a lot but still in mint condition. I asked the Lord, "Where are we?" Jesus smiled and answered softly, "My favorite room. This is where I waited everyday in the rocking chair for you to get up in the morning. You enjoy the fire, so I made sure it was inviting. Notice the bible on the table is worn. Pages are torn because you dug it apart to search for answers. I enjoyed talking to you daily."

"Many times you brought heavy luggage with you to the room. I rejoiced when in brokenness, the old worn out clothes of self-righteousness were thrown out. It was harder to convince you to let Me throw away your heavy loads.[1] Did you not trust My word of casting all your care upon Me for I care for you[2]? Your heavy burdens weren't too heavy for Me. I went beside and helped carry the yoke placed on you because of the cares of the world.

Notice there is no mirror in here, so you can't look at yourself. Once you only saw me, you started choosing to put on the garments laid out daily. I like to call it the garments of praise. Look at your gown you have on. There is no stain from sin. The gown of My salvation is laid out fresh and pure daily. So all you need to do is rejoice at the robe of My righteousness.[3] Wearing the garment of evil containing every sin imaginable to his death, Jesus was buried in my rotten burial clothes. Leaving the filthiness in the grave, Jesus rose with power, majesty and glory. No longer was the apparel of black on me but the garment was white, as pure snow.[4] Wearing the robe of righteousness meant I live guilt free. "Yes," I said, "It is a garment of praise."

I stopped at the chair and picked up the towel. Jesus watched as I rubbed the towel across my cheek. He spoke gently, "That towel has been used many times to dry your tears. As you wept for your loved ones and yourself, your prayers were mingled with sorrow. I heard and answered. Sometimes I just let you sob on my shoulder." Tears welled up, looking at Jesus' robe. The color had been drained on his shoulders as if the tears had a corrosive agent that was meant to reveal the agony that was shared between two friends. Jesus was my friend that was there through the hard times; closer than any brother.[5]

I looked around and up. There was no light in the room yet the room had a beautiful golden relaxing hue that was magnificent. Jesus noticed the interested curiosity on my face. Like a light bulb that was turned on in my thinking, I smiled and pointed at Him. "You are the light[6]. No other light is needed." I began to understand. I was taken to my own personal inner self, the domain that Jesus chose to dwell in with me. As the Lord built the new house within, my life changed. I was going to see the different areas of life where God had been allowed to reside. Where I built the house, labor was in vain. The literal shell was nothing as well as me trying to develop kindness, tenderness, patience and self-control. As the light exposed the areas of my life, I would see what the Father saw. Was I ready for what the "Light" wanted to expose in the dark deep hidden[7] depths of my soul? Jesus saw the fear and shame in my eyes. He took my hand and led me to the rocking chairs sitting in front of the warm inviting fire.

"When you were carrying your heavy loads, you did a lot of pacing." Jesus said. "The path is worn on the floor." Jesus pointed. "There were times you wouldn't even let the load be taken off your back when you sat down." I noticed the chair had been scratched up. "I would convince you to hand the burden over. When done with our morning of sharing, you picked up your load and walked out the door. You didn't hear me say, you can leave that here. I'll throw it out for you." I blushed with embarrassment. He knew I blamed him for robbing me of my one true love? Carrying John's torch of love wasn't a burden. It was all I had left. A cloud of awkwardness was in the horizon of the light in the room, in spite of being in the presence of the king. Curiosity directed the walk to the next room of what was to be revealed.

He took me to the 'room of firsts'. I could see many of the beginnings of life with John. Love permeated throughout the room, as the many "firsts" were with him. As I took each step, recognition of the many photographs on the wall; first love, first marriage, first time in Alaska. The memories came alive at the remembrance of sliding down the snowy mountain in Canada on a garbage can lid. Snuggled in his arms I felt the embrace as we watched and listened to the Northern Lights dancing across the sky. My face radiated as I savored pictures on the wall of John and our life together. Reliving each moment brought back so many of the lost memories due to having mini-strokes. Oh, the joy to have a room of such beautiful loving moments captured through time. To see the display of love so lavishly poured out through so many different important time periods.

Jesus noticed there was barely a glance at the rest of the 'firsts' in the room. No attention was given to when I accepted the Lord. The first day of real life, was a joyous day in the heavens. Yet I acted as if it was a simple thing. In a picture, I was a little girl asking Jesus, The Savior to save me from sin and death. Pain winced in the Savior's heart etching across His face. It was as if the 'firsts' that He held dear, were not as dear to me. Walking past the picture of my baptism, it just looked like I was standing in the water, wet. He watched as I walked past the first soul I had introduced to the Lord. Glancing but not even stopping to look at the face, for there was no recognition. It saddened the Lord, for the soul who needed intercessory prayer from the beginning was forgotten. Within days, the girl had been forgotten because of the clutter within my heart. The participation in the memorial of the bread and wine was noticed for a brief moment but then passed. The room of firsts hadn't stirred my heart toward the things of the heavenliest. The precious firsts of miracles, healing, and praise offerings were over shadowed by the reminiscing of the firsts with my physical realm. With so many precious memories robbing me of thinking on John, it was as if the love was rekindled for him. Jesus understood the deep longing for love. He was trying to get my attention for what He desired for me. He wanted to be the never ending, my "FIRST" love. Jesus wondered, when would I recognize He was my groom? He longed for a depth of love, more than I loved John.

After spending time reminiscing, the Lord encouraged me to enter another room. There were knights in shiny armor standing at attention with different weapons of war. By the gaze, one could feel the power of confidence and control just glancing around. The strength of character was hopefully from the Lord. In the center of this extravagant room there was a swimming pool. The pool looked so inviting, yet I continued to look at the knights holding the different weapons. Intrigued by the unusual looking instruments of deadly warfare, I walked up to one of the mighty men of valor. I studied the weapon carefully. Flabbergasted to recognize the weapon, I covered my mouth. The tongue the knight held on his silver platter was really two tongues. They were sharp and looking like daggers; one mine the other was Johns. Both had used the daggers to help encourage and proclaim love. While at other times the tongues had been used to hurt. I looked on the screen behind the knight. Observing the challenge I promoted at different times. I saw many times John didn't want to fight but after the continued badgering, he would take the weapon that I handed to him. I knew my tongue held power more powerful than a double edge sword. Not willing to have to confront the manifestations being revealed on the wall, I turned away and continued walking. Embarrassed beyond words, I walked up to another knight.

The Bible was being held in his armored hands. My face turned different shades of crimson. I remembered the battles that were fought using the Old Testament against the New Testament. Jehovah Witness verses Baptist faith. With both of us having strong capabilities of using the scripture to prove the other wrong, neither willing to back down. The ripple effects being portrayed on the wall behind the knight was like a video running to the present day. I could see the many battles my children had about religion were because of the seeds of strife due to lifting up a 'religion', both using the inspired word of God.

Then I saw ripples in the pool behind me. I realized this was not an ordinary swimming pool. The pool was a Grace washing one faith, one truth, one doctrine. Not as many things were going into the Grace Pool as I thought would be. When least expected, I would see the battle or a stand of victory submerged into the pool. I couldn't understand why the things accomplished for God had been thrown into the fireplace at the end of the room instead of the pool. Was Christ's righteousness not over my works?

When I took stands that Jesus wasn't an angel, the stand of victory was Grace recognized. Taking the stand against a Mormon friend, who believed Jesus was a brother to Satan it was submerged for it was Grace revealed. Every time I announced things I was doing for God, none of it went into the graced water. Why wasn't it submerged, I was scared to ask? Jesus noticed the curiosity in my face. "When you lift up the things you do instead of what I am doing, it is cast in the fire. Praise given to you takes praise away from my divine working so it cannot last. As your works are tested it is thrown into the fire for it is not lasting.[8]

Works done by the Almighty, showing His power and love was revealed on the screen behind the knight. I could not understand why sometimes when an act was done, I saw the face of an ox, other times I saw Jesus' face. The faces[9] that were being shown on the screen behind the knight, showed the faces of the man, the ox, the lion, and the eagle intermingled with a job I did for him but was not aware anything was done. It seemed to be, when I was not aware I was being used. When a person was talked to and a seed of salvation was planted, the face of an ox was seen on me. Praise to the King, the lion was seen. Sitting at the feet of Jesus learning more Grace, the eagle was seen. Different times of service to people, the face of the servant Jesus was seen.

The scenes throughout terrible lonely time periods alternately changed to a lamb bellowing out. It looked like it was lost. Then I would see the Shepherd. He gently whispered my name. The lamb would frolic back to him. The screen than showed the victory over the moment of confusion. Questions how the sheep know the shepherd's voice[10] displayed the events in my life that brought me to the answer.

The Lord responded not by works; nothing of me except for the asking. Jesus showed the day I began pleading for His voice, without the Bible. Talk to me like you talked to Abraham, Isaac, and Jacob. Suffering from mini-strokes, I lost the ability to move the left side. It hurt to walk. The inability to use the left arm, I fought for mobility. The most degrading aspect of the mini-strokes was the inability to think or remember. All freedom to move, remember or read the Bible was an impossibility. The words couldn't be formed in my thoughts. I had learned direction, correction, and encouragement from the written word. Yet in a moment, all I could remember was Jesus loves me.

Driven by sheer determination that was placed in the heart, the Lord whispered, "Healing is given through the healing in the heart." Harboring unforgiveness and hatred, the anger was faced. The strokes were being brought on because of child-abuse. Believing as my heart was healed by the Great Physician, the gift of mobility would be given. Jesus took one disease of the soul at a time. My testimony is "Amazing Grace" healed me. After hearing audibly it set the heart for hearing more. Jesus whispered, "I love talking to you. You had learned the only way that I spoke was through the Holy Bible, yet I saw you as a friend. I talked to you from the beginning. You just learned to listen.

The Grace Pool was a crimson color as the different events were displayed on the screen the pool could be seen washing the situations with Grace. Right before my eyes the glory of the Lord shown through and faces were seen through the water. Many of the faces I recognized. I had encountered them through my life. I asked the Lord what it all meant. Jesus smiled. "These were the lives that were affected through the tests of your faith. People were watching the physical events and disasters. Their lives were changed by My Glory while they watched Me step into each one of your battles. All things are to My Glory. You heard about the butterfly effect? Your life was on display for the whole world to see. Each battle, each sorrow was seen by others so that in the end it helped softens the hearts and encourages others. My children's lives were changed by watching Me change you. "Jesus said. "I showed you 'Grace' so that you might preach the Kingdom of God to my people who have been burdened down." **The Kingdom of God is not a matter of talk but of power.**[11]

"Much of the service you were doing for the church was not what I had called you to do. I saw your heart and blessed you in-spite of wanting to use you in a different area. I showed up wherever you chose to share with others. Your choices were not always wise than you began to ask for wisdom." I watched the different displays of loyalty to the churches shown. I was embarrassed and ashamed to think there was something I turned down from the great I AM. He was all knowing and all powerful and I chose to listen to man's needs for me instead of His coaxing. I was humbled before the still small voice.

Then I saw the ripples in the pool. Jesus smiled. "I AM in you and through your faith in trusting ME at my every word and action; you learned to trust the heeding of My spirit. You were a challenge because of your strong will but I needed a challenger with boldness and courage to help break the hold of religion on earth. When you came into agreement that My will be done on earth as it is in heaven, I was invited once again into another believers life to rock the world around them. Satan has no hold on you since we are united."

Walking on I saw one of the knights, weapons of war was stone tablets. I recognized the Ten Commandments. Beside the commandments of stone was a heart that had writing on it. Jesus whispered, "I wrote what was important on your heart." The letters written in blood said, "Love ME. I AM The IAM.[12] Love Me with all your heart, all your soul and all your might."[13] The other thing written, I started quoting for I had memorized it years ago." Love your neighbor as you love yourself". Jesus just raised a hand and pointed to the heart. Love others the way I love you. Questioning what was written, He answered, "You won't want to break the hearts of others." You will want the best even for your enemy. With each one of the displays, ripple effects of the manifestation of the battles were revealed. Tradition, religion, and self-centeredness were what influenced most of the decoration surrounding the different knights. The haunting unforgiving past influenced all the battles. I wanted to flee but fell to my knees. The reality of how much time had been wasted on fighting left me speechless.

After a little coaxing, Jesus took me to another room. Entering the 'trophy room', there were many trophies. It almost looked like a sanctuary that had an extension built on to it. I could see a seam line running down the wall and across the floor. It wasn't decorated with the same elegance as the rest of the room by the Master Designer. It held a dark heaviness compared to the rest of the beautifully lit and designed room. Looking at the different trophies, I realized the room was filled with all the wonderful accomplishments. There were crowns and trophies displayed through different time periods. I assumed the trophies were from the martial arts and different activities I had been involved with proclaiming selflessness toward mankind lined up for all to see. Without realizing souls were brought to the Lord. Standing in amazement, my preaching wasn't what changed lives. It was the praise of the redeemed believer that God used to encourage others for something better. The display was extraordinary and impressive. It was nothing of me except a vessel constantly needing protection, direction and miracles. As I looked closer at the different proclamations of excellence, I noticed not one had my name inscribed on it. Each one of the trophies had Jesus name written on it. The trophies had been given to Him by me when I told the world His awesomeness through each battle the family had to confront. Looking around the room the different crowns of glory were displayed. There were crowns to cast at his feet, for He is King of Kings and Lord of Lords.

I saw the crown of thorns and knew when at 9 years old, I allowed him to be Lord of Salvation. I really didn't comprehend how Jesus could die one time for all my sin. Even though I was young, I exhibited the traits of a problem child with many wrong choices ahead. I saw none of the evil things I had done revealed on the screen. I asked Jesus where they were. Jesus smiled and said when I took your sin you became white as snow. Notice the dark stains on me?" I watched the screen and began to sob. The crown of thorns was only understood recently. How amazing was the power of the crown. Shoved on his head the thorns dug into Jesus' pure holy, righteous thinking. The message of love was "Let me exchange your thinking. Give ME your thoughts and I'll give you mine. I rubbed my finger over the sharp pointed dagger thorns that had penetrated the mind of my Savior. The look on Jesus' face showed a sweet sorrow. He knew there was something more to face; the secret in the heart.[14]

Progressing toward the add-on edition, I realized the room didn't have the same peacefulness that the rest of the room held. The darkness beckoned me. With a great sense of fear, cautiously I walked in looking around. The room was empty except for a shelf that was way above my head. What I saw caused me to scream out in horror. Sitting on the shelf surrounded by nothing else was a statue of my precious love. The image of John which couldn't speak or feel, yet the powerful image held a control over my heart and mind. Having no one around to watch or comfort me, the release of emotions poured out which had been bottled up for years. Jesus stood beside His broken child. Facing so many difficult issues He stood beside me with strength and kind words. When ready to talk He would explain to me, the wall and addition built. I was the one who had made an image of a good man to lift up. Teaching the children he was the man to follow, not realizing that the flaws of this man had would bring heart ache. There is none perfect only perfectly forgiven. I had put John up on the shelf above all men. The wall was impenetrable. I had built a high place[15] without realizing it. Jesus knew the room had become too much for his child to handle.

I woke up. I remembered savoring the room of "remembrances" only to have the joy turned to horror. When Christ showed me the wall in the extended room I built with a shelf holding John high above with nothing else allowed in the room. How had I put John on a shelf? Had I not been lifting up Jesus in his exalted glory for years? When had I ever put John in a place he didn't belong? As for the wall, what is that all about? Shaking my head with disillusionment I pondered the lesson that had been given. With shame, I once again considered how much time was wasted fighting. Then it hit me. It wasn't all in vain, for John came to know the Lord. My children had learned to search and question what man taught. To God is the glory for He was the one who allowed John and me to challenge each other's faiths. The result of our searching helped our children tear the sides off the religious God box. The sides were made out of stone. Breaking one law, you've broken them all, made it impossible to enjoy Grace. We all want the ONE TRUE GOD, the author and finisher of the faith. Jesus broke the side walls made of stone. Each one of my family members challenged the faithfulness of love. Jesus didn't use the hammer on us, instead he used the towel on the chair by the fireplace, to wipe our tears.

Pearl Drops of Wisdom

1. Cast they burden upon the LORD, and he shall sustain thee: he shall never suffer the righteous to be moved.

   Psalm 55:22 KJV

2. Cast all your care upon him; for he careth for you.

   I Peter 5:7 KJV

3. I delight greatly in the LORD; my soul rejoices in my God. For he has clothed me with garments of salvation and arrayed me in a robe of his righteousness.

   Isaiah 61:10 NIV

4. "Come now, let us reason together," says the LORD. "Though your sins are like scarlet, they shall be as white as snow; though they are red as crimson, they shall be like wool."

   Isaiah 1:18 NIV

5. There is a friend that sticketh closer than a brother.

   Proverbs 18:24 KJV

6. For my eyes have seen your salvation . . . a light for revelation to the gentiles and for glory to your people Israel.

   Luke 2:30, 32a NIV

7. He will bring to light what is hidden in darkness and will expose the motives of man's heart. At that time each will receive his praise from God.

I Corinthians 4:5b NIV

8. Every man's work shall be made manifest: for the day shall declare it, because it shall be revealed by fire; and the fire shall try every man's work of what sort it is. If any man's work abide which he hath built thereupon, he shall receive his reward. If any man's work shall be burned, he shall suffer loss: but he himself shall be saved; yet so by fire.

I Corinthians 3:13-15 KJV

9. The first living creature was a lion, the second was like an ox, the third had a face like a man, the fourth was like a flying eagle.

Revelation 4:7 NIV

10. My sheep hear my voice, and I know them, and they follow me.

John 10:27 KJV

11. For the Kingdom of God is not a matter of talk but of power.

I Corinthians 4:20 NIV

12. "I tell you the truth," Jesus answered, "Before Abraham was born, I AM.

John 8:58 NIV

13. Love the Lord your God with all your heart and with all your soul and with all your mind.

Matthew 22:37 NIV

14. Shall not God search this out? For he knoweth the secrets of the hearts.

Psalm 44:21 KJV

15. Then ye shall drive out all the inhabitants of the land from before you, and destroy all the pictures, and destroy all their molten images, and quite pluck down all their high places.

Numbers 33:52 KJV

Chapter 12

———— ❧ ————

Call for Love

Hunger pains became intense as I sat writing. As I waited for the food, I found a couple that grasped my attention. The two sitting at the booth in front of me sat quiet. They were an elderly couple, yet they seemed to have what a lot of the youthful couples didn't have. Sitting across from each other they held each other's fingers. The table between the two could not separate what had joined them together. Looking at each other lovingly then glancing around the room, they both turned and looked right at me and smiled. The deep penetrating eyes full of love and tenderness, sent shivers down my spine. Feeling the richness from the depth of their souls, a breath of air fueled a fire for love in me.

The feast set before me was everything I hoped it would be. The tenderness of the steak and the flavor brought all my senses to the fore front. While savoring each bite I couldn't help but look around. Once again my glance turned into a stare, as I watched the elderly couple getting ready to leave. The gentleman was helping the woman to her feet. The compassion and tenderness shown to this woman revealed to the world how much his heart had learned to love his precious jewel. Never seeing or hearing any of the battles, I realized they learned how to love the other more than themselves. As each one did separate offenses learning to forgive ran close behind the battle. With each offense the justification cast blame. How had this couple come out strong without harboring bitterness, anger, or

KINGDOM'S UNVEILED

resentment filtering through their eyes? Are not the eyes the window into the soul? I couldn't help but admire and secretly say to her, "I want that."[1] How many other women hoped their husbands would look lovingly at them.

As he held the coat for her, she slowly put her arms in the sleeves. I realized patience had been learned for the woman moved extremely slowly. It did not seem to bother the groom in the least. The smile she gave him, when she turned around and he started buttoning her long coat, could melt even the coldest of hearts. The man bent down and kissed his bride of many years on the cheek. I smiled and said hello as they walked by my table. The savory meal had lost its appeal. I craved what this couple had, love. The passion to grow old with someone who would love with the tenderness and loving-kindness that was shown by this man to his beloved wife had stifled any appetite that was there.

Drawn to the ocean, the moon's reflection danced on the water. The sound of the waves washing up on the beach, brought with it calm within my spirit. The pressure was as if my head was in a vice. I could feel the tightening in my thoughts but didn't really know how to fix the situation. I was lonely but didn't really know why I couldn't welcome any man into my life. The cool water surfaced at my feet, washing of tenderness seemed to be starting ever so slowly to rid the poisonous toxin labeled 'extreme loneliness'. Particles of pain would surface than drift out to the deepest darkest depths of the sea. Jesus sat beside me on the shore. As I took deep breaths of the salt air, he smiled. I remembered the attitude when I first moved to Ocean City. I couldn't stand the fishy smell. Now I embraced the scent of the sea and the salt.

Noticing the rocking motion as I held on to my legs, Jesus knew the next lesson would be harder than the last one. I hadn't accepted the last healing session very well. The knights holding the different weapons were not bad weapons. All able to defend or attack, the weapons had the ability to heal or destroy. Having to face the different knights holding the weapons of choice that I had so often used, the realization had been overwhelming. Concentrating on the defensive and offensive tactics that were "Terri" used, instead of allowing the Holy Spirit to use, pierced clear to the soul. Jesus wiped a tear from his face. He knew I needed to face the battle, for the future battles could be won using the different weapons. If courage and humbleness would have been welcomed, the righteous weapons I was using properly for spiritual warfare would have be revealed. Instead, I was beating myself up over the 'sanctuary in the high place' I had built and the realization I was still pushing the religious works. The weapons the knights were holding were not the problem. When Jesus was ushering toward the knight holding the vials of selfless prayers, I looked back at the knight holding the love letters (His Word) I had used to condemn and judge. I couldn't forgive myself.

Jesus understood the broken humbleness. He saw me like the bird, I continued to try to coax all summer. "A lesson using a cherished pet would reveal more to her," thought Jesus. I didn't understand He wanted the religious mold to stay broken in my children so that they would continue to preach only Grace! They saw Jesus in a greater proportion. Running away from what I had taught of law and Grace, to the one who would teach abundance of Grace and His righteousness from His heart.[2]

Jesus smiled a soft smile. Even though I didn't really go and gaze upon the tray of praise, he knew that was the one I used most. With every opportunity, praise for Him supernaturally ran in conversations. Continually I was accused of not being able to carry on a conversation without putting Jesus in it. Praise through song and testimony continually rose from deep within. That was His favorite weapon I used, although I wasn't fully aware how powerful the weapon was against the underworld. "Many ripples are going out of a heart singing forth praise to the King," Jesus whispered, "They watched you but remember the melody within their hearts is of Me.[3]

*   *   *

Jesus asked, "How long before she understands I want to be the groom that looks lovingly in her face as she grows old?" The Holy Spirit whispered, "I am prompting her heart. She will understand. Recognizing the position of bride is one that takes time. I will continue to woo her heart through your unfailing love."[4]

Pearl Drops of Wisdom

1. What man desires is unfailing love.

    Proverbs 19:22a NIV

2. He will teach us His ways, so that we might walk in His paths.

    Micah 4:2 NIV

3. May my lips overflow with praise, for you teach me your decrees. May my tongue sing of your word, for all your commands are righteous.

    Psalm 119:171-172 NIV

4. Though he brings grief, he will show compassion so great is his unfailing love.

    Lamentations 3:32 NIV

Chapter 13

Freedom Screams Break Free

The bright new day brought with it a fresh new hope. After spending several hours writing, the moment of relaxation in the hot tub was exactly what was needed. It was amazing how relaxed, for there was not a care in the world. The thoughts of yesterday day were no longer burdens. While enjoying the moment, I drifted off to sleep. The moment was right as the Lord had prepared the next step to healing. In my dream, I was on the beach where most time was spent when I wasn't working. It didn't matter what time of day, the place had become a place of solitude. Waves gently washing up to the shore, I leaned back and took a deep breath of fresh air. The seagulls were flying, swooping down then soaring up as if they were striving to impress the onlooker. In awe and amazement, I was caught up in the moment unaware it was a dream.

I looked for the bird that I loved. It was the only one that seemed to show it had been caught in a snare and managed to survive. The seagull stood on one leg. With the other leg broke off at the joint, the bird had won my affection. Having respect for the bird that chose to continue to compete for the scraps of food being thrown out. With the great announcement from one seagull a multitude of birds would arrive willing to do whatever to obtain the meal sent from the King, by one of his curious servants. The broken legged bird tried hard, only to be beaten by another. He learned to watch me closer. Throwing a piece of bagel out far away with one hand, I would set a bite down on the wall. It was far enough away that the seagull felt like it could trust me. He flew up and ate the cherished morsel. As I threw more out for the others, I continued to give "Stumpy" his tidbit bringing him closer to me.

Was Stumpy out here now flying around? Could she spot him amongst the other seagulls circling around? There was a bird calling out extremely loud in the air. Calling to a seagull that was trying to fly but there was a chain around his ankle. The seagull calling in the heavens screeched so loud it was beginning to bother me. The bird struggling on the chain kept being pulled back so he couldn't soar. With agony pouring forth the bird showed he was being tortured. The desire for freedom was obvious but looked like impossibility. Wanting to show compassion on the seagull, I walked toward the bird. Extreme fear culminated from the fear of being snared and unable to get away. I recognized him. Stumpy began struggling and fighting the chain that held him captive as an excruciating wail flew out of the bird's mouth. I saw the bird fall to the ground. The seagull's leg broke right at the joint. The remainder was left behind still caught in the chain. Tears poured down my face as I listened to the wailing pouring forth from the broken seagull. I walked slowly to the bird to try to help. Out of fear once again the seagull strived to do what it knew, fly. Feeling extremely hot, I woke up. What was he chained to? I forgot to look and see what held the bird from having the ability to fly. The words "break free" rang in my thoughts.

Then I saw a huge wall in front of me. The wall was made of bricks which separated the room. Nothing could be seen past the wall. I could hear a man's voice but there was no way to reach out to the man calling me. The pain and sorrow in his voice left an impending doom in my spirit. Calling out in the spirit for the man that was behind the wall I asked the Lord to pour out His unfailing love on him. I could see the need but did not realize the depth of redemption needed. I knew that God would explain all the details but He would start working on my own issues.

The bird snared with the chain unable to fly was me. The chain was fear that a part of me had died when John died. The Spirit of Fear held the chain all the way from the depths below which would pull up more from the core of my being. With the Spirit of Loneliness working beside the Spirit of Fear, they held a grip that no man could break. With my own memories, I had allowed a dead man rule over my thoughts and heart. Hoping never having to experience losing someone I loved beyond words again. How was I able to break the chain? I didn't want to break a piece of my heart that held the love I had experienced. The challenges John and I had shared together had been used to build character. God had used each event to develop a faith walker. What would break if I didn't trust the one willing to help take the chain off? If I was as terrified as the seagull, would I lose a gift being given? Unwilling to accept help from the onlooker, fear controlled the entire being. I knew Jesus wasn't just an onlooker. He was the One that could take it off. What was my part in being willing to let go? Had I not tried to move on? I had already left everything I knew and moved to Ocean City.

*   *   *

In the heavens, the great crowd watched with anticipation at the revelation of the bird breaking free from the chain. God directed her to the words "escaped like a bird out of the fowler's snare; the snare has been broken."[1] Jesus continued speaking to the crowd. "I don't want her to just run as Moses ran to work for me. I wanted to use Moses in a powerful way. He charged in, and Terri has the same determination to free those in bondage. Time is of the essence. She must be willing to submit her ways and thoughts to my ways and thoughts. As I reveal, she will let me take the chain off.[2] She will answer my call for her life. Terri will understand the vision of the wall. All in the heavens knew she only saw part of the vision. She had no clue she was praying for the man that would preach God's grace in immeasurable proportions. Though his preaching would be only for a short time, he would be used to share Grace the way he had experienced it; immeasurable.

They could already see the man that knew nothing of Grace except salvation. God's gentle hand of mercy was leading Greg to a place where he would recognize and accept the hand of the Almighty holding salvation, healing, and redemption from a life of destruction. Running as fast as he could leaving behind destroyed lives, he hoped to leave his past behind. Hoping to stay under the authority's radar, he hoped his old life could be buried. The man being directed to Ocean City had belonged to the Pagans in biker and religion. Leaving home at the age of fourteen this teenager turned into a man overnight. Not appreciating the rules of protection that had been set, he moved in with a family member with ties to the Pagans. Feeling loved and accepted the group was willing to teach this young teenager the way to live. The demonic influence infiltrated slowly and decisively and was carefully cemented with an extreme hatred for Jesus. Not knowing any better, he believed the lies he had been taught. Jesus wanted something better for him. He accepted the LORD in 2002 but struggled with much of what he heard. When the message of substance was given Satan used the oldest trick in the book. The tired weary spirit would help him sleep. So the ears would not hear the message that could break the chains forever. Once again God wanted something grandeur for His child. He would run into one of His anointed children of God and his life would be changed forever. God was orchestrating[3] his plan into action using not only a prayer warrior but also a praise warrior. The two would stand united against the dark sinister spirit beings that had manipulated his thoughts and actions from a young age.

Then Jesus spoke softly," I need to show Terri the wall she has built. Her wall must be broken in order for her to be able to help this lost and confused man. The crowd watched as she listened to the gentle comforting voice of the Mighty Counselor,[4] known also as the Prince of Peace. "Terri, write down what stops you from even considering love in your life. Write from your heart not just your mind. You need to face your fears. Each time you have written something down, put a square above it and write the key word in the square," Jesus whispered softly. I began the tedious task. Facing my fears, I became weary and discouraged. After finishing the project that had been laid on my heart, I looked at the first piece of paper where the chart had been started; stunned when the picture was a solid wall of fear. Each one of the squares held the word fear. The wall of fear was a fortress built around my heart. Was the impending doom I felt going to be because I hung on to fear, instead of grabbing hold of a gift of love from the Father?

I began to cry once again. The second day of vacation was as powerful as the first day. The vacation was literally a spiritual retreat given by the Great Physician. Though it didn't seem like healing at that moment, I knew that digging down into the depths of the soul it would dig up the root of the problem. Now, what? The Lord didn't say a word. I looked at the list, how pathetic. One or two I could have faced, now I felt like a real basket case. I didn't hear another word. "Lord, how do I eliminate the wall?" I pleaded. I didn't hear a word. Was I to face the list alone? Why had Jesus left me? So began the fight in the battle of my thoughts.

PEARL DROPS OF WISDOM

1. We have escaped like a bird out of the fowler's snare; the snare
    has been broken, and we have escaped. Our help is in the name
    of the LORD, the Maker of heaven and Earth.

    Psalm 124:7-8 NIV

2. Free yourself, like a gazelle from the hand of the hunter, like a
    bird from the snare of the fowler.

    Proverbs 6:5 NIV

3. In his heart a man plans his course, but the LORD determines
    his steps

    Proverbs 16:9 NIV

4. Trust in the LORD with all thine heart and lean not unto thine
    own understanding; in all thy ways acknowledge him, and he
    will direct thy path.

    Proverbs 3:5-6 KJV

Chapter 14

Redeemed Off the Highway to Hell

Heading over to the biker's bar, Terrance's twenty-first birthday was one to be remembered. Slowly befriending many of the different people there was sincere concern for the bartender, Charlie. With 3 jobs, he was always working and didn't ever get a break. He was of middle age and his face showed he had experienced more from life than what he cared to share. Dropping kernels of Grace to different people, I wanted to show the biker my God of unfailing love. Not wanting to chase them away from God, I didn't preach. I would drop kernels of Grace through my conversation with them. The Lord opened the door for witnessing, when a man with a deformed hand was healed. Every biker wanted to know this God of healing. The Lord impressed the bikers and Charlie so a biker ministry was being done in a Pagan biker bar.[1] Drawn to the sound of the pipes, I found a strange but awkward feeling every time I went. Assuming the feeling was because of all the burdens I would feel for the people, I would pray knowing I was literally walking into a territory that was heavily controlled by the underworld. It was known Pagan territory.

I wanted to give Terrance a present that couldn't be offered anywhere else. I walked around asking the different bikers to give my son a twenty-one engine salute. The bikers heard the story that was presented. His father and he rode together on his Harley. John passed away from Agent Orange after serving two tours in Vietnam. Would they be willing to bring the joy to life by the sound of the pipes? In some twisted way I hoped my son could feel the presence and love from his father. The young man had faced many battles that had stemmed from the same attitude his father had taught him; Live hard—Ride free. With veterans in the crowd and the general attitude of the biker, eighteen bikers revved up their bikes in unison. In the group of bikers, there was one that impressed Terrance. The proud seasoned biker took his bike to dangerous levels in the Harley's RPMs. Knowing too much gas could destroy the engine the man continued to push his bike to the extreme. The power and heat flowing forth the man showed he knew the limits of his Harley. Understanding the repercussion of pushing his vehicle of deliverance to the limit, the biker hoped he had set the standard for the future of one who held the same passion of the sound of the pipes.

Terrance sat beside Tiffany at the picnic table in utter amazement. The rumble and the roar sent up through the crowd drew many onlookers. Why would these total strangers be so willing to oblige an outsider? Terrance watched as the one biker revved his engine to the danger zone on his bike. The humble brother in the Lord, demonstrated a gift from the heavens that left a major imprint in this young man's life. Yes, some of them knew his mother but she was more of an acquaintance. The Father used the perfect gift to instill more lessons into this young man's thoughts for going to the extreme for others. The birthday present sung from the pipes was followed by different bikers expressing their good wishes. Terrance chilled with several of the bikers after the hoopla. They shared stories of the different rides that were taken. Not all the stories held glamour; some were how they had wiped out or how they had totaled their bike. Speaking from experience each biker wanted to share the love for the bike: mechanics, the sound, the feel, and the general working of the bike. Each one wanted to pass on the knowledge and passion for what they stood for; live to ride, ride to live.

A woman came and sat down by Terrance sharing advice on what to avoid. She gave a testimony of how drugs and alcohol had led her down a path of destruction. She then shared how God had made a difference in her life,[2] the bikers bar had turned out to be a place of exposing the web of deceit through a dangerous lifestyle. With the woman's words of advice the young man was given a subtle message of wisdom and discernment. One of the radical family members of God had experienced the ride to live but didn't want to see a brother go down the same road. He didn't need to sell his soul to experience freedom. The sowing of wickedness would only reap the sorrow she had experienced. The anger surfacing from the biker gangs would destroy any chance of living free. She instructed him in the snares of the paths of wickedness if he chose to follow man's ideas which covered the wicked heart's intent. Directing him to the ride that is sweeter since she met Jesus, she steered him on the highway that brings glory to the kingdom.[3] God hadn't taken her pleasure, he enhanced her life so that she could enjoy the pleasure more. She was the wife of the biker, who took his bike to the extreme for Terrance. He, too, proclaimed the Redeemer had redeemed his life from destruction. Sharing more about the joy of his bike the subtle message left was; know your vehicle and the limit. Listen to the sound, you will hear when it is not running right. As I listened to the biker, I realized that was somewhat the walk of a believer.

We should have a joy as we talk about the vehicle we run on. Are we running on the vehicle of Grace or some other message? Do we realize with Jesus there is no limit? Jesus is not a God of limitation, so there is no boundary restricting His amazing works,[4] if we listen, we know when something has been added or taken away from the perfect sound of the melody of undeserved kindness. In the glories, the rumble and the roar rising to the heavens brought the redeemed bikers off their seats. Mingled with praise for King Jesus the group couldn't help but reminisce on their rides. Each one remembered and savored the ride for freedom. With excitement the different men shared stories of places they had been and the experiences. Everyone turned when Jesus entered the banquet room. He smiled at the group who had accepted his invitation to the banquet that had been laid out just for them. He smiled as he spoke, "I love the sound of the pipes too. I knew the only way to find you guys was to go to the highways and the byways. The road you all traveled was tough. Some of you stayed on the highway to hell till the last hour. When you were prisoners of your thoughts and actions, the drugs and alcohol dulled your senses so you couldn't hear me calling your name. It took time for me to persuade you that I could release the torturing spirits because you didn't trust anyone. You guys were "super tuff" to convince that I really loved and cared about you, but I'm glad you all made it here. My Grace was realized after severe street lessons. I am delighted you all chose to ride on the King's highway desiring to bring your comrades with you to the feast that I graciously prepared for you. Each one of you rode hard and fast to be living free. You are free indeed.

As the friends ate together, they listened to the bikers and friends sharing advice to Terrance. Jesus told the crowd of his biker friends, "He will use the sound of his pipes soon to win spiritual battles. The sweet melody from his spirit joining with My Spirit will bring harmony into the heavens and the angels will sing with him as the biker's world changes in Ocean City. Terrance is a praise warrior. I will send him soaring in the physical realm as he begins living free. The more he praises Me the more pagan walls will tumble down. "

Pearl Drops of Wisdom

1. And he said unto them, "Go ye into all the world, and preach the gospel to every creature."

    Mark 16:15 KJV

2. Through Jesus, therefore, let us continually offer to God a sacrifice of praise-the fruit of lips that confess his name.

    Hebrews 13:15 NIV

3. The highway of the upright is to depart from evil: he that keepeth his way preserveth his soul.

    Proverbs 16:17 KJV

4. Is any one of you in trouble? He should pray. Is anyone happy? Let him sing songs of praise.

    James 5:13 NIV

Chapter 15

Journey to the School of Grace

Glen felt the humiliation of being thrust out of my apartment. Even though I explained to him, he couldn't understand why I was so mad. He was a professing Christian but didn't want the message of Grace going out to the undeserving, a young black girl. I am an ambassador for Jesus the Christ, the Son of the Living God. He never differentiates between the races, offering to all forgiveness and love. Walls of hatred, mistrust, and prejudice would have to be torn down. Lord, let him understand a bigger picture of Grace after salvation. Glen didn't consider himself prejudice but would have nothing to do with any other race beside "white" and neither would his girl. Supposedly he had quit associating with the Pagans but could never leave them. Glen had belonged to the religion as well as the biker group and was classified as a protector. I asked who he protected. He was unable to divulge any information. All he would say was that he used to love a literal witch. She was dangerous to all and especially to those who opposed her in thought and action.

Wallowing in his self-pity, he went to a friend that maybe could make sense of it all. She gave him some valium to "chill" him down. His best friend, alcohol, continued to be poured down his throat as he drank his sorrows down. He felt rejected by the woman he loved for what, God or the element that he despised? The Spirit of Loneliness tightened the chain about his chest strangling the air, revealing his broken heart. Anger was set ablaze in his thoughts that haunted him. He tried to comprehend the difference between him and his love.

He wondered what wall I was talking about that had to be torn down. How could he get answers? He would search the world over so that he might understand the deepest thoughts of this girl that was tearing his heart into little pieces. With confusion the voices in his head screamed, "She says she loves you, this isn't love. You should feel elation. Happiness was felt when you met for a brief moment in time. Yet, now all you feel is pain. That's not love! Why would you want a woman who doesn't know how to satisfy your needs? You had a woman who loves you and knows what you want! Go back to what you know!" The Spirit of Judgment screamed. A soft gentle Spirit spoke, "She hasn't said a word against you. The message she brings is one that I want you to hear and understand. "I am the one that you asked to save you. I love you! She wants deliverance from your tormenting thoughts. My healing is needed for your broken heart. No woman could ever attempt to direct complete healing and satisfaction. What you long for is in Me."

The Spirit of Condemnation spoke," You aren't deserving of this woman. Your karma brought you what you deserve, pain. You hurt so many others that now you will understand the greatness of the pain and suffering you put them through. Glen cried out, "Just the thought of torture to a woman brings agony to the spirit within me. I stopped a rape that was being done to a woman. Every fiber of my being has been to protect the weak and vulnerable." He was not sure where he had learned that value. He just knew he was to protect. "Why would you throw an accusation like that out?" Suddenly Glen had an overwhelming fear. Did she wonder if he had observed blatant atrocities? The appalling cruelty displayed would leave a wall between them. Did she actually believe he would sit by? The Spirit of Justification piped in, "The insatiable appetite brought to women by men driven by sexual cravings and control issues in your biker realm, made those women willing to share themselves openly. Terri knows the thoughts of the biker realm." The Spirit of Condemnation began to condemn with the Spirit of Judgment's help," The women lost all dignity to those that were in control. Man was so easy to persuade to do evil. The demonic entities laughed their sinister laugh in unison. The sexual desire as well as submission to the controller was taught through cruelty. The insatiable appetite that man had was now deeply rooted in the women that belonged to their biker colors. You can't get rid of those thoughts. You learned how to please women by the training taught to you. The screams of the abused spirits of those that you watched in different situations are what haunts you. Many biker organizations were like the Pagans that abused the women sexually transferring demonic spirits.

Terri knows the biker realm of rape due to losing her virginity to a biker rapist. So this already sensitive landmark in her history will make her wonder if you would have watched or helped? Not protecting those in need, yet you call yourself the "Protector". What are you protecting? It wasn't the innocent. Your actions portrayed your thoughts. You found a woman that you respect and love, yet she has a discerning spirit that can see into your soul. She sees the real man."

The soft gentle Spirit, whispered, "She isn't judging you. She hasn't said a word against you. She saw My protection through you in your eyes, nothing else. With sympathy, she understood the loss of your virginity at the age of 12. You were a victim when your friend's mother came in and raped you. You didn't see it as rape you saw it as a good thing. You were brought into manhood by an older woman. Lust of the flesh robbing you of your innocence allowed the enemy of real love to plant the seed of artificial gratification as being loved and wanted." The voice of total love and forgiveness spoke, "You professed to being born again. She does have my gift of discernment and recognizes the deliverance needed. The torture within your thoughts she understands for she had experienced the same bondage. She is offering you the greatest gift; deliverance of wrong thinking. She wants you to have peace of mind that only I can give".

Glen held his head in excruciating pain as the spirits continued to fight the battle. Only knowing the battle in the streets, he sat defenseless as the battle raged in his head. The jabbing pains in his physical body became increasingly alarming. Facing the battle field in his head, it was as if his body had been projected to the actual fortification. As the enemy stood with great strength armed with pain, Glen felt like he was being pulled apart. Satan intended to fortify the wall of defense that he had carefully constructed. Glen could not understand the battle going on inside his physical body. He had no idea the torment of his allies that had helped him fight in the Pagan world seemed to be raging war for his soul. He heard the voices fighting. He could decipher the words, "already forgiven, let him go!" Then he heard, "He doesn't want your way, he finds it impossible to follow. He only knows what he has been taught." Glen understood both sides wanted his loyalty. He was at a battle where he seemed to have no weapon of defense. Hearing the two kings wanting him for their bidding, he was afraid of both. No one was his master; neither Satan nor Jesus. He trusted no one. He had learned he could only trust himself and his instincts. Glen felt like he was a good man, he voiced out loud, "I haven't killed anyone." Raised up young with the Pagans, he never had to prove his loyalty by killing someone. Satan screamed, "You didn't use a physical weapon but you were my weapon to go out to maim and destroy. You belong to me!"

*   *   *

A trumpet sounded and a war cry went out. In the heavens, the crowd of witnesses could see Terrance and me driving down the road. The sounds in the car were joyful as Terrance gave a word of knowledge after I shared the burden on me heart for Glen. He professed to be born again and yet, there were obvious spirits of oppression tormenting his soul. His thoughts were not the same for Jesus as mine. How could these well-fortified walls tumble down? The Spirit of Knowledge spoke using Terrance, a vessel that had once been under the same bondage as Glen. "Sing, mom. That is what will break the chains. The prison will open and the wall will tumble down!" [1] The shout in the heavens rang forth as Terri and Terrance began to sing forth praise. The partnership of the earthly realm and the heavenly realm was in agreement. Jesus prayer, "Thy kingdom come thy will be done on earth as it is in heaven," [2] was now agreed on by two claiming the victory for the one who knew salvation but nothing of the power of the resurrected Lord. The songs of praise continued through the night and into the next morning. [3]

Neither one of us was aware the School of Grace had an immediate opening. Glen was going to take a crash course that would stop all the infiltration that could disrupt the flow of the words of Grace. The instructor was one who understood shame and embarrassment. He carried scars of torture and abuse all over his body. The strength in his demeanor could be seen by the students that entered the school of training. Entering the class with an attitude of arrogance and pride, students became humbled. As the study progressed each came to the realization of how unworthy they were to be in the presence of the Master. Each one received personal instruction of the courses offered. Glen was to be brought immediately to the School of Grace at Snow Hill.

* * *

Glen finally couldn't fight any longer. He was sure he was at death's door. With the natural instinct to survive, he needed help now. The agony in his physical body was so extreme he didn't know which worse; the head, heart, or his body. The combination of the alcohol and pills was tearing down the vessel of the blood bought man. After texting and calling for my help with no response, he asked his friend to take him to the hospital. I went to bed not knowing Glen was trying to reach me. The IV slowly dripping in his arm and the bright lights, suddenly made reality quite fearful for the already fear driven man. With an insane madness, Glen pulled the IV out of his arm. Running out of the hospital, he ran to his best friend again. The bottle gave him comfort and strength. Calling more friends, he continued to try to find someone who could understand him and his girl.

The men gave their thoughts which only caused more grief. The alcohol which was poisoning him began to take its killing effects to the breaking point. Glen found himself at the hospital seeking help once again. Recognizing the man who had sought help than ran out sent up warning flags. A search was done and a warrant was found in another state. Under guard, Glen was driven to the "School of Grace" at Snow Hill held in the jail.

Driving to Public Landing Road, where the criminals of society were locked away from victims and loved ones, a sign was noticed that advertised Furnace Town Road. With a firm hand the hard headed and rebellious are given lessons stripping the offender of all dignity and pride in order to teach respect for rules and authority. With shame, each one of the prisoners is allowed one phone call. The call is placed letting people know they're in trouble. The pleading for help is urgent! Then the heat is turned up for the prisoner like a furnace. With extreme lessons the guards bring the criminal to a place where they must consider what they chose over freedom. Their actions would go through the furnace. Each one would find that their actions were but ashes. Glen was there at the King's bidding. Going to get help from the drugs and alcohol, he had searched for healing not knowing his sickness was one the earthly physicians had no cure for. At the King's request, mercy would be brought to him in a place where he would meet the Great Physician. Glen knew he was sick but knew nothing about the diseases of the soul. Jesus was going to diagnose the problem and cure the different diseases inflicting His precious son.

The building holding the prisoners showed heart conditions. The prison grounds covered with snow and ice was in no comparison to the cold self-centered iced over hearts the prison held. As each one of the prisoners experienced their own public landing, they lost their freedom. A territory filled with others who had the same weaknesses and diseases of the soul. Glen knew fear showed weakness, yet as he faced the fiery furnace he couldn't help but be afraid.

Pearl Drops of Wisdom

1. About midnight Paul and Silas were praying and singing hymns to God . . . . Suddenly there was such a violent earthquake that the foundations of the prison were shaken. At once all the prison doors flew open, and everybody's chains came loose . . . he was filled with joy because he had come to believe in God, he and his whole family.

   Acts 16:25-34 NIV

2. Your kingdom come. Your will be done on earth, as it is in heaven.

   Matthew 6:10 NIV

3. Be sober, be vigilant; because your adversary the devil, walks about as a roaring lion, seeking whom he may devour:

   I Peter 5:8 KJV

Chapter 16

Key of Praise

After my quiet time with the Lord, I checked the phone. Glen had called and left texts. The day before was spent praying and praising Jesus. The hatred that was blatant against not just race was also against God. The desire to have a possible relationship was exciting for a couple of weeks. The Lord had continued to show the real man. The attitude I realized was against hearing the Word of God. Casting out the legions of demons required more; a fasting, praying and praising heart. The need for light to separate darkness was being asked, on everyone Glen went to for advice. He hadn't gone to wise council concerning one of the anointed children of God. Instead he went to the Pagan's high priestess. Would all involved see the right hand of God at work? Deliverance was at hand.

God brought to remembrance the vision of the man on the other side of the wall that I couldn't see or get to. The voice calling out was the man she loved and wanted to share her life with. With deliverance the man would be powerful for the kingdom. What should I do next? How much would bail be to get him out? Was bailing him out a part of God's plan? I didn't want to step in the way of the Author and Finisher of the faith. Jesus was about His business, where could I help? I called to find out the information needed to find out about bail, visiting hours, and the arraignment. It was resolved without my hand involved at all. No bail for he was wanted in another state. Visiting hours were Saturday. I was to pray earnestly for the battle would be difficult, for Glen would have to tear down a mighty fortress.

The ground covered with ice and snow held a beauty that somehow encouraged me. The unusual beauty shed a different light on Ocean City welcoming a white Christmas. The joy Glen and I had putting up a tree, now left loneliness in my heart. Joy and peace was sent down from the heavens in the large snowflakes. Watching the quiet soft falling snow reminded me how there is a beauty in transformation of life when the cold has been experienced. Praises flowed from my lips. Writing and preaching Grace, the man I married had to understand and comprehend 'more Jesus'. A different picture began to emerge. Glen's heart was cold toward God and mine was hot. Foolish pride and the false teachings separated the two of us from what was critical; Christ Jesus' leadership of our lives. Was the man whom God called by name, the one that I was to help but not necessarily marry?

I went out to watch the sunrise. It was dark accept for a road of crimson breaking up from off the water shooting straight into the sky. It was amazing to see just a crimson road. As it widened, a golden hue ebbed on the edge of it. It was still darker on one side of the road, but the golden hue widened where it began looking like the golden lines created a sea-shore extending around one side of the sky. The blue setting in between the golden hues had white wispy clouds that looked like waves. It was like looking at Ocean City from a different picturesque view.

The territory of interest literally lit up the area which held so much darkness. I saw an image that looked like a person walking on the road of crimson. Walking the road that extended like a rainbow, I was brought up out of the dark lonely night. The golden hue, etching its royalty and blending the colors, led the way of the walk. The sun's radiance infiltrated the sky swallowing up the darkness without the help of man. ELOHIM separated the light from the darkness.

The message given; He wanted to lead the journey chosen for his servant. He was walking with me on the crimson road that would travel from one end of the sky to the other. Golden hues were the power of Grace to be recognized throughout the jail in Snow Hill then continued. Wherever my foot trod, the territory would be opened up with victory. The light of the Holy Righteous One would bring light to the darkest and loneliest places displayed on the public landing.

*   *   *

In the heavens, Jesus was delighted to see the message was received that he had especially prepared. He used her words, "Bring a man up to me out of the sea. Terri had been joking around when looking at the great ocean. Jesus smiled as he saw her earnest desire in her heart. She wanted a man who would understand the deep Sea of Grace. This union was not to be married in the physical but in the spiritual realm. He was to be a part of the bride of Christ in his last hours. He would be totally submerged in the Sea of Grace.

Jesus heard a joyful sound as he heard in unison Terri and Terrance singing forth his praises. Terrance was at his home and Terri at hers. Yet the sound of the two as it was filtering through the blood of Jesus sounded forth a praise offering that brought joy to the heavens. As the melody from the earth rang in the heavens, the angelic voices began to sing. The great multitude sang forth songs of redemption. Jesus began working in the heavens by removing the chains that had held Glen so powerfully. Jesus began bringing to light the vision Terri received before; of the bird calling. Glen was being encouraged by her to soar to the heavens. He was chained to the many false beliefs that had been taught to him. Not realizing the Pagan's teaching was so deep in his subconscious, he had to break the chain of unbelief as well as crush the stones of the altars of Satan and self-idolized worship.

As the wickedness of Glen's training through life was exposed, the leg he had adamantly stood on was broke. Laying in wretchedness, Jesus in His unfailing love showed tenderness and compassion unraveling the entangled chains one by one and removing them from his thoughts. The chains constricting his breathing also broke loose. The inhaler Glen had to use was not needed. The "Great Physician" watched his son take deep breaths. His eyes were opened to total deliverance. Fear was replaced with adoration when there was no judgment or condemnation only gentleness and underserved kindness.

Glen went home to be with the Lord 4 weeks later, a week after he was let out of the education from man's iron fist training of jail. With no way to pay the child support debt due to the economy, the lesson could be a future thing once again. In the "Graced Kingdom", he learned lessons of the Father's love for the child. The "Heavenly Father" paid his child support clear to the death, so he could be reborn of the Spirit. A lot of questions were answered about the things surrounding his grounding in the Pagan world. He found the majority of the world belonged to the Pagan belief without desiring to join a group advertising 'Pagan". With boldness he had proclaimed the condition of his heart. At the School of Grace he proclaimed, "Redeemed". The group he had associated with declared you can't leave the group except through death. In the School of Grace, he found he escaped the second death no matter what happened in the physical death. He not only learned lessons of God's amazing love but turned around and planted seeds to others caught in darkness.

The irony of the street signs that were named by man held so much food for thought. The culmination of signs of direction in the physical realm also gave the path of changed lives if so desired in the spiritual realm.

1. **Snow Hill** - all climb a cold mountain that lifts up themselves as important. The separation from God causes the coldness. Self-worship has been programmed into the thoughts of man. When the cold broken heart realizes Jesus wants to be Lord of their lives, it requires stepping down and trusting His leadership. Many are not willing to give up their position.

2. **Public Landing Road** - every individual eventually ends up on the landing where they are exposed of the wretched person they really are. Some realize their need for help and hope. They seek redemption from destroyed lives. While others turn to further themselves in the ways of this world.

Those seek praise from man because they look like they are living right.

3. **Furnace Town Road** - The Lord tests the heart. He tests in the furnace of affliction, [1] as the heat is turned up in life, who do you turn to? The choices are so many but there is only one that helps, strengthens and gives the miracles.

4. **Basket Switch Road** - after making the choice of submission to the LORD of Lords' leadership, the basket is filled with fruit from the Holy Spirit, [2] every second spent with their Lordship, the more good fruit is produced by the Holy Spirit, not by man's effort. The enabling of the Spirit would fill to overflowing the power of God working in his life, through God's love.

Taking out the Bible, the Spirit began to teach Glen the fruit being offered from the two different baskets. Exposing the things contained in the basket he was used to indulging in, a stench of rottenness permeated. The old basket of fruit offered by Satan and man left the taste of bitterness in his soul. He found he was dying from the poisonous silent killer fruit. This basket held nothing that brought joy to his heart and peace to his spirit.

The other basket contained things that were given by the Spirit: Love, joy, peace, patience, kindness, gentleness, goodness, and self control. Glen realized he didn't have the ability to do any of these on his own. [3] The more he studied, the more he realized it was received from God through Jesus. It was like he was starving for what was served out of the basket. It contained only things that were pure, lovely, and true. He recognized salvation years before but hadn't experienced victory over his wrong thinking till now. Glen found that his mind, body, soul, and spirit were healed. He was a new man. Glen was a vessel full of praise and worship toward the resurrected Lord. His face like a mirror was reflecting the Spirit that dwelled in him.[4]

Pearl Drops of Wisdom

1. See, I have refined you though not as silver; I have tested you in
    the furnace of affliction. For my own sake, for my own sake, I do
    this. How can I let myself be defamed? I will not yield my glory
    to another.

    Isaiah 48:10-11 NIV

2. But the fruit of the Spirit is love, joy, peace, patience, kindness,
    goodness, faithfulness gentleness and self control. Against such
    there is no low.

    Galatians 5:22-23 NIV

3. Humble yourselves before the Lord, and he will lift you up.

    James 4:10 NIV

4. Submit yourselves, then to God. Resist the devil, and he will flee
    from you. Come near to God and he will come near to you.

    James 4:7-8a NIV

Chapter 17

<hr>

Hide 'n' Seek Grace

'D' made his way across the country seeking what, he did not know? There had to be more to life than what he was living. With every move he was sure someone was out to get him. Having to always be on guard he became tired and discouraged. He had burned so many bridges along his way in life there was not to many he could depend on now. Who could he trust? Who would have his back? Considering the trail of failures and enemies, he rubbed his hand over his hidden pocket. He felt his friend beside him. The loyal friend had helped him out of many scrapes on his journey through life. This was the only one he could really depend on. As he continued to run he headed for his "brother's" home. The bro had been there through many of his dealings in life. Their friendship was one that rang true. He would stand by him once again. 'D' decided this time he would try to be different. Settle down; maybe find a woman who would love him. He needed to be accepted for what he was; a nice guy just down on his luck. All he needed to do was make some fast money.

The great multitude in the heavens watched the man running once again for his life. They had heard prayers from one of his loved ones asking the Lord to introduce amazing grace to 'D'. Tears were mingled with sorrow for the whole world knew the shame and embarrassment this man had caused his loved ones. The pleas sent up were made with urgency for God to intervene. God in his mercy directed the man to Raintree Apartment Complex. Jesus smiled as he opened doors for this man who was seeking refuge from his past life. The direction was Spirit led. A child of Grace had been searching for peace just months before. Kaylie had just been directed to the same place in November. Those with financial needs were housed there. After being in a marriage leading to disaster, Kaylie chose to submit leadership of her home to the Lord. She wanted God's mercy and goodness on her and her son.

Jesus knew the lessons that needed to be brought to this rebel of a man. The discipline that needed to be brought to the one who wanted no rules or correction wouldn't be taught by man. 'D' needed to go to the School of Grace. Having heard about Jesus, but not wanting to walk on the road to Golgotha, Jesus knew the soil was tilled and ready for seeds of Grace to be planted in the mind of this weary traveler. The manure was deep in his life so the plant coming forth from the Grace seeds would be strong.[1] The gentle warmth of kindness shown by others would slowly melt the ice that was protecting a heart that had iced over. Everyone would observe the heat turned up on the furnace at 'D's' public landing.

When I went to visit Kaylie, the change was noticeable. Her speech proclaimed God's goodness over her life. Her spiritual walk was starting to show that the rain of righteousness had been turning her desert into an oasis. Peace and rest could be felt when people came to her home. The broken hearted were encouraged and the lost were shown the way to Grace. It was as if the finger of God was pointing and nudging them to one who had pearl drops of wisdom mixed with a heart full of compassion so that they might hear His abounding love.

'D' showed up with his "bro". The conversation turned toward God and His Amazing Grace. Bro listened attentively to Kaylie's excited conversation. Every time Kaylie and I came together the depth of the conversations were in a level that most people couldn't understand. Kaylie was intellectually gifted. God had used the fascination of quantum physics and science to teach her. The depth of conversation was a challenge to comprehend. Grasping science itself proved man is minute compared to the expansive display of the universe. When any one part of God's creation goes out of the created plan of order, the chaotic effect throughout the galaxies are caught in a spiral in order to correct the imbalance from the alteration. Explaining in great depth how the earth had shifted at the north and south poles, she explained in lengthy detail how the shift had changed our planets weather. The upheaval in the gravitational pull was creating the chaos of proportional magnitude. The tsunami's, tornados, earthquakes and flooding were all of greater destruction. It was as if she had literally been taken to a mountain and was shown the massiveness of God's creation. With the view she had been given she could see the results of one part of creation falling out of alignment. Man was just one thing God had to intervene in and fix, had all his creation begun to rebel? Man rebelling against a Holy Righteous God? Creation rebelling[2] against man for they were trying to control the weather. I met a man in Tennessee that had shifted storms after given orders in the military. Had the rays shot from the earth changed not only the weather but also altered our Universe?

Days turned into weeks of "Chilin" with Kaylie. The seeds of God's love and His powerful deliverance over her life of destruction were planted into 'D's' sub-conscious. Miracles of the Miracle Worker were expressed over and over. He was a sponge that seemed to be absorbing the living water that he had never before been able or willing to hear before. With ears that were dull of hearing, it was as if the fresh new view of this awesome powerful God had touched his mind. The training of Grace had started and was about to turn his life up-side down.

I received a call Friday morning from Kaylie, "Mom, you coming this week-end?" 'D' came knocking at her door in the middle of the night needing a place to stay. She asked me to step in so he didn't take up residency on her couch. Concerned that Kaylie had let him stay the night with her and my grandson, I would be there. Kaylie had a big heart and knew people would try to take advantage of her kindness. After arriving, I began lecturing the man on why he shouldn't be there. Offering to take him job hunting and house looking the next day, surprised even Kaylie that I would be willing to help rebuild his broken life. 'D' willing accepted. Shortly after the conversation he left Kaylie's humble abode. The next day rolled around and there was no sign of the man needing help. There was more to this man than what Kaylie or I knew. Hoping he wasn't embarrassed or ashamed, we were genuinely concerned for 'D's' well-being. The weekend passed with no sign of the man seeking a place to sleep.

Monday afternoon, I came back from the Laundromat. Who was there again, acting like he lived there? 'D' and Bro had come over to chill. When Bro left, 'D' stayed with no inclination to leave. Uneasiness crept in as I considered, was he planning on moving in when I left? Folding clothes, Kaylie and I neither one said a word. Both knew Mom would take care of the situation. I just didn't want to ruin Kaylie's friendship with Bro. Choosing my words carefully, 'D' was told to go. The man became upset and said he wouldn't come back. He told Kaylie goodbye and then left the apartment. I apologized to Kaylie if it cost her friendship with Bro. Kaylie said she was okay with it all. She would talk to Bro later.

Ten minutes later, there was a knock at the door. The neighbor from upstairs came in all excited. There were police everywhere. Kaylie and the neighbor headed to the door to go out and watch all the hoopla. When she opened the door fear instantly set in. U.S. Marshals were standing at Kaylie's door with shields up and guns pointed at her. The one in charge screamed at her, "Where is he?" Charging into her house, they ordered us out of the house. Kaylie stepped out then said, "what about my baby?" They had her go get the little one taking a nap. Nothing was making sense as they could hear things being shifted and moved. One of the marshals held up a picture. "Do you know this man? Where is he?" Both of us said we didn't know. Together, we explained what we knew of the man named, 'D'. The agent asked, "Did you know he was a wanted man? Did you know he is on America's Most Wanted list?" Flabbergasted both of us shook our heads. Neither one knew.

'D' reportedly broke out of prison with a weapon that the U.S. Marshals were searching Kaylie's house for. The escapee was captured in another building complex. The ones that had showed kindness were shocked that their families' lives were put in jeopardy without any consideration from those that wanted the man hidden. The secrets of past criminal involvement were kept confidential leaving a threat of expulsion to those who had opened their homes because of a friendship with Bro.

*   *   *

In the heavens, Jesus told the great crowd of witnesses, "This man isn't just wanted by the U.S. Marshals. He's wanted by Me, too. He's done many offenses. The greater the stain of sin the greater my Grace will be recognized. He was directed to where he could hear amazing love, goodness, and forgiveness. His capture now and here was orchestrated by Me. He will be sent back to man's prison where 'D's' training will continue in the School of Grace. He will have others, watering the seeds that Kaylie has planted. My hand has been guiding him to where he would be willing to call out for help. I touched Kaylie's heart. With her spiritual eyes open and her ears sensitive to my voice, she let 'D' in. With no knowledge of My goodness, mercy and love, I wanted to send 'D' to a servant that had been in the state of desperation and saw My redemption from a life that held sorrow and destruction. While he is imprisoned, he will grow because of My love for him. He desperately needed to see a heart full of compassion. Kaylie threw the pebble of selflessness in the Pond of Grace and the ripples of My goodness and mercy[3] touched other people's lives around her."

Pearl Drops of Wisdom

1. But where sin increased, grace increased all the more, so that, just as sin reigned in death, so also grace might reign through righteousness to bring eternal life through Jesus Christ our Lord.

    Romans 5:20b, 21 NIV

2. We know that the whole creation has been groaning as in the pains of childbirth right up to the present time.

    Romans 8:22 NIV

3. Surely goodness and mercy shall follow me all the days of my life, and I will dwell in the house of the Lord forever.

    Psalm 23:6 KJV

Chapter 18

∽∾∽

Master's Degree at the School of Grace

A student in the School of Grace for many years, I wanted to help others that were struggling with the journey. I understood, undeserved kindness could only really be taught by Jesus the "Grace Rabbi".[1] So many believers were caught in the grasp of the iron hand of the law. I had stumbled on a verse that left me questioning? It said, "The LORD abhorred [2] his inheritance." Did Jesus abhor His or did He look at it different because of Grace? Jesus knew this training would be a lot harder for me than ever imagined. The training field was in a well saturated Bible preaching territory.

Field Experience 1:

It was a beautiful Sunday morning and my training class was being held at a church. I looked forward with anticipation as I walked into the church a few minutes late. The music brought forth from the piano player was to stir the hearts into praise and worship. We have a reason to sing, [3] our God should be highly exalted. The congregation didn't sing along with the choir. No one smiled. Assuming it was just a choir piece, I could hear a woman singing faintly behind me. A smile broke through on my face from the joy of hearing her faint melody of praise from her heart. The preacher announced it was victory Sunday and welcomed everyone. The sound of praise was sung but once again no one joined the choir but the elderly woman and me. I sang loud hoping the voice of two would encourage another. Had the people not understood the meaning of 'victory' Sunday? In between one of the songs, the preacher stood up and proclaimed, "Someone is supposed to say something." No one said a word. "Maybe a testimony, "asked the preacher? Still no one said a word. Looking around the room, I saw sorrow, weariness and discouragement.

The preacher stood up to give his sermon, "The Lord is coming soon. No longer will we have pain or sorrow. That will be the day of victory." As the message continued, I understood why there was no victory. The message was victory in the future not victory in the "today". The hope of tomorrow just kept the people struggling to reach something in their today, but what? In the middle of his sermon the preacher said again, "Someone is supposed to say something" No one moved including me. A visitor in the church, I wanted to see someone testify to God's marvelous works within their life today. As the sermon was brought to a close, the emphasis was depending on their works being necessary to receive the blessings of heaven. If they wanted God's blessing, they needed to quit a list of things. Ways to fight their battles victoriously were not given. Nothing was said of Jesus and His finished work at the cross. No encouragement or hope was left for the weary discouraged Christians. I felt a terrible burden within my spirit combined with nausea.

At the altar call, the musician began to play the piano. Suddenly the preacher blurted out, "Somebody is supposed to say something. Speak forth! There was irritation heard in the voice. "Hurry up and say it! We want to go home and eat!" With a brief moment of pause, I stood up. "Does it matter if it comes from a visitor," I asked? With a sarcastic tone in his voice, the preacher said, "If you are the one to speak, do it!" Speaking at other churches, I always felt welcomed but feeling intimidated and awkward I begin to speak.

Total forgiveness and trusting the faithfulness of the one who loves them was spoken boldly. As I spoke the heaviness in the room was deafening. The piercing looks from the leaders of the church were as if there were daggers ready to attack. One woman in the crowd seemed to understand the message of total forgiveness, greatly blessed and deeply loved. The smile on her face coaxed and encouraged me to finish the word of God's blessing on them. With stares that were of coldness, I walked out of the church. No one welcomed me. I was somewhat surprised no one picked up stones. Instead they just parted and let me pass without a word. The sadden spirit was hidden deep as I asked for courage walking to the car.

Field Experience 2:

I was invited by a believer to a special prayer gathering at a high school. It was the same town as the other church I had gone to. The town's churches were trying to win back their school and town, from the demonic influence. The young people were in the chains of addiction, seeking comfort from drugs and alcohol. Peer pressure was in the forefront but the Spirit of Condemnation followed close behind each one. The parents were watching the family unit being drug through the mud and mire, judicially as well as medically. Teens were dying. Believers were willing to pray to take back their community. Gathering once a month at different spots they were united in their desire. Arriving early, there was a good crowd gathered. The number of concerned citizens was 92. No longer would Satan destroy what they held dear. Preachers were recognized representing the different churches including a preacher all the way from Belize.

In minutes the prayers were sent up. Then the group dispersed. Once again the spirit within, began bothering me. There was more socializing before the prayer then the time that was spent interceding for the town. No praise offering was sent up to the heavens. Unable to bridle the tongue, I asked a group chatting cheerfully around me, "We're not going to sing forth praise?" "No, we just pray and leave, "said a woman. Out of the well spring deep inside, I reminded the group of Paul and Silas. The two had every reason to question the suffering they were going through after preaching the message of Jesus. They were beaten and then thrown into the prison under heavy chains. Treated like criminals, the two messengers of hope acted on what they believed. Rejoice in all situations: good and bad! I continued to speak forth truth. As they praised God, [4] doors opened and chains fell off. Lives were changed. The guard and his family came to know the One who gave peace and joy through the suffering.

The woman stood for a moment then answered, "You're right." The women around shook their heads in agreement but no one started singing. The group turned and started talking amongst themselves. The Spirit within the deep of my soul became sorrowful. I spotted the preacher from Belize and walked over to him. I felt a stir within my heart.

Curious to know what this man of God does in his country when needing to go up against his powerful enemy Satan, I asked the question. The man took a deep breath, choosing his words wisely so as if not to offend. "We would just be starting the meeting," he answered. We would sing [5] in praise of the Victor Christ Jesus. "Then sing," I said. "Sing in your language." The gentleman laughed, "We speak English." I said, "Please sing! If I know the song, I will join in." The man began to sing forth praise. I didn't know the song but knew the heavens were rejoicing with me, for he sang with love and adoration for his Redeemer. After finishing the song he told me, to sing. I sang. The man of God joined in for he knew the song. We both sang loud, "Lord there is none like you." It only took a spark to get the fire going. A girl standing with four others around her was faintly singing too. Smiling and putting a hand to my ear, I went over to the bashful but courageous girl. I said, "If I can't hear you, can the heavens hear the song of praise?" The young adult sang louder and the group of friends standing with her joined in with those that were breaking the chains through praise, to the King. After singing the melody of praise, the group introduced themselves to the other believer's in this circle of victory believers. A little boy came up and said, "Sing it again." The group sang louder forgetting the group of leaders and elders that still chose not to join in. The Spirit was moving through the small group that wanted to see lives changed in their families and friends.

One of the singers stepped back away from the circle and began dancing [6] unto the Lord. The LORD's face shined down on her. She radiated as the motions from her physical joined with the Spirit of the One who dwelt in her. The people, who chose not to sing or dance did stop and watch the Spirit led daughter of the Lord lift her heart's adoration to the King who sat on the throne. Those humbling themselves at the footstool in praise and worship caused the redeemed in the heavens to sing and dance before the Holy King of kings. The heavens and the earth were in agreement for a brief moment in time. The Spirit moved through the small group. Suddenly, a man called out to the preacher from Belize, "We need to go!" The joy that had been on his face was stricken as if he had been slapped. The brother in the Lord whispered, "He is my ride. It has been good." The rest of the people scattered quickly leaving the group of five and me. Sharing and testifying the small group acknowledged what God was doing in their lives. None wanted to leave for the praise wasn't finished.

Field Experience 3:

The next part of my training required trusting God's leadership and provision and not leaning on my own understanding. Still in the town where professing Christians were displaying the works in the name of God, there was an elderly gentleman. He had been asking for God's help. He was lonely and discouraged for no one seemed to understand the position he was in.

Visiting Ralph, I needed to use the bathroom. He had a toilet that had been leaking and shifted a lot when sat on. I was concerned it could go through the floor, yet knew the gentleman had no financial resources to fix the leak. I wondered how expensive a flange might be. Studying the throne of humbleness, I heard God say. "There is more wrong than what you know." Looking deeper into the project ahead, I noticed someone had cut plastic carpet guard and screwed it to the actual toilet. Why would anyone bolt plastic around the base of toilet over top the problem? Whoever had tried to help really didn't have the understanding of how to correct the leak. I heard again, "There is more wrong than what you know." Digging around the plastic runner, I could see the wet moldy carpet. Was the rottenness soaked into the wood? I heard, "you will need help."

I hoped the daily food kitchen had plumbers that were retired or out of work. As I drove the faces of different people would pop into my head. Each one the words "not that one" came out. I finally blurted out, "Lord, show me which one you have to do the job. Direct me to the man you want to do the job."

Beans, cornbread and collard greens were what was being served that day. There was no jalapeño pepper cut. Using my fingers, I tore the pepper in small pieces dumping them in the bowl. A few minutes later I was not able to eat. Unaware I touched my eyes, severe burning set in. Weeping because of the burning I lost my appetite. The swelling and blurred vision due to the foreign substance I knew I needed to wash out my eyes. Pushing the tray to the gentleman in front of me, I asked him to empty it. With blurred and burning vision, I only wanted to get to the car. The man who emptied the tray blurted out, "She got mad at me!" I asked, "Who was mad at him? Why?" "The lady said I wasted food," the gentleman said. "I tried telling her it wasn't my tray but she let me know I wasted the food." No matter how excruciating the pain was, there was a need that was much greater. The man had been unfairly misjudged. With swollen, red and crying eyes, I found the lady that had judged the man. I tried to explain the situation of why it was my food that had been dumped. The woman didn't care whose tray the food was, if we weren't willing to eat the food served, don't eat. With anger stirring inside, I took off my glasses. The weeping eyes would surely show the woman the desperation for compassion. I once again began explaining what had happened for me to leave the desired morsels. Once again the woman showed what was important to her. "You wasted the food. Next time don't take a tray if you don't plan on eating it," was the woman's arrogant answer.

Leaving the building, I was mortified to see the example of a cold and insensitive heart. If her spiritual eyes were open she would have seen the need for compassion. To have an ice pack offered would have been plenty to comfort the wounded sister in the Lord. I tried hard not to judge but wondered if the glasses she wore on her face was strong enough, then realized there was a lesson here for me. Do I get wrapped up in what I think is important for another, yet my spiritual eyes are blinded? Are my ears dull of hearing, missing what is critical to the individual being served. Living in the physical moment of service, could cause an insensitivity overshadowing the real need at that significant moment? Lord, may I be sensitive to others needs. Give me a tender compassionate heart. Open my spiritual ears and eyes [7] for you know the need of the injured soul, whether the need is physical or spiritual.

After driving a short distance, I started laughing. I had forgotten to look for the man God wanted to help with the bathroom. Had He made it so I wouldn't see what I wanted to see? Yet, showed what He needed me to see and learn from? While I was joking around with the Lord, I heard the Lord loud and clear, "Terrance". Terrance is in Virginia. The Lord said, "Ask if he would be willing to go to Tennessee. "The response was what I expected, "How much would you pay me? I laughed and said, "How much you going to pay him Lord?" The pay was set at $50.00. Gas would be paid both ways. The next issue was critical. The finances weren't there for all the building supplies, gas and pay. The Lord told me to go to the bank. "Lord, I only have $24.00 in the bank." The Lord again told me to go to the bank. With unbelief at the amount sitting in my account from the ATM, I walked back to the car. How can it be $402.00! Impossible! I walked into the bank and went straight to the bank teller. The teller handed me a balance sheet and asked if she could help anymore? I walked out to the car dumbfounded. Sitting in the car in amazement I asked, "How can it be?" The Lord responded gently, if I have a job to be done, I will provide everything needed to complete the job. [8] Now, are you going to take money out to send Terrance gas money?"

Field Experience 4:

A celebration of praise music in the park was set in the town that wanted to claim it back for the LORD. Blood bought believers looked forward to the day where Jesus was honored. The leaders of the celebration were sponsored by 23 churches. I looked forward to the day of praise and worship. Musicians playing Southern Gospel, Christian contemporary and Christian rap were hoping to stir brothers and sisters hearts, to break out of their shell and worship Jesus openly. The gatekeepers welcomed the people in the morning with joy and thanks. As the volunteers would drive up to the gate, the greeters told them thank you for being a servant to the King. Whether the volunteers realized it or not, the greeters at the gate were encouraging the tired and stressed servants. Some responded with grunts, where others responded cheerfully. I desired to have the Holy Spirit come like at Pentecost in people's lives in this town that continued to strive to take back their town for the Lord. When I greeted a couple of people with "May the spirit of Pentecost fall on you", they responded with, "Now you're talking!"

As the morning continued, the demonic realm also entered the premises. Professing Christians followed by Spirit of Judgment and Spirit of Condemnation entered with them. The gatekeepers would ask those attending and serving to park on other streets requiring them to have to walk to the event. Parking inside was reserved for EMS and handicap. With righteous indignation people would say, "I 'm volunteering. Why do I have to walk?" Some volunteers were bold enough to say, "That wasn't meant for me." The gatekeepers allowed some to go ahead and park inside, just because they didn't want the attitude to escalate. The attitudes of some servants' were worse than those that came just to see what was going on at the park. Walking was nothing to those who wanted to come and "check out" the bands. Hearing about the praise event all week, they were looking forward to the full package that went with free food. Churches and the media made it sound like it was going to be something extraordinary.

As the lost and confused entered for the free food, the Holy Spirit interceded with the burdens sent up to the heavens by the prayer warriors. The angels rejoiced when a soul came to know the resurrected Lord. Multitudes of ministering angels were sent down to those gathered in the park. Those that attended the celebration came from the King's highway and the byways. I talked to a gentleman professing to be a Christian. George was upset, instead of rejoicing the park was being used for furthering the Kingdom; he saw it as a ridiculous display of religion. How could city officials approve anything like this in the park? If they wanted this kind of stuff, they should go to church. Pride was heard in his voice as he proclaimed he went to church every time the church doors were open. He said twice, "If they want this kind of hoopla to be put on, do at one of the churches. I wondered at the way he said "they". Those that cared about the lost and dying were the body that belonged to the "Bride of Christ".

George was just waiting anxiously for the rapture so he wouldn't have to see the evil any more. Was George so preoccupied with his future destination that he had forgotten the Lord's plans for his life today? This man proclaiming love for God did not seem to share the same heart of God. Closing the door of his heart to those that were in need in the park, implied the church building was more important. Did Jesus not show up in the park and find the searching lost child? I couldn't help but wonder if it was held at his church, would the "Christian Rap" group be welcomed to play at the event?

If the Lord returned at that moment of his refusal, would he have been spared since he didn't want those in the park spared? If he wasn't excited about Jesus' visitation at the park, which was welcomed by new family members, where was the concern and courage to go out and fight for others trapped in snares? Leaving the comfort zone of the 'religious churches' and accepting the challenge of ministering on the streets full of violence and fear, required something different. Convinced the people he was watching were evil, where was the burden for the soul going straight on the road to hell! His judgmental spirit wanted nothing to do with seeing the lost redeemed. Would he be held accountable for the souls that he should have talked to but chose not to? The park was filled with others that agreed with him. His friends and he socialized every day at the park. They gathered to enjoy the peace and quiet. Their argument was this music wasn't praise, it was noise. I wanted to laugh for the Christian contemporary music playing was praise. What would their comment be on the Christian rap? They couldn't sit together and talk because there was noise and confusion? What would happen when they were in heaven with the multitude of angels singing?

*   *   *

The four lessons that were displayed for training left an overwhelming sorrow inside me. Three weeks of the fruit of the church left despair and discouragement. What had filtered through in each lesson, left me in an emotional state where I just wept? Unable to control the brokenness inside, I hid from the world. I didn't go anywhere or meet with anyone. I read and studied the Bible which made me cry even more. The passages I was reading exposed the crumbling foundation of the doctrine of truth. Doctrines led by demons [9] left man and his churches lifted up. Knowing the lesson was needed in order to continue ministering, yet it left me devastated spiritually. Where was the joy and victory? I called a servant of the Kingdom of Heaven who has the gift of deliverance. I needed to know if something had attached itself to me for the sorrow was so overwhelming. Rejoicing usually poured forth through my lips but now weeping. As the woman listened to the burden on my heart, I felt like Jeremiah the weeping prophet. After laying the burden down, I asked if there was something taking root? She came back with, "There is nothing in or on you except the LORD. JESUS is weeping in you. You are feeling the broken heart of Jesus. The agony the church brought in His name causes the burdens to be heavier for those searching for the truth." Stunned by the words, I waited for her to say more. "Let the Holy Spirit teach you."

Pearl Drops of Wisdom

1. But be not ye called Rabbi: for one is your Master, even the Christ; all ye are brethren.

   Matthew 23: 8 KJV

2. When the LORD saw it, he abhorred them, because of the provoking of his sons, and of his daughters.

   Deuteronomy 32:19 KJV

3. "Sing to the LORD for he is highly exalted . . ."

   Exodus 15:21a NIV

4. About midnight Paul and Silas were praying and singing hymns to God, and the other prisoners were listening to them. Suddenly there was such a violent earthquake that the foundations of the prison were shaken. At once all the prison doors flew open, and everybody's chains came loose.

   Acts 16:25-26 NIV

5. O sing unto the LORD a new song; for He hath done marvelous things: his right hand, and his holy arm, hath gotten him the victory.

   Psalm 98:1 KJV

6. You turned my wailing into dancing; you removed my sackcloth and clothed me with joy, that my heart may sing to you and not be silent. O LORD my God, I will give you thanks forever.

    Psalm 30:11-12 NIV

7. For this people's heart has become calloused; they hardly hear with their ears, and they have closed their eyes.

    Matthew 13:15 NIV

8. Trust in the LORD with all your heart and lean not on your own understanding;

    Proverbs 3:5 NIV

9. Now the Spirit speaketh expressly, that in the latter times some shall depart from the faith, giving heed to seducing spirits, and doctrines of devils.

    I Timothy 4:1 KJV

Chapter 19

Fat Swallowed Double Edged Sword

The classroom was full in the heavens. The graced class had many eager students wanting to learn from the Master Instructor. When Terri chose to take the extra-curricular class in the field training, many of the redeemed in the heavens also wanted to learn more of Jesus' heart. All had experienced his unfailing love but few understood the emotions in His heart. For centuries, churches beliefs and doctrines watered down the message of the Kingdom of Heaven. Instead of powerful in faith, believers had become weak. Instead of hot and bubbling over with powerful praise because of Jesus' finished work at the cross, many had become lukewarm. How many understand Faith[1] is the substance (being sure) of things hoped for, the evidence (certain) of things not seen? The great gathering waited for the "Great Rabbi of Grace". All heard He was meeting Terri in her hidden class room, curious to find out whether Jesus would say he abhorred His inheritance or not. With all the weeping that was done in the last three days, Terri was finally ready to sit at Jesus' feet and learn.

*　　*　　*

In my quiet time of searching and asking the Holy Spirit to teach, what was I to learn? I knew the time of weeping was over. Now I was to be equipped for a battle. Sitting at the feet of Jesus, I wanted to know what was next for the Kingdom, to be shown such a powerful hypocrisy in the church toward the Almighty. Then the Lord showed a passage to be studied.

Eighteen years the Israelite people were under the iron hand of Eglon, king of Moab. The Israelites had done evil once again in the eyes of the Lord. With the intense burden that was put on them, the people cried out once again. They wanted delivered from the cruel slavery that the king forced on them. The God of mercy turned his face on Israel again and sent a servant carrying a secret message. With tribute, the Israelites sent Ehud to present it to King Eglon. Hiding a double-edge sword that he made a foot and a half long, Ehud made his advances to the king. After he had passed the idols, Ehud told King Eglon there was a secret message. The king in all his pride and arrogance dismissed the servants that attended him. The message of death was delivered personally by the hand of Ehud. He pierced through the fat to the center of his belly. Being enormously fat, the sword was swallowed up by the excess, clear past the handle. Ehud locked the door behind and escaped without being noticed. The servants noticed the door was locked. Ehud once again passed the idols, then informed the Israelites the mission was a success. Blowing a trumpet in the hill country, he led the Israelites to conquer their enemy. Ehud told them to follow for Jehovah had given victory over their enemies.[2]

The Lord continued to speak, "That day they struck down ten thousand Moabites. Even though the warriors were strong and vigorous, they still had to fight to take out the strong force that held them captive. The victory was not already obtained just because the evil king was taken out. I said, "Lord, I don't understand. What are you trying to tell me?" The answer left me more confused than when I started the passage. Jesus answered, "The church has become lukewarm. [3] I will spew it out of my mouth. The sins of Sardis have brought the sleepiness of the church to this age. Wake up! [4] My bride has been crying out to me but does not realize why there is no victory in their lives. There are warriors willing to fight for their freedoms but they do not understand what they are up against and what to fight. With an abundance of fat surrounding the core of the problem, the double edge sword must be used to kill the spirit in control. You will go out to my people. Daily put on the full armor of God. [5] Walk in My light and truth, I will expose the things that have been done in secret, succumbing my children once again to darkness and slavery. The church has been deceived by seducing spirits which you will see and expose. The glory of conquest will be Mine. None will hurt you for I AM in you. With confidence in the Lord that he would teach me as I walked, spiritual eyes were opened afresh and my ears began listening more carefully.

I encountered a man who opened a thrift store for the homeless using the title "Reverend". I was told by the Lord to help the man proclaiming to love Him. After several days of working with him, I saw fruit that questioned his conversion and his ability to direct the guidance needed to help the growth of the faith. The evidence of the Holy Spirit was not there.

I was asked to sit in on a counseling session, with a soon to be married couple, with him. Counseling the two desiring to be married, the preacher acted bored and kept yawning at the woman who had many issues. Having issues with rape and marital abuse the woman showed signs her past hadn't been dealt with. Fear wasn't just in her speech, but in her face and body language. Battle of the past, was still being fought in the present. The more that was shared the more insensitive that preacher became. The burdens fell on deaf ears. The Holy Spirit within, revealed the self-proclaimed preacher did not have the ability to help. Worse, he was insensitive to her spiritual needs, laughing at the sorrows that were happening even while having sex. I was surprised the preacher wasn't against the two having sexual relations before marriage. Deliverance was not available to the couple needing to rid themselves of the diseases of the soul.

I went in to the thrift store the next day to visit with the preacher. Upon entering the store, there was a beautiful table and chairs set that I stopped to look at. There sitting on the table was a book of incantations. Mortified to think a professing Christian would have a book of witchcraft being sold from his store made me nauseatingly sick. I walked around the store and spotted other occult possessions.

Items were all donated to the store. Nothing had to be received. Instead of throwing out the occult items or preferably burning them, the blatant display of evil was promoting witchcraft. Feeling the evil in the room, I turned around and walked out. Angry, there was no dividing line on the Christian based, I had to go back and talk to the owner. Judging the sin and not the sinner somehow seemed impossible at that moment. Praying in the Spirit was critical before I went back in. Powerfully but subtly, the occult had infiltrated some of the churches in the area. With courage and boldness, I talked to the preacher and his wife. Forgetting the reason I had went into the store in the first place, I expressed firmly; they had to make a choice. Their business was either for God or against him. You cannot say you're a believer and sell things that are evil in God's sight. The Lord specifically mentioned witchcraft. We are to utterly abhor [6] the detestable things not of God. The two expressed they didn't realize it was evil. What? Surprised at their answer, I explained the different things in the store that were not of God. They said they would remove it. Halloween was coming. It tied in with the theme; celebrating the day of the dead. How appropriate their comment; celebrating the day of the dead. Witchcraft doesn't give life and they were telling the people we support the holiday. Here is the book to follow to solidify the death.

The day came when the truth was revealed. The gentleman came and asked me to do the counseling with him. With his business sense and my wisdom, we could go far. The couple he had counseled wanted me there. Mortified to think of my own wisdom, I heard the Spirit say "no". I turned him down. I asked him how long he had known the Lord, wanting to know his salvation experience. He accepted the Lord in prison 2 years ago. Never reads the Bible. Isn't sure he believes in it. How did he become a "reverend"? He smiled, "Over the internet. I wanted to marry people. There is money to be made there." He was striving to lead people by the golden rule; do unto others as you would have them do unto you.

Once again in the classroom the Lord began teaching me from the experiences that I had encountered. The acts were based on the same principle; the appearance of Christ centered. Standing on the fundamental basic word Christian, where was Jesus in the equation? The compassion intended was for the poor and homeless Vietnam veterans. Believer and non-believer alike care for the ones who suffered because of the meaningless war in the name of "freedom".

Based on the "reverend's" limited knowledge and choosing not to pick up the Word of God the man was slowly leading the flock straight to the slaughter house. Allowing the objects of witchcraft in the celebrations offered to the world, no one had to miss out. All things were acceptable as long as you care about one another. Jesus reminded me, "I hate rebellion as much as witchcraft." Refusing to pick up the written word is a form of rebellion. [7] Looking to one's own understanding rebels against My wisdom and understanding. [8] Woe to the teacher who is self-indulgent and full of greed. [9] Be cautious!

The church, you attended was a sleeping church. I talk about the Church of Sardis, look it up! The appearance of attending was noticed but I was not noticed. There was no praise for they see nothing praise worthy. Woe to the teacher who shuts the Kingdom of Heaven [10] in men's faces. Not revealing the victory in their today closes what I opened up for them. They need to wake up. Strengthen what remains and is about to die. My children showed no life because they are full of dead man's bones. But do notice there are a few who have not soiled their clothes.

Those gathering to pray for the town had hearts that desired to have their town given back to God. Jesus asked me the question, "Did the prayer leave the grounds of the high school? The need is great. There are many wood cutters and water carriers but few carry oil. They carry dry moldy bread.[11]

Confused at the lesson, Jesus took me to the scripture where a group gathered and prayed around an altar. Elijah had challenged those not worshipping the true God. They had left the purity of the faith for the beliefs infiltrated from the false religions through the leadership of King Solomon. The God that brought down fire was the one to be worshipped. They cut themselves hoping to bring forth the answer of prayer. They continued the frantic prophesying till the end of the day. There was no response. Their god was Baal. [12] Did I understand what I was being told? How could it be that the churches of today were being accused of Baal worship? Jesus continued teaching me, "You were taken to different places proclaiming to be the family of God. In these situations the Holy Spirit revealed the lack of power, joy, discernment, wisdom and knowledge. The Great I AM moves without any restraints. Continue the journey I have sent you on. The Holy Spirit will teach you the hindrance of His moving powerfully.

As a son of Zadok, remember the good news you carry. Practice the important neglected things of the laws; justice, mercy and forgiveness. Continue to stand on My faithfulness of love. You carry the presence of the great I AM. Humble yourself and submit. Comprehend the Holiest of Holies' desire to be full and over flowing as He uses you.

I will show you those that are white washed tombs that haven't risen from the grave. The one's holding the coffins the dead are trapped in, are entombed themselves. They cannot answer but with empty selfish words. Terri, you must understand, "Woe to those who build tombs [13] for the prophets and decorate the graves of the righteous."

PEARL DROPS OF WISDOM

1. Now faith is the substance of things hoped for, the evidence of things not seen. For by it the elders obtained a good report. KJV Now faith is being sure of what we hope for and certain of what we do not see. This is what the ancients were commended for. NIV

   Hebrews 11:1-2

2. Once the Israelites did evil in the eyes of the Lord . . . . cried out to the LORD and he gave them a deliverer—Ehud . . . The Israelites sent him with a tribute to Eglon, King of Moab . . . Ehud made a double-edged sword . . .

   Judges 3:12-30 NIV

3. I know your deeds, that you are neither cold nor hot. I wish you were either one or the other! So, because you are lukewarm-neither hot or cold-I am about to spit you out of my mouth . . . You say I am rich; I have acquired wealth and do not need a thing. You do not realize that you are wretched, pitiful, poor, blind and naked.

   Revelation 3:15-17 NIV

4. I know your deeds; you have a reputation of being alive, but you are dead. Wake up! Strengthen what remains and is about die, for I have not found your deeds complete in the sight of God.

   Revelation 3: 1b-2 NIV

5. Put on the full armor of God, so that you can take your stand against the devil's schemes . . . . Stand firm then, with the belt of truth buckled around your waist, with the breastplate of righteousness in places . . . .

Ephesians 6:11, 14 NIV

6. Do not bring a detestable thing into your house or you, like it, will be set apart for destruction. Utterly abhor and detest it, for it is set apart for destruction.

Deuteronomy 7:26 NIV

7. For rebellion is as the sin of witchcraft, and stubbornness is as iniquity and idolatry. Because thou hast rejected the word of the LORD, he hath also rejected thee from being king.

I Samuel 15:23 KJV

8. Trust in the LORD with all your heart and lean not on your own understanding; . . . .

Proverbs 3:5 NIV

9. Woe to you, teachers of the law and Pharisees, you hypocrites! You clean the outside of the cup and dish, but inside they are full of greed and self-indulgence.

Matthew 23:25 NIV

10. Woe to you, teachers of the law and Pharisees, you hypocrites! You shut the kingdom of heaven in men's faces. You yourselves do not enter, nor will you let those enter who are trying to.

Matthew 23:13 NIV

11. "This bread of ours we took hot for our provisions from our houses on the day we departed to come to you. But now look, it is dry and moldy."

Joshua 9:12 KJV

12. You have abandoned the LORD's commands and have followed the Baal . . . If the Lord is God, follow him; but if Baal is God, follow him . . . Then you call on the name of your god, and I will call on the name of the Lord. The god who answers by fire-he is God.

I Kings 18:18, 21b, 24 NIV

13. Woe to you, teachers of the law and Pharisees, you hypocrites! You build tombs for the prophets and decorate the graves of the righteous.

Matthew 23:29 NIV

Chapter 20

Unexplainable Activities in the Spirit Realm

Directed by Jesus' mercy and love, He taught me to trust his faithfulness in provision and his leading for furthering the kingdom. I was taught to heed moment by moment not just day by day. He said, "Wherever my foot trod, [1] the territory would be given to me for His beckoning. Daily my prayer was, "Lord, may you direct [2] my day with your love, so that at night I might sing forth your praises." The uniqueness of the individuals' that I met left imprints of traditions, faith, and values. The essence of the American people could be seen in the behaviors and speech. The different religions and traditions had filtered through leaving confusion to many. Some held biblical grounding with the shadows of faith, while others mirrored [3] the image of the resurrected Lord in their lives.

I came to a territory full of history. Pursuing freedom, the slaves ran through tunnels in the hill-side. Some meeting death in their quest. Once again the words from the Russians, Israeli's and Americans, expressing concerns of freedom, rang through my thoughts. The oppression people shared was the same; bondage under a cruel hand of control.

My guide, Nicole, drove around showing all the points of interest in her town. Driving past the middle school I noticed a wall built out of stone surrounding the grounds. Withstanding battles, it now protected the school on the hill. It stood as if it was a fortress worth protecting. Closed, heavy metal, gates were leaving an appearance of control and protection to those passing. Could these doors hold the power to intimidate those being sent in to learn from the school masters?

Driving through the town, I was amazed to see the Yuengling Beer Brewery. The old building was still being used even though it had been in commission since 1892. The passed on cravings for the time aged brew had not been extinguished through the ages. The ale had survived because of meeting the needs of the people. Those that had mastered the proper blend of flavor had experienced the effects of the Civil War, the Great Depression and other climatic events in history. The company had endured the test of time. The building was empowered by the determination of those who held shadows of loss but with everything to gain; wealth.

Continuing the tour, we drove past an amazing house. In spite of the majestic grandeur the old mansion held, it was not inviting. Supposedly it was a haunted house, yet I felt drawn to it. The shutters were closed not even welcoming the new season to touch its windows with warm sunlight. There was eeriness about the premises that sent a sensation through me. Mustering up the courage, I climbed the old broken steps. Walking across the porch, I headed toward two heavy wooden doors. The looming entrance with heavy hinges turned the house into a fortress that seemed impenetrable. Knocking, no echo could be heard. A voice answered through the closed door, "What do you want?" I explained I was from out of town and would like to see her house, if it was okay. The woman's voice came back with, "You're not welcome here." Disappointed I walked away, but was determined to see the place again, only from the inside out.

The town, rich in history, seemed to have left a distinct mark in the people's lives. The twisted stories of the slave underground, in the hillside to the house on the hill that was supposedly haunted, left me with an extreme curiosity to the different sorrows, joys, and pains that had been felt thru the centuries. The guide's curiosity was not peaked at the places that I had found intriguing. The mysteries of the past left many legends traveling through time. What tales of freedom or slavery would be left for the next century of Americans? Would this country still be considered the land of the free? Was courage seen with the imprint, continuing the legacy of freedom for my loved ones and those that I had been given the opportunity to meet? Little did I know the twisted past would expose the labyrinth in the lives today. Jesus would unravel secrets of great deception brought on by the "great deceiver", himself.

The next morning after sharing intimate moments with my precious Jesus, I stopped for a cup of coffee. Turning around, with the coffee in hand, I noticed someone coming up the stairs and down the hallway. I assumed the bathroom was in use by the grandmother who lived in the basement. Without hesitation, I grabbed another cup for her. She never came out. I went to the bathroom. It was empty. Nine o'clock in the morning, grandmother came up the stairs. I mentioned to her about the cup of coffee poured for her earlier. The woman looked at Nicole. The look on both women's faces left me in bewilderment. Grandmother spoke up, "that was my son." "Oh?" I said. "I didn't know anyone else was downstairs." Nicole filled in the blanks, "her son is my dead husband. His ghost watches over the family." These were women professing to believe in Christ. The son had professed to love the Lord. Was it really the husband's spirit?

As I drove to a new destination, my thoughts wondered about passing spirits. Were they demons like some people believed or were they the spirits of loved ones? Many said they saw their loved ones spirits for only a brief moment then vanished right before their eyes after passing. Bonnie had seen her loved one sit in a rocking chair beside her. Kathy saw her twin for a brief moment going across the room. They felt like God had given them a gift, a moment, bringing closure to the one needing comfort. A final goodbye, that intimate moment that no one else had been given. I can understand the intimate closure, but questioned a Christian spirit choosing to leave the heavens to watch over physical beings.

As my husband, John, was leaving the earthly realm there seemed to be a moment where he and I experienced something not seen by the rest of the family. He had lost the ability to speak the last four days of his life. The heavenly Father allowed John his treasured request; to say goodbye to his family audibly. I saw and heard the cherished words of love and encouragement, yet when reading "Tears of the Father" my children said he hadn't talked audibly. They just saw him drowning from the fluid in the lungs. What really happened that I was able to see and hear the cherished good-byes?

Kaylie wanted to experience the uniqueness that seemed to follow my walk with Jesus. She had expressed to me the desire to see the things He had let me see. Inexpressible joy was felt when she voiced the desire to see the face of God. Jesus had directed the hunger craving for His glory. Miles passed as I contemplated God's vision for my daughter.

*   *   *

In the heavens the great crowd of witnesses observed with much curiosity. Two real close friends walked up to the group talking. Elisha and Elijah listened. Neither one of them said a word for a few moments. Would anyone really understand what God had shown the two of them? They exchanged looks and smiled. The experience they had encountered was truly unique and never happened again as far as the two of them knew. Why had the Almighty conceded the experience of a supernatural event together? The two stood separately with boldness against false prophets worshipping Baal. With powerful faith in the faithfulness of their God, Elijah and Elisha had seen God send fire upon request. Elisha said calmly to a group listening, "Asking for the revealing of the majestic power of the Almighty is never wrong. When Kaylie is ready the Lord in his faithfulness will reveal an eye opener that will forever change her thinking." I wanted to receive a double portion of God's spirit after seeing Jehovah work through my mentor and friend. Elijah had such great faith in the Almighty, EL SHADDAI."

"Kaylie wants the same thing. Her mentor and friend's faith in the EL SHADDAI through the name of Jesus challenges Kaylie to want more. Watching her mother take God out of the 'box' that religion put him, God impressed Kaylie. The Great I AM works better with no limits or boundaries. The Lord will equip Kaylie for the desire to be used is from the Father. Ancient legacy of faith is being shadowed by the ideology of worshipping Jesus for what He did and man works. She has to learn the servant's heart toward the Master's heart." Tears welled up as he realized once again the Israelites had turned their backs on the Almighty God. "Terri worked for Jews that were not of God. The reign of terror was one she knew nothing about really. She saw the angry attitude of Esau toward the different ethnic groups as they came into the store but was unaware how deep the hatred was for the races that stood on Jesus the Messiah. She saw a Christian dismissed quickly when she preached Jesus' redemptive blood. The spiritual deliverance wasn't what the Jews were looking for. They still want someone with power in the physical realm. Using the love for the Jew, Terri was used by EL SHADDAI to show the Jew the power of Jesus. No one could question miracles that were seen."

"As a servant washing Elijah's hands, I was taught the servant's heart." Elisha, with humility continued speaking, "I saw the pain in his face when man's arrogance challenged the Almighty God that he worshipped and trusted. With the basin sitting at his feet, I would pour water onto the filth that had accumulated. Rubbing the dirt off, I sensed the washing of the defilement of the Israelite people. Tears of anguish were shed before a Holy God for an unholy people".

Not wanting the focus to be on him Elijah changed the subject. "Wow, it was great though to see your face when I was being taken up," laughed Elijah. "You thought I was going to be like Moses with his grave never to be found? [3] When I stepped on the flaming chariot, [4] I have to admit I was in awe myself. That ride was sweeter than any of the kings' chariots on earth that I ever saw. I could not imagine why the King brought the best chariot to escort me to His presence. As many times as I had asked to catch a glimpse of His face, I really never imagined how I would meet His Majesty, my LORD. Humbled by His presence, I couldn't look on His Holiness. King Melchizedek, priest [5]of the Most High came and extended His hand. He called me by name and lifted me up. What was strange, He said to me, "well done my good and faithful servant. You trusted EL SHADDAI with the little things in your life and depended on His faithfulness in the big things that you requested. You hated evil. Idol worshippers you abhorred. When you called for fire to consume men if you were a man of heaven, the EL SHADDAI affirmed you belonged to him. You desired to see power, strength, and victory over your enemies and situations". Elijah replied; "Now, I understand **JESHUA** is the High Priest of power and indestructible life. The perfect sacrifice given by the High Priest is King of Righteousness."

There was silence for a moment as Elijah remembered how he waited to hear the voice of God. He was in a cave watching the wind storm that took out a mountain. God wasn't there. There was a major earthquake. God didn't appear then either. He found God when he heard the soft voice. [6] Elijah knew the still soft voice was calling to another; Kaylie.

"If God was planning on taking you in the flaming chariot, why did he have you go to Bethel and Jericho first?" asked little Atreyu? "Little One, Bethel means House of God," commented Elijah. "It was the place to humble oneself before the presence of the Holy God. After an encounter with God, there was great magnitude of fear and respect due. Sacrifices were done by Abraham and other men of faith. A portion of the excellence of the Glory of God, the stairway to the Gate of Heaven was revealed to Jacob. Humbleness was ensured as God talked to him there.

Jesus whispered softly, "Terri needs to go to Bethel. It is time for her to understand who I AM." Jesus smiled as he remembered the fear that was on her face when she met an Amish man. "He was quite extreme in his beliefs of works. Terri felt evil standing in his presence, just as Eli held reverence for Me. She brought praise of Me and healing miracles from Me into his world. Now is the time for a greater gift to be shown to her. The broken humbled vessel of clay will be filled with power, for she is not afraid to preach the gospel." No one heard Him for they were all listening to Elijah.

Jesus listened as Elijah continued speaking, "I was sent to Jericho, where Jehovah had shown His power to take down walls of strength against a mighty fortress. It was not by power or might of man, but by the Spirit of the Lord. Praise was sent up to the heavens as the power of the Lord came down on our enemy. I went to relinquish all that I was and everything I knew of God to receive something greater. The limitation of God is because man has quit gleaning after the Ancient of Days.[7] Man must become an empty vessel to allow a

Holy God to make something greater of them. Crossing the Jordon showed the journey of walking faith was finished." Elijah said, "I was to cross into a land flowing with so much greater. The God of Israel called me by name to His Presence. I took off my cloak to be exchanged for something better. I touched the water with the cloak and the waters parted. When the chariot stopped for me it was on dry solid ground."

*   *   *

Terrance and Tiffany had opened their home for family, when Kaylie and I went to visit them in Ocean City. It had been months since Kaylie saw her brother. I watched as the brother and sister interacted with excitement and laughter. Missing each other immensely, the two shared their life's' trials and joys. All in the heavens could see the joy that emulated from the hearts in the room.

The great crowd watched as Jesus touched my eyes, which left me speechless. I saw a golden hue surrounding Terrance, Kaylie and Tiffany. With a heart full of joy, I realized the growth that had been done. With a grateful heart, I praised Jesus for His faithfulness in changing hearts and lives within my precious loved ones." Jesus spoke with direction, "Terri, get down!" I didn't move. Then Jesus said again, "Get down!" I excused myself and went to lie down in the bedroom.

*   *   *

The heavens were opened up to me. The Brilliance of Righteousness sitting on the throne was resplendent, I couldn't look straight. While lying down prostate before the throne, my face was tilted to the side. The crowd watched as my fingers were open so I could look upon the Righteous Radiant King. His resplendent appearance left me speechless and unable to stand. Everyone in the crowd remembered the first time they saw the Glory of the Lord. Unworthiness before the magnificence of pure righteousness left humbleness and awe.

I didn't look around the room for there was absolutely nothing as beautiful as the King sitting on His throne.

Whether a dream or vision I cannot tell you. Unable to explain in logical reasoning why I was in the heavens, the experience was one of peace and serenity. Hearing my children in the other room, I also saw them standing in Jesus' presence. The crowd marveled as the speech flowing through their mouths, holding sweet melodious music from their hearts, held the listeners captive. In robes of white their appearance made them look pure and innocent. Adorned with splendor and glory they were shown honor, as they stood in the presence of the King. They weren't in the back of the room but were standing close to the throne itself. The glow about them seemed to come from the inside out. They were unaware that their conversations were being heard in the throne room. Those in the heavens listened to the words pouring forth from their mouths. Then I realized why, they were also in the throne room. They were praising the LORD as they were exalting the marvelous works they were seeing him do.

I noticed an angel was sitting close to the King and he had a pen in his hand writing something down on a long scroll. What was being written? Were names being written down in the Book of Remembrance, [8] or was it the acts of the Lord that they were testifying about? I watched the Lord laughing and enjoying the conversations, with all the dramatic charades, even though they were not contemplating being in His Presence at that moment.

I tried to stand up but my body would not cooperate. A strange cold came over the physical body as a large black hand stretched across holding my body down. I recognized the Angel of Death, as the cords of death were entangling me. The physical body was shaking out of control, yet I experienced no pain, only an amazing peace, as King Jesus walked toward me. I heard my children enter the room, expressing concern in the physical realm. I asked, "Am I dying Lord?" There was no fear just peace as I watched the thrashing on the bed below. The eyes of the Father, which held only gentleness, had my full attention. There was no fear as my physical body seemed to be fighting to survive. The crowd listened and watched as Kaylie's hand touched my back. In the physical realm not a word was uttered, but in Glory she was pleading for the LORD to help her mother. The crowd heard Jesus ask me if I was ready to come home. The crowd was surprised when I asked for a little more time. As Kaylie continued to pray, Jesus lifted the dark hand off of me and threw it through the floor. Peace was revealed to Kaylie. The crowd watched as she covered me up and left the room.

Jesus lifted me up. Face to face the joy and love for each other was recognized. The crowd watched as Jesus touched my head. A shaft of light surged through my body, starting from my head to my toes, igniting a fire inside. As the healing progressed a glorious radiant light exploded into what looked like a fountain. The flood surging through my body left me feeling totally alive for the first time. With an undeniable awe and respect, I had never felt so much peace. Love had refined and purified me from the core of my being. Dedicated to the Spirit of Love, freedom consumed my heart, mind, body and soul.

The tears of overwhelming joy flowed as I whispered, "Thank you for showing me a glimpse of Heaven." Jesus whispered with tenderness, "You are my Bride. Lean on my bosom. You'll stay close to my heart." I was the Bride! I looked lovingly into my Groom's eyes.

PEARL DROPS OF WISDOM

1. I will give you every place where you set your foot, as I promised Moses.

   Joshua 1:3 NIV

2. By day the Lord directs his love, at night his song is with me—a prayer to the God of my life.

   Psalm 42:8 KJV

3. . . . But to this day no one knows where his bones are.

   Deuteronomy 34:6 NIV

4. As they were walking along and talking together, suddenly a chariot of fire and horses of fire appeared and separated the two of them . . . .

   II Kings 2:11 NIV

5. Then Melchizedek king of Salem brought out bread and wine. He was priest of God Most High, and blessed Abram, saying, "Blessed be Abram by God Most High, Creator of heaven and earth. And blessed be God Most High . . . .

   Genesis 14:18-20 NIV

6. . . . Then a great and powerful wind tore the mountains apart and shattered rocks before the LORD, but the LORD was not in the wind. After the wind there was an earthquake, but the

LORD was not in the earthquake. After the earthquake there was a fire, but the LORD wasn't in the fire. After the fire came a gentle whisper.

I Kings 19:11-12 NIV

7.   . . . The Ancient of Days took His seat . . . .

Daniel 7:9 NIV

8.   Then those who feared the LORD talked with each other, and the LORD listened and heard. A scroll of remembrance was written in his presence concerning those who feared the LORD and honored his name.

Malachi 3:16 NIV

Chapter 21

Words of Prophetic Knowledge

I was directed to a Spiritual Deliverance Meeting. The simplicity of the group gathered left me wondering what ministries were involved, for all were in leadership positions. Battles I had encountered left a craving for stories of the victories they had seen the Lord do. As the group gathered the Spirit of the Lord also walked into the building of worship. As the songs of praise poured forth through mouths of the redeemed, the Spirit moved through the believer's souls and spirits. The worship of song lifted off different burdens that the believers had, as they worshipped in Spirit and Truth. Everyone in the meeting room was seasoned Grace Believers, understanding it was not the efforts of service that merited God's Amazing Grace. Undeserved kindness was a gift given by **ELOHIM**, the Mighty Creator, to those who had accepted the gift of ransom through the atonement of Jesus, His Beloved Son. The group of anointed leaders and believers lifted up the One who was creating something new. When finished, He would present the Bride of Christ to the Father.

Jesus looked into the faces of work worn servants. Tears welled up for his tired workers who had been fighting faithfully. The heat from combat against Satan and his manipulative, conniving demonic spirit warriors had brought them to the King seeking encouragement and deliverance. Some of the anointed ones were fighting for those in prison. Others were battling for those caught in addictions hoping to find relief from the imprisonment in their thoughts. Jesus could see the demons that had leached on to powerful Grace Warriors of the faith. He heard the prayers sent to the heavens. Burdens for others, the prayer warriors cried with great agony from deep within their spirits. The redeemed in the heavens heard the moaning from the Holy Spirit, as He interceded on the behalf of the saints.

The crowd listened to me pleading for Henry and his broken heart. The elderly gentleman lost his beloved wife. Spirit of Depression, with the help of Spirit of Loneliness tortured him daily. The man didn't stop to consider the Spirits of Anger, Bitterness, and Unforgiveness had bound him in chains, leaving mixed emotions toward his grandson. Henry, a man of God, wanted to display the attributes of compassion, forgiveness and unconditional love toward a rebellious self-centered young adult. The teen had left a trail of sorrow for this grandfather, who only wanted to give what he had in order to help this child who really did not comprehend love. Justin's father had died and he was left with a mother who didn't want anything to do with him. Introduced to the drug realm, he lost not only his innocence but also the ability to feel emotions. The rebellious youngster would do anything for the next fix. Grandfather continued to bless, as the grandson continued selling the gifts for drugs. Vehicle after vehicle was traded for the desired "high". The grandfather did not realize he enabled the boy's actions. Loyalty for the grandfather was shallow, compared to the self-centered desired substances. Tears would flow and the question of love would surface if Henry said, "no" to anything. Knowing about God and seeing his grandfather's life did nothing but torture him when he was denied the pain release. His twisted thoughts haunted him in the day, leaving anguish through the night. He stole hearing aids, stereos, televisions and even the bed that his grandfather slept on just to be able to indulge in the treasure of his heart, relieving the suffering of his soul.

The day arrived, when the grandfather became a constant reminder of the self-centered life of indulgence and addiction. A drug deal had gone sour. The young adult pulled a scam on two unsuspecting pill seeking boys. After exposing the falsity of the desired pills acquired, the two young adults sought revenge. The 'burned' boys traced the dealer to his home, which was shared with his grandparents. Not considering that the dying woman and Henry might be in the house, the lads threw rocks into the windows; shattering the picture window. Henry wanted revenge by ripping the young men from limb to limb. The terrified woman began screaming leaving the important thing at hand; consoling the dying woman on the couch. Knowing his grandson was involved, brought Henry to his breaking point. Holding close the frightened woman till she fell asleep, Henry gently laid her down and then began picking up the shattered glass. Each piece began to expose shattered feelings he felt for his broken life. The depth of brokenness turned to resentment for Justin didn't want love. The Spirit of Anger came alive but was hidden for the Spirit of intimidation was stronger, as Justin manipulated Henry.

Henry's eyesight was not very good yet he strove to find every piece of glass. Totally exhausted, the grandfather laid down on the couch. Waking up with pain, piercing shards had penetrated through his skin above his 'good' eye. Several pieces were left buried under the skin. The doctor wouldn't try to take out the slivers of glass for they were too close to the eye. The piercing shards left a festering sore. Having the physical injury become a constant irritation, the shards internally oozed resentment in his mental and emotional state, too. Not only did grandpa have to be concerned about the physical eyesight, his spiritual vision had become foggy.

In the hour of deliverance, I had taken the situation of Henry to the throne. I took the man's burden and laid it on the altar of the Lord. I pled for God's faithfulness in mercy and healing. With tears pouring forth, I asked the Lord how to help this man who had been so willing to help his own flesh and blood in spite of the constant cruel and abusive mockery. The great crowd of witnesses watched as the Spirit of Guilt whispered, "You knew! Why you didn't step up a year ago? Why did you wait till now?" The crowd saw guilt press down on me as the light exposed the things in the darkness. They listened as I confessed to Jesus. I knew all involved but wasn't aware there was an injury. Jesus spoke softly and tenderly, "You would never have known about it, except I had you go visit Henry. You brought my Spirit of Comfort to him. I was encouraged as you encouraged

Henry. His attitude of sorrow turned to joy for he was laughing and sharing stories of My power. It was good to hear My son laugh again. It had been a long time since I heard him laugh."

Jesus continued speaking lovingly," He laid the request of, "Heal me" before you. I watched your face as he shared the story of how he received the injury. I saw the darkness of guilt and shame attach to your thoughts, as well as anger, the more the details of the night of deceiving and revenge unfolded. Your spirit was pierced with the shard that was intended to cause diseases of the soul." With a fresh boldness and cleansing within my heart, I began to pray for Henry again.

* * *

Satan knew the battle was great but did not expect what he saw when he walked into the little hidden sanctuary. He walked around with pride until he saw one of his demons thrown across the room. He recognized the Spirit of Depression. He saw the Spirit of Condemnation be tossed up in the air. As he walked closer he heard the voice of the Holy One. The crowd in the heavens watched Satan cower behind the Spirit of Fear. He wasn't ready to face his enemy. Jesus and His angels stood their ground and continued to fight for those who just rested in Jesus' faithfulness and worshipped him. With cheering on from those who loved him, Jesus was encouraged as he fought against the many demons. Jesus could hear Satan challenging the Spirit of Fear to march forward against this mighty opponent.

The praise and worship was permitting Jesus to take leadership in each warrior's battles. Jesus cried out in a loud voice, "Satan, I command you leave this place. You aren't welcome in My Presence." At the command of Jesus, Satan gathered up his long robe and covered his face. He could not look upon the beauty of the One he despised. With only the Presence of the LORD in their midst, the worshippers exalted Jesus.

* * *

As the deliverance ended, the prophesying began. As the Spirit spoke through a woman, I found myself questioning, "More?" I was told, "Spend more time with the LORD". I thought, "Lord? Do we not spend much time together?" The woman said, "You are going to need more. Drench yourself in His love." A gentleman then spoke, "Satan is going to go up powerfully against you." The tone was strong and very direct. No fear was recognized in me, only the Spirit of peace and courage. The only way to go against this aggressive and powerful foe is to concentrate on the "I AM". Learn and understand who He is for you. Begin praying with the names of God through Jesus. There is power that is unleashed when you make a request using the names that Satan comprehends. The different names showed the capabilities of the EL SHADDAI. "God" is generic but when you understand the depth of YAWAH, in the flesh of Jesus, your formidable foe will have fear and trembling when you pray using these names. Walk in a victorious way with courage. Satan will try to influence your thoughts and take you off the path that the Father has chosen for you. The path is simple: **love and trust Him more.** The more you sit at His feet; the clearer the path becomes. Satan doesn't want you to stay directed by Jesus' Lordship. You are causing an uprising in his realm and he isn't going to hand it to you. The souls you are fighting for are the ones that he has held onto for years. Satan will try many different attacks. His attacks will be more cunning and more subtle. Be wise as a serpent but harmless as a dove. [1] His kingdom is starting to crumble because of your faithfulness and obedience. Stay alert. Judge the spirits [2] with wisdom. Discernment is yours for the asking. You may not know the demonic realm but they are created beings under the great I AM. Jesus is with you, so don't be afraid. Remember, at the name of Jesus every knee [3] will bow including Satan. Jesus' name is a strong tower; [4] so run into His strength and protection. Courage must continue to fight against the lord of evil."

*   *   *

I then saw myself standing inside of a large tower. [4] The walls were enormous over my head. There were windows and a winding staircase so that I might look out on the territory. There was only one door with a knob that could turn if I chose to go out. I heard, "Stay in the tower." I turned but saw no one. The illuminating light shining within was brighter than words could express. I fell to my knees when I realized I was in the presence of the great "I AM".

*   *   *

I heard the man say, "I cannot say enough, know who you are in the great I AM. The victories are yours because He dwells in you. "I was mind boggled as I was about to go sit down. Yet, the Lord wasn't done giving the messages to me. Called for a purpose, the anointing of His Holy Spirit was to be revealed through another woman in the congregation in a fresh new way. A woman in the audience hollered out, "Wait! I am to tell you something." The lady spoke with authority as she blurted out. "You have wanted the blessing of your own home church. You wanted them to anoint you with oil and bless you as you went out to minister. You don't need to look any longer to man, I AM all you need. You have the blessing of these anointed ones." With a fingertip of oil put on the top of my forehead the lady put out her hand. She blew air on me. A rush like a mighty wind started at the top of my head then circulated through to the bottom of my feet. A woman who had been touching my shoulder felt the Holy Spirit move through her body at the same moment. Both of us were caught up in the rapture of the Holy Spirit coming in a powerful way over me. The woman touching me gasped out, "Oh my goodness," but didn't remove her hand. The washing of the anointing of the Holy Spirit flooding through me, left us in awe and wonderment.

Jesus smiled as He watched the Holy Spirit set the two women in a celebration of praise and awe. The breath of air surging through fanned a flame that was already burning bright. Leaving the women with a gentle touch from the heavens, He sent the sisters in the Lord out with power. The kiss of the Groom to His Bride left the two women speechless. The gift had been ordered from ISH, (the husband) on the throne.

Pearl Drops of Wisdom

1. . . . Be ye therefore wise as serpents, and harmless as doves.

    Matthew 10:16 KVJ

2. Beloved, do not believe every spirit, but test the spirits, whether they are of God; because many false prophets have gone out into the world.

    I John 4:1 KJV

3. that at the name of Jesus every knee should bow, in heaven and on earth, and under the earth.

    Philippians 2:10 NIV

4. The name of the Lord is a strong tower; the righteous run to it and are safe.

    Proverbs 18:10 NIV

Chapter 22

Wisdom Over Improvising

In the deep caverns below, Satan sat concocting a plan that would help deceive this hated ambassador of the King. In the eyes of this evil master of disguises, he saw the whole travel of Grace like this play script that was prewritten. Jesus, the director of the script, orchestrated her comings and goings. She was receiving pieces of the satanic puzzle everywhere she went. If she put the puzzle together she could expose his hidden agenda planned throughout the centuries. Simply stopping and talking to people, Terri was becoming a hindrance in the caverns below. Satan knew he couldn't stop God's healing touch, but could he detour God's plan by Terri's own choices?

The mighty vindictive hold Satan had on the Redeemed Ones was no longer. The chains of religious bondage were falling off. Terri's attitude of joy and peace was contagious; like a disease that people wanted. The hungry and thirsty, tired and weary Christians were now starting to partake of the same water that she had been drinking of. Satan suddenly had shivers run down his spine as he remembered Ezekiel prophesied about water. As the fresh water [1] empties into the sea of salt, the water becomes fresh. Swarms of living creatures [2] will live wherever the river flows. Satan finally understood the statement Ezekiel had made. As Terri and other Grace Believers share the fresh message of Jesus being the Spring of Living Water, the salty water of religion was changing Christians who had learned the law and self-empowered works. Terri was one who was chosen to help others receive a drink of the fresh water. How could he have been so blind? Was the script **EL SHADDAI** had wrote, inscribed on her heart? Satan wanted to look at the script and see if there were some changes he might be able to insert.

Satan sat at the table surrounded by his demonic followers. Each one was given a tablet to write their ideas of demise for this spirit filled, spirit led believer. The Demons of Pain and Agony wrote down, car wreck. Attack her spine and neck. Just the fear of the crash would cause her doubt that she was in the Almighty's hand. With excruciating pain, there would be the need of pills. As he was writing, the Spirit of Agony saw the Demon of Dependency looking over his shoulder. Without saying a word, an evil grin broadened across his face. The Spirit of Dependency would write the same idea that would support his crippling demise. It may not stop the grating voice of praise but it would slow her down.

The Spirit of Manipulation devised a plan that would use Terri's God given compassion for the veterans and the elderly. No longer would the giving heart be able to operate when exposed to the disguised carrier of the Legion of Spirits. Sending a candidate that demonstrates joy and peace harboring concern for other's needs, Terri would be slowly drawn into a web of deception. As the group sat writing their different ideas, Satan looked around the room. The sinister group seemed to be enjoying the demise of the target that was intended. It was time to seize this powerful warrior for the underworld. With the excitement in the caverns below, Satan was convinced there was no way they would fail this time. She could be swayed or be killed.

Satan did not consider God's plan invincible. Using the gifts given by God, could she be swayed toward the darkness? Manipulating her strengths, she could be valuable for his endeavor of deceiving mankind. Satan smiled a sinister smile, as he pondered his position. He was the director of the screenplay of this world. Satan laughed at the unsuspecting fool. As the demons laid out the different attacks against the faith walker, the plan of action using the Freemason and Illuminati twisting together with the Zionists the pieces of the puzzle would become a labyrinth as she meets my powerful demons. The twisted winding passages of her travel would succeed in diverting her gaze off Jesus, toward what is important, self-preservation. With the plan of attack laid out, he grimaced at what had to be done.

*   *   *

Lucifer quivered slightly in his steps as he walked into the courtroom. He had to get approval from King Jesus before he could go up against one of His blood bought children. In his thoughts, Satan wondered why it was so hard to go before him. Having to get permission from EL ROI (the God who sees) was just wrong. He knew whether Terri would break or stand. The hedge about her seemed invincible but she could choose not to follow Jesus bidding. Something powerful was holding Terri to the loyalty of Jesus, the King of Kings. Hatred and anger began boiling inside for the anointed class. As he approached the throne Satan felt intimidation creeping in for the presence of the Righteous One could be felt.

When King Jesus entered, Lucifer fell to his knees. [3] He tried not to bow and humble himself but could not stand in His presence. Inside Jesus was the presence of ESH OKLAH, the Lord of Consuming Fire. Satan knew Hades; the Lake of Fire was created by God for his final destination. With fear and trembling Lucifer felt the eyes of the angels that used to be his friends looking at him. The pride he carried was stripped of him every time he entered the room. Lucifer looked around. The angels were not even looking at him. All were bowing before the King with honor.

King Jesus spoke, "Lucifer why are you here? Why bring your evil presence before the throne?" The King spoke with justified anger for he knew why Lucifer was bringing dishonor before the court. The tempter stood. The angels could see the twitching in his face. The power of the One on the throne left this arrogant praise-seeker with a trembling in his voice. "I see the hedge you have around Terri," Lucifer uttered. "We will see the truth as she is put through the fire." As Lucifer, the angel of light presented the challenge of Terri's loyalty; the elders watched the face of the Lord of Righteousness. The angels that were guardians of Terri knew the formidable evil dragon was pushing his limits. Jesus loved His Bride. He also knew the depth of love Terri had for Him. Jesus knew her testimony proclaiming His unfailing love for her and her family. Lucifer waited for his answer. King Jesus said, "It is allowed. You will see where her loyalty lies. I am embedded deep within her heart and the Spirit is leading her. As the light goes before her she will expose the dark secrets you have tried to cleverly hide. Woe to those proclaiming to be the "Enlightened Ones". The Illuminati will lose its power over my children for Terri will reveal the many levels of twisted evil deception. Now leave my presence before I cast you to the fire that has been awaiting you for years. Your time is almost here but there are more chains that need to be taken off my children and cast to the bottomless pit for your 1000 year bondage. I despise the torment you enjoy thrusting on my children. Soon you will experience the pain and agony that you brought to others. Depart from Me!" The guardian angels escorted the dragon Lucifer from the face of the Lord of Hosts.

Two hours after arriving in Tennessee, Pat from the Daily Bread was laid on my heart. Listening, I went over to visit with her but she wasn't there. I sat down and began eating with those already feasting. A woman came and asked for a ride home. She had back problems and just recently had surgery. Pulling up her pant leg, I saw the wound left from knee surgery. I prayed for safety taking this stranger home for I felt uneasiness. Not knowing the territory very well, I also asked for Him to help me find my way back to town. As the woman and I rode to her house, we visited. The conversation was simple, but heaviness was felt in the car. I didn't really understand what I was feeling, but my senses were on red alert. I slowed down as I approached the driveway of the woman's home, which was on a curve. Suddenly, I was slammed forward hitting my forehead on the steering wheel. A vehicle came around the curve and slammed into me. Not able to pull my thoughts together for a few minutes, the passenger with me had to take control of the situation.

I tried to get out of the car and take a step, but my back brought me down. With my head spinning and my back screaming out in pain, I knew I had been brought to a standstill. Not questioning God or man I sat totally stunned. I listened to the man explain the wreck, from his point of view, to the police. Everything sounded correct until he said he was going to go around but the white car in front of me hit its' brakes. Both my passenger and I disagreed. There was no white car. He was insistent. Thinking upon the white car, took my mind off the bumps the ambulance kept hitting sending excruciating pain. That could only have been the Lord. What was he trying to tell me? Was the presence of the Lord seen by another? Why hadn't I been shown the vehicle so I could steer away from it? A sudden jolt shot through my body as we went over railroad tracks bringing me back to the situation at hand. I wanted to laugh because I had asked the Lord for help back to town. An ambulance, as my transportation, never entered my thoughts.

I had been warned and put on guard that Satan would come up against me. Was there more to this story? Was the key, the mysterious seen and unseen white car in front of me? Was it Satan or God who was in front? I considered the "I AM". I had been told to find out who the "I AM" was for me. Being a prayer warrior, I had begun to pray using the many names of God. Had my vengeful foe Lucifer and his hosts of fallen angels also noticed the answered prayers?

In the heavens, the crowd of witnesses watched the scene in the emergency room. Love could be seen on the face of Jesus. He allowed the wreck to be done for He knew my heart. I had learned to trust His love. He recognized the Spirit of Fear standing on the side of the road with his friends, Bitterness and Doubt. Jesus smiled for my first thought; it was a sign. I was to stay put for a while in Tennessee. Evidently, the Lord had work that needed to be done. Tired and weary believers were supping at the Daily Bread. As the physical hunger was taken care of, so would the spiritual food be given. As I waited to have x-rays done, tears slowly trickled down my face. Jesus watched as all seemed to walk by me as if I wasn't even there. He heard my pleas for Him to touch me. He reached out his hand and touched my cheek. He caught the tear drop that was ready to drop on the bedding. He whispered, "You're not alone. I am here beside you. Do you want to talk?" I had to ask the million dollar question, "Lord, were you the white car seen in front of me or was it Satan who likes to masquerade as an angel of light? Jesus smiled. Then He said, "Who is the 'I AM' for you?" I knew YAHWEH SHAMMAH (the Lord was there) in my car with me. "Thank you Jesus. There is no one else here for me." Jesus whispered to me, His precious Bride, "There is no other place I would rather be, I will never forsake [4] you. I love you."

*　*　*

Satan seethed as he watched the two in the hospital. The love shared was one he could not understand. There was no anger or resentment. Jesus sat with Terri. The girl was in definite pain and yet she wasn't hateful. Satan made sure no one helped her for hours so that the anger and resentment would set in, but it didn't. He saw that Jesus had taken her in His arms and there was only a peace.[5] The Demons of Fear, Resentment, and Anger was not able to touch her. Her thoughts automatically went to the One that held the passion of her heart, mind, and soul. As the group of demons watched, none had the courage to go up against Jesus who held her. The demons asked their master with disgust in their voices, "How did she see past the hidden disguise that you had put in front of her?" Satan huffed!

Pearl Drops of Wisdom

1. Can both fresh water and salt water flow from the spring? . . .
    Neither can a salt spring produce fresh water.

    James 3:11-12 NIV

2. . . . . There will be a large numbers of fish, because this water
    flows there and makes the salt water fresh; so where the river
    flows everything will live.

    Ezekiel 47:9 NIV

3. that at the name of Jesus every knee shall bow, in heaven and on
    earth and under the earth.

    Philippians 2:10 NIV

4. . . . for he has said, I will never leave you, nor forsake you.

    Hebrews 13:5 KJV

5. And the peace of God which surpasses all understanding, will
    guard your hearts and minds through Christ Jesus.

    Philippians 4:7 KJV

Chapter 23

Pawn's Revealing Dream

Using the Daily Bread, Satan considered the place a great opportunity to deceive this faith walker. If Terri thought her abilities were needed desperately, she would be sucked into a greater scheme. She would help him win back his kingdom. If given the opportunity to serve with very little time to think and pray, she would fall in the snare of deception. Jesus was always staying by her side so he knew he had to direct this character himself. As the play began to unfold, there were pawns in the earthly realm that were willing servants for the underworld. Satan sent a servant to sit and eat with others at the Daily Bread. The servant had the appearance of a woman that was 51 years old. She was a pretty woman with a beautiful smile that could melt hearts.

* * *

I walked into the Daily Bread to eat. Befriending many of those who were fed, I spotted a woman who had a glow about her. The woman shared stories of how she had been in the military and was put through experimental testing. The conversations were filled with sorrow and grief. Yet, worsened as she talked about her family robbing her of what was rightly hers. The more she talked the more her conversations didn't make sense. Throughout the discussion this woman's mind would jump to talking about spirit beings in other dimensions. The robbery was also done in the heavenly realm. Was she saying Jesus had robbed Satan of his throne? The thought of demon possession crossed my mind. Not through with the conversation, we sat outside in my car after eating lunch. The woman shared several dreams with me. Every time I had tried to witness, the door was shut tightly. So after listening to the dream, I offered to interpret the hidden message to the woman who held so many secretive thoughts.

The dream had a man beaten to death. With fresh blood dripping off, he was standing on the shore across the river. While she walked, the dead man walked a little bit in front of her. His hand which had a slight hint of a glow, was reaching out toward her but she didn't want to take the extended hand. She arrived at a cabin. She looks back for the man who was nowhere to be seen. With fearful hesitation, she opened the door of the cabin. A man sitting at the table, with a long rolling list, was calling out names. The woman started to step in. The gentleman at the desk lifts up his head and calls out her name. In fright she turns to run, for there at the desk is Satan himself. She wants to escape Satan, who laughs wickedly. He is delighted. There is another soul who was willing to heed his voice and submit to his direction. She started running on a path beside a chain link fence which never ends. Her thoughts tormenting her as she runs, "I'm not bad. Why am I here?" There is no light, just total darkness which screamed out to her wanting to swallow her up. With no hope for any light she just runs, it seems for eternity, in total darkness. With fear directing the darkness, her screams seemed to echo through the madness without end. Still able to hear the wicked sinister laugh she finds there is no place to run and hide.

This was the interpretation given to her. Jesus was the man, who had walked with her on the other side of the river. He had been broken and beaten, taking her punishment to His death.[1] Jesus went to the depths of hell obtaining the key to let her out. She saw Jesus' hand reaching out to her, yet died in her darkness of sin. She chose not to accept the Hand of Forgiveness. Instead her eternity would be wrapped in darkness with her chosen master, Satan. He welcomed her when she arrived at death's door, with no way out. She recognized his voice for she was trained to listen to his lies. Hunting for the way out would haunt her, and the screams from Hades would last through eternity, for she chose not to hear the Plan of Salvation and Deliverance while she was alive. The name Jesus would never be forgotten; for Jesus' fresh dripping blood had been offered to her.

As I started talking about the blood of Jesus, the woman's eyes began to roll. Words that came out of her mouth surprised me. The evil spirit inside of her said, "You know nothing of us. There are many of us. You think you can write about us, yet you know nothing." I noticed the "us" in the evil spirit's conversation. With boldness I ask, "How many are there?" The question was totally ignored. The spirit continued, "You are too strong for me, but there are many of us and we are coming against you. You will be destroyed. We have already started the masterpiece of your demise. YOU WILL BE DESTROYED!" The demon roared. I spoke with boldness," You have no control over my life except what the Father in Heaven allows. I am not afraid of you for the Blood of Jesus is what I stand in. I will live for Christ for He died for me. If I am to die, I gain. [2] To see my precious Savior, Lord, and Master would be joy, for I have only been able to believe through faith. I am in His hands. In Jesus' name you must obey, so you cannot touch what is His without His permission. Again I ask you, how many are you, a legion?" The demon once again ignored the question that had been thrown out.

Changing the subject the entity talked in riddles how they had been at 9/ll. It said they didn't have to do anything except plant destruction and greed in the hearts of man. Man followed the plan that had been masterminded by the Illuminati leaders thru the guidance of the "Enlightened Ones". The destruction was planned long before anyone knew. The entity continued to talk in riddles, some that made sense and others left me bewildered. I knew nothing of the Illuminati and naturally assumed the 'Enlightened Ones' were demons. Turning its head toward the Daily Bread, it then spoke against it, "This place is going down. The plague is coming soon. Many will spend eternity gnashing their teeth. We convinced many the truth was a lie. Shame will be the cup they drink, when the wrath is poured out. We have many followers in this place, carrying the appearance of good. Trust no one for they work for us."

I spoke, "In the name of Jesus, you have no control here. When the Lord removes his hand then it will be done. This place is a sanctuary for many. The physical food is nothing compared to the food that is being given to them daily from the Lord, Himself. There are many servants for the King. You are not going up against them. You are challenging the One they serve, Jesus Himself. Walls are being torn down and chains are falling, off not because of them but, because the Presence of the LORD is here." The woman shook as the demon squelched, "You are too late. There is no hope here." Talking to the woman instead of the demon, salvation was brought to the fore front once more. As I talked about the blood of Christ for forgiveness of sin, the woman seemed driven to hurry out of the vehicle. She opened her door and jumped out. I followed suit. The woman was nowhere in sight. I was absolutely dumb founded. Looking around the empty parking lot, I wondered what I had been talking to. Was she a possessed woman or a demon in the appearance of a woman? The confrontation with the underworld left me somewhat in a state of shock. I began a search to find out about the Illuminati.

* * *

In the caverns below, the demons were being raked over the hot coals. The spokesman for the group had divulged information that was not to be given out to anyone and especially to an anointed child of God. Satan had watched Terri's face as the tidbits of information on the Illuminati and 'Enlightened Ones' had been given. To disappear before her eyes; how foolish were the demons to show their capabilities. Knowledge of the underworld was coming into light. Terri had been praying to ELOHIM to separate the light [3] from the darkness. Evidence showed that God was doing just that. In foolishness, they offered information she should never have known. Satan was not ready to throw out the script that he had adjusted. Terri will get caught up in the family business. Little does she know what the business really involves? Satan would send another who would be more subtle. He rewrote the script using more of the kindness of Terri's heart. The snare would be one brought on because of compassion. The demons watched at a distance the determination of Satan up against this blood bought, Spirit led believer.

Pearl Drops of Wisdom

1. Seeing what was ahead, he spoke of the resurrection of the Christ, that he was not abandoned to the grave, nor did his body see decay. God raised this Jesus to life, and we are all witnesses of the fact.

    Acts 2:31-32 NIV

2. . . . and he separated the light from the darkness.

    Genesis 1:4 NIV

Chapter 24

The Plot Thickens

Weeks had passed since I had been at the Daily Bread. Seeds of Grace had been sown in Ohio, Virginia, Pennsylvania and Maryland. With such an interesting situation the last time I was in Tennessee, I knew to be on guard at all times. Jesus opened doors to minister continually. Before sending me out, He reminded me, "Watch out for the wolves in sheep's clothing. [1] Satan wants to destroy you, be on guard. Snares and traps that have been set, I will expose." I wondered how many times I was told by people, "watch out." Was the Lord speaking through them? I smiled when Jesus whispered "Every time." The assignment set by the Lord was to do street ministry for next two days. I had helped Howard clean out his beloved wife's clothing. The gift of love was to be passed out to the women in need at the Daily Bread. Jesus desired the physical need be met first. When the opportunity opened up, I would witness to those wanting to be fed spiritually.

Enjoying the fellowship with the people, I felt a tap from Jesus on my arm. I looked up and saw the woman of interest. She was talking with an elderly woman. The conversation looked like it was intense, as they were staring at me. Guarding my thoughts, I hoped my face did not reveal the questionable involvement the elderly woman had with the possessed woman? I continued to lay out the clothes for the women shoppers, who were thrilled to be receiving the much needed clothing. With delight the women would go tell others about the garments that were available for their choosing. Gifts from Howard, the servant of the King, were being received willingly and openly. The clothing was in mint condition some even had the tags still on them. Discouragement was seen on the faces when not all were able to receive. Without having all the sizes needed some left empty handed. I felt the desperation of the women who would put their children first and had nothing for their own bodies. I asked the Lord to let me give out gifts from Him, again to others. The joy it brought to the women was unimaginable.

While serving the people, I was asked more than once "Why are you doing this?" I would answer, "Jesus saw your need. He promises to take care of those that He loves. He loves you." I didn't ask if they knew the Lord, it was more showing the act of God's faithfulness for all those who were in need. The doors would then open to their hearts and the different street preachers began to preach God's unconditional love. The street preachers all lived with the same issues of poverty; yet spoke with boldness that even made me smile. God was working in a powerful way. The message of no drinking, dancing and drugs was never brought up. Only words of God's unconditional love and forgiveness flowed from the lips of Ministers of Grace.

While ministering to one of the women, I felt a tap on my back. I turned around to see the elderly woman. The woman wanted to look in the clothes. As she gathered a pile of clothes for herself, I watched the woman in need. When she had finished gathering, she asked me, "Why are you doing this?" I answered, "Jesus saw your need. He promised to take care of those He loves. He loves you." The woman whispered to me, "I need to talk to you." I followed the woman to a quiet spot where she proceeded to tell me the story of her life. The whole time I was wondering what she really wanted. I heard desperation in Jenny's voice as she divulged the story of her husband, a World War II veteran. The agony he suffered due to the many gruesome things he had experienced was revealed. Night sweats combined with the haunting nightmares left the veteran with no desire to sleep. Her husband had been buried alive in the war. It left him unable to deal with darkness or closed in places. Mental anguish from the physical torment was a constant torture that caused him to go insane. He longed to rid himself of the agony within his thoughts, praying to die.

Jenny began to cry when she told me he had killed himself in front of her. Mortified by the information, I really didn't know what to say to the grieving woman. I held Jenny, who was weeping on my shoulder. What was I to say to console the broken hearted woman? No words seemed to sound appropriate for the sorrowful occasion. It was still vivid in Jenny's thoughts as she explained the details of the night of horror less than a year ago. Which brought us to the reason for the meeting? She wanted to open a home for vets and wanted me to manage the home. The elderly woman lived in Tennessee, yet had broken down property in Virginia? Why did she live in Tennessee? Jenny wanted me to go look at the property with her. She said there was a lot of destruction done because her family was vindictive and wanted to hurt her. As she continued to share from her heart, she exposed family problems. They had stolen the property from her. She needed my help to get that back for her also. The more it went the more uneasiness crept into my soul.

Jenny said she was a blood bought Believer. That was how I proclaim belonging to Jesus. Had she been blood bought by Jesus' atonement? Her needs seemed endless but familiar. She demanded, "You WILL help me get what is rightfully mine!" I detected a hint of anger in her voice. All I could say was, "Let me pray about all these things. Can I ask why you are asking me? You don't know me at all." The woman smiled and said, "I see into your spirit. You have a kind, giving spirit. The vets have been forgotten. Their burdens are great and you care about the vets." A red flag went up. I hadn't said anything to this woman about the vets. The possessed woman she had talked to knew. Had she recommended her to Jenny? I asked the woman how she knew the pretty blond woman, pointing to the woman. The elderly woman said she was family. Jenny said she would trust the woman with her life. She had helped guide her through situations before. Shivers ran down my spine. The Spirit of Discernment whispered, "Silence." I asked, "Is she a Christian?" An adamant "NO" shot through her mouth. Jenny continued, "Her family was church people but she wanted no part of it." The way she said 'NO', threw another red flag. It was as if "Christian" was a bad word to this woman who said she was a blood bought Believer.

I left that day and began to pray for the elderly woman who had lost her husband, her property, and her life. The uniqueness of the whole situation left no peace in my heart. I asked the Lord to reveal the bigger picture. In the dark scenario what was the truth? I asked the LORD, "Should I help this woman? You gave me a heart for the veterans. Why isn't she living in Virginia if she has a place there"? Question after question popped in my head.

I spoke at a church the next day. It wasn't just any church. The service was tied in with a second-hand store which helps young girls. Girls were sent there by courts, family, or of their own free-will. Each one had lives that were destroyed somehow, whether by drugs, violence, or man problems. Man sent these girls here for one more chance to try to correct their problems. God was using the place to help restore lives from destruction. I felt like it was an honor that they would ask me to speak that night. As I was preparing for the message, I heard the Lord ask for the ceremony of the bread and wine to be done in remembrance of Him. Before the service started, Jenny entered the church. She said," I have to speak to you." Once again I followed the woman thinking it must be something urgent. Jenny said, "We can open up a place like this. I have the money right now to start it. You can run it." I declined but noticed another red flag. What was it about this lady that I kept feeling like something wasn't right?

When the bread and wine [2] was passed out, everyone waited to sup together except Jenny in the back row. It sent shivers down my spine. I felt as if the moment of remembrance was a gesture of mockery permeating eeriness from this woman. The token of bread, representing Christ's body broken for man, was treated with the same disrespect as the wine which was taken like a shot of alcohol even though I asked for all to wait till the prayer was said. Before the memorial service was over, the lady quickly walked out the door without looking back.

Was this another wolf in sheep's clothing? What was the game being played? Why would a woman who wanted a home for the veterans in Virginia want with a second-hand store in Morristown? What was the urgency to have me be a part of her situation in life or business? There was no peace the more I encountered this woman. The woman was trying to manipulate circumstances in order to obtain my services. Why?

While driving to see my children in Virginia, I prayed earnestly about the situation. Listening to Messianic praise music, I became caught up in worship of EL SHADDI. Knowing Jesus literally cared about every burden and care brought joy to my spirit. I sought wisdom whether or not to check out Jenny's house. I noticed the sky became very dark out of nowhere. The wind tried blowing the car off the road. Sheets of rain poured down making it almost impossible to drive. I exclaimed, "Light my path Lord. [3] I can't see." The LORD spoke, "You can't see for truth isn't in it. If you go with this woman you will never see your children again. Stop and consider. The story seemed familiar. Both women have proclaimed their home was stolen from them, after fighting with family. What you are hearing isn't all a lie. There was a great battle in the heavens. Stolen? No, Satan was cast out of the heavens. He wants your help in restoring the house that is crumbling around him. You have brought truth and grace into his territories. You witnessed Psalm 103:1-5 and shared it with the people at the Daily Bread. Your testimony of My salvation and healing is causing a disruption. The message of Grace redeeming the lives of destruction is making it so that Satan is losing control over the minds that he had held for so long. Satan is trying to manipulate you so that you follow his leading, instead of Mine."

"Stay true to the message of Jesus' loving kindness and tender mercy. People are receiving the message. They see the fruit of the Holy Spirit.[4] The hungry are being fed and the thirsty are receiving drink. Continue to seek My wisdom. My face is shining [5] down on you." As fast as the storm hit, the dark rain clouds moved out. The message exposing the darkness surrounding Satan's satanic web was displayed by creation. After hearing the words of Knowledge, the sun came out shining.

Pearl Drops of Wisdom

1. I am sending you out like sheep among wolves . . . .

   Matthew 10:16 NIV

2. . . . "This is my body, which is for you; do this in remembrance of me." In the same way, after supper he took the cup, saying," This cup is the new covenant in my blood; do this, whenever you drink it, in remembrance of me."

   I Corinthians 11:24-25 NIV

3. . . . The LORD is my light and my salvation—whom shall I fear? . . .

   Psalm 27:1 NIV

4. But the fruit of the Spirit is love, joy, peace, patience, kindness, goodness, faithfulness, gentleness and self-control. Against such things there is no law.

   Galatians 5:22-23 NIV

5. Make your face shine upon your servant . . . .

   Psalm 119:135 NIV

Chapter 25

Badge of Courage

I felt the unquenchable desire to go back to the house that held so many mysteries in Pennsylvania. Was the house really haunted? Was the whole town holding hidden secrets that even the people living there knew nothing about? I remembered the ominous feeling the last time I was in town. Curiosity drove me back to Pottsville. As I drove to the town that had hidden the African-Americans in the tunnels, the past enveloped my thoughts. The story of Mr. Biddle came to mind.

Nick Biddle was of African descent living in Pottsville. He was born a free man, in the North, fighting a fight that took him to Washington D.C. endeavoring in the quest for freedom. No man should be owned by another. The Civil War had divided the Pennsylvanian's families for not all agreed with the northern thoughts as the southern ideals were considered practical by some. Was he aware other races had suffered slavery? I shuttered, thinking of my ancestors with the Irish and German descent. As I passed another boarded up hillside, I considered how many people had run in these hills. How many were hidden and starving as they struggled not only against man but also the elements. As cruel as the weather would be, the cruelty left by man was stronger.

I was impressed with the willingness of Nick Biddle, for he went the extra mile. He chose to fight for others freedom. He was brutally attacked and beaten by an angry mob. Nick sustained a gash in his head. After tending his own wound by wrapping it with a cloth, he put on his hat, then boarded a train headed to Washington. No injury was going to stop him from presenting his case to President Abraham Lincoln. Very few Americans knew Nick Biddle had the first blood spilt in the Civil war. On his arrival in Washington, the crowd greeted him differently. With banners waving, the people accepted him with respect and cheered him for his stand. His brand of patriotism was shared among the people of Washington D.C., freedom for all. His military honor badge was a visible deep scar for all to see. His trophy of courage exemplified the distance he was willing to go for others.

How many people in the Pottsville area remembered the man? Did they know Biddle Elementary School was in honor of his stand against slavery? The tour guide, Nicole, went to the school but never was told the significance behind the name. I couldn't help but think about the man who received battle scars for freedom. As the generations passed, was there any acknowledgement from the younger generations? Would his legacy as a freedom fighter be known? All those who knew the character of the man had passed away, so the depth of his devotion would be buried with those who understood his passion.

With the thought of the battle scar, I pondered about the distance Jesus went to give freedom to mankind. Has the legacy of the deep scars in his forehead from a crown of mockery [1] been watered down so much that the passion is no longer seen in the church today? Can we see the depth of His devotion when we consider the deep nail print scars in His hands[2] of healing and feet that carried the message of peace? Choosing to be the servant, He was pierced for our transgressions [3] in order to bridge the gap that separated mankind from the Father in Heaven. To leave His position in glory[4] to embrace with open arms, the lonely walk to Golgotha in an ultimate face off with the god of this world. He had to win the keys to death and hell in order to receive the souls belonging to the Father. Beaten to the place of unrecognizable distinction, He still continued on the road to Calvary. Could He hear any pleading for His innocence, as the crowd was cheering the guards to crucify Him? Was it the faces of fear and sorrow, pushing the Lamb being led to slaughter? [5]

I considered the conversations that I had with Natali, Aviel and Esau. They saw Jesus as a heretic. They didn't believe Jesus was even a Jew. Born of a virgin was totally made up. The only thing that bothered them was they wanted their temple grounds back. Why couldn't they build in another part of Jerusalem? Faces mortified! They had to have possession of Palestine, for the Mosque of Omar was sitting where their part of their temple used to be. The part critical for a Jew to be able to worship correctly, they needed the Holiest of Holies spot back. I couldn't help but wonder if it was because of what happened to Emperor Julian. He went in to rebuild the temple. After much expense and considerable time of construction, was compelled to halt any building on the site due to flames that burst thru the foundation. The eruption killed workers. Was the Ark of the Covenant hid there? No longer, was the presence of God contained in a box made of wood and gold. He put His precious countenance within the temple of flesh, Jesus. [6] Humiliated and bruised with our iniquities the redemption for vile creation that made a mockery from the day He gave his life to present day.

* * *

The Mohammedan Mosque, now called the Mosque of Omar contains high on a wall an inscription saying:

> **Praise be to God who has no son or companion in his government, and who needs no helper to save him from dishonor . . . The messiah Jesus is only the son of Mary, the ambassador of God . . . God is one and far be it that he should have a son.**

The System Bible Study Copyright 1933

* * *

Were the angels angered or sickened by the cruelty done by the Almighty's creation? Watching the principalities of darkness join with hearts of stone, did the angels of the heavenly realm understand the picture of redemption being given? They knew Jesus' Kingdom was not of this world, [7] but did they know the thoughts of God. Did they weep, as they watched the suffering of the One that won the battle in the Heavens for them? Could Satan not understand prophesies any better than man? The Islam faith displayed the mockery from the depths below when they listened to Lucifer make it look like the Almighty was dishonored because of the wickedness of man. If he would have comprehended the perfect permanent stain in the heavens; Jesus pure sacrifice was announced in the Garden of Eden, but thought of before the beginning of time. Jesus had exchanged the Heavens of praise and worship for punishment in order to bring us peace with God.

The week before the display of injustice, Jesus rode into Jerusalem with palm leaves waving. The Jews were lifting him up as a king. Rejoicing in the miracles that he showed, their admiration was expressed with dancing and jubilee. The worship of Baal and Molech intertwined with Judaism had never brought healing or deliverance. The people were impressed with Jesus' abilities to fix things in the physical realm. Believing he was the promised Messiah. Jesus rode the unbroken ass knowing this exaltation was only a brief moment in time. Hearts of praise would be brought to halt. Once again Jesus exchanged praise and worship so that he could be rejected and hated by man in order to do his Father's will.

It was raining outside. The darkness was so great I couldn't see any longer. It was as if the heavens were crying with me. Rain was pouring down in sheets making it so the wipers couldn't keep the windows clear. The road was flooding as a dense fog hung in the darkness. The dark clouds that covered the skies emptied the sorrow that I felt in my heart. Unable to drive for the powerful rain was flooding the road, all I could do was weep. Under the blood is where he put not only those fearful followers but also the angry Pharisees. Jesus saw past the mocking soldiers and guards thoughts, to the need that screamed louder, REDEMPTION. Jesus walking past each face in the crowd whispering in His thoughts, "This blood is for you."

As I considered the exchange, I noticed a circle of blue that started to emerge in the dark clouds. There were white stringy clouds, outlining in the circle edged with a fine line of gold. It looked like a simple crown. The storm was replaced with a crown of peace leaving me in awe. The extreme difference was noticeable as the beauty of the sun began to shine forth its rays down on the dripping trees.

How many showed the battle scars for the Kingdom? Martyrdom was known throughout the world. With hidden messages and common sense renewed how many Christians were being martyred in order to stifle the secrets being programmed to generations of youth to control their nature instead of Jesus? What happened through the centuries that people went back to their own works instead of the ultimate work at the cross? Hatred was strong, by those walking on the boardwalk, against the artistry displayed in sand of the life of Jesus the Christ. Considering my hand compared to the hand of Golgotha; Jesus took it all and gave it all. His scar is the Badge of Courage and Love. All God's wrath and punishment was put on Him. Yet, my hand held life when He wants to use it.

I gave a woman a necklace. It was a circle within a circle, with no obvious beginning or end. Words were written thanking God for letting the two paths cross, so we could be friends. The gift given from the heart was received with elation then turned to hesitancy. Amish custom does not allow jewelry. The necklace was hidden under her clothes, hiding it from her husband and family. I understood when she took it off to go in public. Though precious to the woman, the gift could not be seen or she would be excommunicated from her religious ties. Are Christians today any different than this woman? Professing to love the gift of life, but loving the things of this world more? How many people hide the gift so that they are not ridiculed or judged? The depth of Jesus' passion for the believer is not hidden in the heavens. He isn't embarrassed to carry the Forgiveness Badge.

I thought of Moses. Sharing intimate moments with God, Moses glowed in the face,[8] the people were afraid, so he covered the evidence he had been with God. The crowd chose not to see the glory of the

Lord on Moses. Was the godly radiance a constant reminder of their choice of separation from God?

"I will not hide Your Righteousness in my heart or conceal Your Love and Truth. As Moses radiated your presence when he came down off the mountain, so may you shine through me! May I radiate the joy of the Lord, for I am not ashamed of the Gospel [9]of Christ?" I prayed.

PEARL DROPS OF WISDOM

1. The soldiers twisted together a crown of thorns and put it on his head . . . .

    John 19:2 NIV

2. Then he said to Thomas, "Put your finger here; see my hands. Reach out your hand and put it into my side. Stop doubting and believe."

    John 20: 27 NIV

3. But he was wounded for our transgressions; he was bruised for our iniquities: the chastisement of our peace was upon him; and with his stripes we are healed.

    Isaiah 53:5 KJV

4. And no man hath ascended up to heaven, but he that came down from heaven, even the Son of man which is in heaven.

    John 3:13 KJV

5. He was oppressed, and he was afflicted, yet he opened not his mouth: he is brought as a lamb to the slaughter, and as a sheep before her shearers is dumb, so he openeth not his mouth.

    Isaiah 53:7 KJV

6. In the beginning was the Word, and the Word was with God, and the Word was God. And the Word became flesh, and dwelt among us, and we beheld His glory, the glory as of the only begotten of the Father, full of grace and truth.

    John 1:1, 14 KJV

7. Jesus answered, "My kingdom is not of this world. If My kingdom were of this world, then My servants would fight, so that I should not be delivered to the Jews; but now My kingdom is not from here."

    John 18:36 NIV

8. When Moses came down from Mount Sinai with the two tablets of the Testimony in his hands, he was not aware that his face was radiant because he had spoken with the LORD. When Aaron and all the Israelites saw Moses, his face was radiant, and they were afraid to come near him.

    When Moses finished speaking to them, he put a veil over his face.

    Exodus 34:29, 30, 33 NIV

9. For I am not ashamed of the gospel of Christ: for it is the power of God unto salvation to everyone that believeth.

    Romans 1:16 KJV

Chapter 26

Twisted and Intrigued

I was drawn to the entrance gates of a large cemetery, in Pottsville. The sun was just coming up, yet a silent golden hue, draping down from the heavens, shined on the grave stones. They were commemorating loved ones, who had passed, dating from the 1700's and 1800's to present day. It was as if the Lord wanted special notice given to those He had touched with a believing heart. As I looked at different monuments, intrigue was left to the personage of those whose names were written in stone. Some had written in lengthy detail, others only one word. I noticed one headstone had no name, only the appearance of a woman's face. Amazed, it was as if the stone was calling out for me, to listen to the messages [1] within the garden of rest.

The silhouette, with high cheek bones, displayed a strong strength of character; the tilting of the head upward, declared respect, as she lay beside other notable and infamous people. Some had only a small stone honoring the passing of the loved one, where others showed the prestige by enormous structures signifying the importance of the deceased. Sitting here beside the tomb with the weather worn face, King Solomon's writings entered my thoughts. A time to live and a time to die, [2] death happens to us all. I noticed heritages gathered together. The difference of race in life, no longer mattered in death. This garden of rest held all bones equal. The racial, religious and financial situations through life, no longer mattered. The effort of obtaining money and power was no better than the one who lived peaceably with only a piece of bread. They both ended up in the same place, the grave. The restful place was holding all till the sound of the trumpet call of God, when once again the culmination of bones would separate. The dead in Christ would receive their bodies leaving the other bones for the White Throne Judgment.[3]

I wondered why the woman's face exhibited intense suffering on the stone. What generation had the woman come from? Had she been one of the women who had suffered from the potatoes famine in 1840? Had she migrated to Pottsville from Germany or Ireland? Maybe she was an African American who had been born a free woman, or was she possibly a woman who through courage ran in the tunnels for freedom. I thought, "If only the tombs could speak." Wandering around the different tombstones, glancing side to side I noticed clues left for future generations. Family trees were traceable as the plots held the different family members. Information left behind could be seen spiritually, as well as physically.

One family was set around a tree that was made out of stone. The branches were cut off at the top leaving a lot of room for the family tree to grow. There was a vine made of the same material, winding around the tree. The vine was broken by design, as if signifying the separation of one critical to the life of the vine had been broken by death. There was a vessel laying down on its side and broken, with the contents spilled out, leaving those who looked upon it to realize another broken vessel was emptied of life. Was the message to future generations: Here slept a family member waiting to be caught up in the rapture? Was the vine representing the Vine [4] of Christ? Broken was a part of the vine but the main vine was still seen by brothers and sisters in the Lord. I was curious about the life the family members had lived. Had they left behind a legacy to their children's children of faithfulness to God and servant hood to man? With the tombstone displayed, they left behind a message to look to the Vine and the Vinedresser. Had they taught that to their children?

The broken vessel that was spilled out left much to my imagination. Was the spill because of the death of the loved one, or was it leaving a message of greater depth? Christians are vessels that are broken that God wants to fix and fill to overflowing. [5] Curiosity of whether the pot represented the believer had broken at death and the filling was no longer possible? Maybe the picture was, here lays a broken pot[6] that never was filled with the overflow that counted. As I took pictures of the stunning masterpiece left in honor of those laying at rest in this spot, I wondered? Were the members of this family all believers? Twelve bodies would rise at the trumpet sound.[7] What joy would be pouring forth from the graves? They would be saying, "Man that was a good nap. Hallelujah to the Lord for bringing our bodies back to our spirits." Just the thought of the dead in Christ rising first sent shivers down my spine.

I noticed a tombstone that drew my attention, once again. There was nothing fancy about it. The burial monument did not stand high or lift up the one contained within the vault, but left me trying to figure out what the words were that were written in stone. Some of the letters were worn badly because of the age and the weather. The grave was for a woman named Sarah Fowler. She was born March 1818 and passed away August 1888. The words that were etched in stone left the message, "Why do we mourn for dying friends or shake at deaths alarms? Tis, but the voice that Jesus sends to call them to His arms".

I sat beside the woman who left the note of encouragement to those who would take the time to stop and hear the message sent from the garden of rest. Here was another sister in the Lord. Her gravestone was proclaiming from the grave, a tender reminder to those who believed in Jesus, the promise of hope. I found myself looking forward to the day when I would meet the sister of encouragement. What miracles had she seen and testified about? The loved ones, she left behind, left a picture of what had been exemplified by Sarah's life. She wasn't perfect but was perfectly loved. As she had spoken hope and love, so was it spoken in stone for those needing encouragement.

While writing notes of the different monuments and names of historical interest, a man walking his dog stopped and asked me a very peculiar question. "Are you the lady that brought back the plates?" I told him I didn't know what he was talking about. He heard on the news, a woman from Tennessee found name plates off the tombstones of that particular cemetery. Was I the one that found and returned them? I did find the situation quite interesting, for I am from Tennessee but let him know it wasn't me.

As I pondered on these things, I noticed a church that looked quite old. Walking toward the chapel, set amongst the tombs, curiosity sparked within my spirit. Studying the structure of the old place of worship, the walls were made of brick. The stain glass windows were still beautiful to behold. As I walked around the magnificent structure, I found there was an open door. Walking in to the quaint historical church, I noticed two men sitting at the table. I couldn't help but notice the old picturesque interior of the basement in the old gathering place. With slight hesitation, I began talking to the men about the history of the church. Question after question poured forth, as answer after answer was shared between the three. The passion for the restored building was felt amongst the history buffs.

Bob and Tom were the ground keepers. They maintained the outward appearance of the buildings and the actual gravesites. It was their job to maintain a beauty in the garden of rest. Whether it was to do carpentry work on the building or mowing the cemetery lawn, the two showed a respect for the dead and the living. The attitude of the two was vibrant. The history shared, was in no comparison to the actual visual tour that I was taken on. Even though the building was historically old, it was in outstanding condition. There was a certain pride seen, as the men showed me the inside of the church. The pipes and original organ were able to be seen in the loft, from below where I stood. Breathtaking as the organ and pipes were, they were not able to be played. Money was needed to fix the pipes that once bellowed the melody of praise.

The conversation then turned to a somewhat grim picture. The stories of ghostly apparitions began to unfold. Unsure how to take the divulged information, I listened to the men share their ghostly encounters. Growing up in a Bible believing home, I was taught ghosts were demonic spirits. Bob was painting a house that dated back to the 1800's. He had been made aware the place was frequented with ghosts, but succumbing to any available work for the physical needs of his family was more important, he was not hesitant about doing any job. He told me ghosts were a common thing in Pottsville. He let me know everyone had a ghost story. I was curious, why the spirits were so prevalent in this territory. As he was painting in the bedroom upstairs on the third floor, he heard voices coming from down stairs. Bob was working the job by himself, so knew there should be no one else in the house. He started to go downstairs and the voices continued, although he couldn't make out what was being said. When he walked through the kitchen, the front door slammed shut. He opened the front door. To his surprise, there was no one there. Looking around the property, there was no sign of any person within his visible range. I was amazed at the calmness within the man's appearance. Had the people learned to accept the presence of those from another dimension? I asked if he was scared. His response was, "As long as I wasn't bothering them, they wouldn't mess with me."

Tom held his tongue, as Bob spoke of his different encounters with the ghosts. When he spoke of his encounter there was tenderness in his voice. His was more of a personal nature. His wife and he had bought the house of a woman he knew. She had passed away. He saw her ghost for a brief moment. Tom saw it; the woman wanted to take a glimpse of her home and make sure it was being taken care of properly. He never saw her again. He assumed the woman was content with the respect being shown to her home.

I was not quite sure how to respond with all the different spirit entities. I had my own paranormal encounter in this town staying at Nicole's, so I knew it wasn't just the people's imagination. I didn't want to accept the paranormal as the rest of the town people. Why would the spirits from another dimension, be willing to live amongst the humans? Were the spirit beings, demons? Were they deceiving the people of the town by using their family or acquaintances in order to stay without confrontation? I talked to a girl who had been partying with friends, one night. They heard joyful children running and playing in the cemetery. There were many who said, they had seen a man carrying a lantern walking in the graveyard.

I walked around in another state curious to know what people thought about ghosts. I developed and distributed a questionnaire to obtain feedback for my curiosity. The Virginians left impressive opinions. Some saw it as projecting images from deep within their own thoughts; whether turmoil or peace. Some said, "People live with their own realities. Visualizing what they hope to see." Many in Virginia had seen their loved ones, shortly after passing away, if they weren't able to say goodbye. It was brief then never again. Majority of those were professing believers and their loved ones were also professing Christians. One question that I asked on the Virginian questionnaire was, "If the loved one that passed away loved Jesus, why would the spirit choose to leave the presence of the Lord to go to the physical realm of wickedness? One little girl made the comment, "If they knew Jesus, they would want Jesus to go to them. Jesus is "bigger" and "badder" than anyone!" [8] Out of the mouths of babes the answer seemed so simple. The believer would want to have the powerful, tender and compassionate Jesus watching over their loved ones.

Writing pertinent questions after reading the history of names off the tombstones, I saw hidden mysteries. Intriguing details were like puzzle pieces challenging me to look deeper. As I went to other towns and states, another piece to the puzzle would be given. An Amish woman named Mary informed me the house that drew my attention was haunted. She wanted to know why I had to go to the haunted house. It is strange. Why was I drawn to a town, house and cemetery that have the living sharing their lives with the dead? A town entangled with the shadow of death and destruction strangling the life out of the people gripped in sorrow and despair? The Bible says not to dabble in the things of the demonic realm, but the Almighty God had directed me to a town that seemed like the living was dancing with the dead. Their world seemed to be so intertwined with entities, from another dimension, that left their town with secrets. Jesus Christ dwells within me. He is the light that exposes the darkness.

The cemetery ground keepers shared how they had moved the oldest tombstones to the main cemetery, leaving the burial vaults. Bob said the town needed space to grow. The families didn't care the grave markers were placed in the old cemetery; as long as bodies weren't disturbed. He went around with a pole trying to find the different burial vaults that were not lined up with tombstones. As he searched, death blew its stale stench into his face. He punctured through one of the caskets.

I wondered if the soul belonged to Satan. Would his spirit be screaming out? "Go to my loved ones and tell them I was wrong. All-I-had-to-do was BELIEVE in JESUS and His underserved kindness. He is the way, the truth, and the life!" The soul screaming loudly, "I saw what I could have had. I turned down His WAY in abundance, His TRUTH in abundance and His LIFE [9] for ME in abundance. The stench of religion escaped out of my tomb. I followed Lucifer's teaching of my works being seen. Faith without works is dead. I didn't realize it was; Faith without JESUS' WORKS SEEN in me is dead. My soul will be in torment for eternity!"

Why is there so much confusion of the teaching; Faith without works is dead. Jesus answer somewhat startled me. "There is a mixture that is not pure and true. Look and see what is buried in the vaults below their foundation? By His answer I knew there was something dark and sinister restraining the pure undefiled powerful teaching of Grace. I whispered softly, "Lead the way.

Pearl Drops of Wisdom

1. ... death is the destiny of every man; the living should take this to heart.

   Ecclesiastes 7:2 NIV

2. A time to be born, and a time to die ...

   Ecclesiastes 3:2 KVJ

3. The rest of the dead lived not again until the thousand years were finished . . . Then I saw a great white throne and Him who sat on it, from whose face the earth and the heaven fled away . . . The sea gave up the dead which were in it, and Death and Hades delivered up the dead who were in them. And they were judged, each one according to his works. Then Death and Hades were cast into the lake of fire. "This is the second death." And anyone not found written in the Book of Life was cast into the lake of fire.

   Revelation 20:5, 11, 13-15 KJV

4. I am the vine, you are the branches. He who abides in me, and I in him, bears much fruit; for without Me you can do nothing. (notice He brings fruit)

   John 15:5 KVJ

5. ... You anoint my head with oil; my cup overflows.

   Psalm 23:5 NIV

6. . . . I have become like broken pottery.

Psalm 31:12 NIV

7. For the Lord himself will come down from heaven, with a loud command, with the voice of the archangel and with the trumpet call of God, and the dead in Christ will rise first.

1Thessalonians 4:16 NIV

8. That Christ may dwell in your hearts through faith; that you, being rooted and grounded in love, may be able to comprehend with all the saints what is the width and length and depth and height—to know the love of Christ which passes knowledge; that you may be filled with all the fullness of God. Now to Him who is able to do exceedingly abundantly above all that we ask or think, according to the power that works in us.

Ephesians 3:17-20 KJV

9. Jesus saith to him," I am the way, the truth, and the life. No one comes to the Father except through Me."

John 14: 6 KJV

Chapter 27

Accomplishments of Enlightened Confusion

In the deep caverns of darkness below, Satan welcomed the legions, the Spirits of the Air and the Spirits of the Underworld. The lord of the underworld acknowledged the demonic spirits that roamed the earth, bringing the world together in utter chaos. The yearly demonic convention was being held once again in the Bohemian Grove. The Demons of Ancient Canaanite, Luciferian and Babylonian mystery religions were assembled together sitting at the tables. The cups were full of the blood of the saints. In a year's time, many had been martyred for their faith. Some sacrificed without their knowledge.

Ceremonies in the earthly realm had welcomed the demonic spirits every summer. The leaders were hoping the spirits would usher in their wisdom and guidance for their countries economic forums. The nations of the world had been divided into 10 empires under the New World Order. The selected group in leadership belonging to the Illuminati, were requesting direction from the" Enlightened Ones" of the Universe. Dancing with the demons leaving Care or Dull Care, as the men liked to call Him, in ashes. The ceremony displayed Dull Care (Jesus) as a cruel taskmaster. The "elite" group of leaders along with the demons chose to run to the "pastoral precinct of the grove". All gathered could escape the responsibilities that Care placed on them. The men gathered could replace the tyrannical standards with a simpler way of life for a period of time. The world's leaders made up by the Illuminati and Freemasons were exposing their nakedness, dancing in the rituals of the pagan gods with the origins in the worship of Molech and Baal. Beelzebub, prince of the demons, was lifted up by man as well as the legions of demons that he ruled over.

The demonic controlled men, belonging to the "elite" group on earth incinerated the effigy of Care as the demons below lifted Beelzebub up on his throne above their heads for worship. Having called for the spirits, the Freemason who carried the title "Lamp of Fellowship" kindled the fire on Care to show an end of the tyranny that had been required. In the caverns below Care's enemy Ease and Beauty mocked Care, "Jesus died for them? Look, see what they think of him! What the Almighty planned for me they are doing to Jesus." With a snide in his voice, Satan knew Jesus was watching the whole show. The men on earth were celebrating their freedom. None of the Christians would see their idolatries in the high places. [1] The sexual immorality was allowed to those of leadership for they were following the desire of Ease and Beauty. Satan didn't need to do anything, for man's heart desired to do evil.

Since the beginning of worship Satan had tried to convince the world "true light" was dark and darkness would appear as light. Those following the "elite" believed the Illuminati had received the truth from the "Enlightened Ones". With the worship of ancient mystical religions, the incantations summoned the demons. Men in leadership all around the world wanted guidance in order to achieve the New World Order. The control of finances, power, and media would be controlled as Satan rejoiced in the secret evil manipulation over the weak minded. The hidden messages within their own U.S. currency revealed the agenda of the Freemasons and those over them, the Illuminati.

With the dancing of the demons surrounding Satan, no one noticed the fiery coals that were dropping around the cavern. With a hot coal landing on the table of celebration, a chain also fell down, clanging as it hit the goblets knocking them over. The blood of the saints ran across the tablecloth. Another blood bought saint had received deliverance from his thoughts. Once again what was loosed in the heavens was loosed on the earth. Another chain was hand delivered by the angels. The chains were being sent back to the true cruel slave master. **The blood bought, anointed by the Spirit, believers are few in numbers, but definitely receiving power from the Heavens above.** What was rocking the coals of fire, this time? As he looked around the world searching for the problematic chaos, Satan saw the **Spirit led believers** at work. **In the darkness, the believers radiated a light through them so he knew they were not regular 'religious' folk. Satan knew he had no authority over these vessels for their devotion was to Jesus' love for them. They recognized, they were the Bride of Christ. Love for their Groom was obvious. Their eyes had been opened to His Righteousness over their unrighteousness and His Righteousness over their righteousness. His Righteous works accomplished things in the supernatural, beyond their imaginations, leaving them praising God continually. The power of the "GREAT I AM' that dwelt in them continued to be the light revealing their paths. The power of the "Black Maria" was no longer feared by them.**

The "Black Maria" was a vehicle announcing death or injury in the physical realm. The vehicle of death was known through the centuries as it visited it's presence on those dying. In the spiritual realm, the greatest vehicle of death was Satan's favorite, religion. With an agonizing torment the tortured soul would leave the earth to an open sepulcher of the grave. The tormented spirits were screaming out waiting to be judged before the White Throne judgment.

The Spirits of the Children of God, belonging to the Kingdom of Heaven were no longer visited by the sorrowful wailing. They were welcomed by Jesus personally before the physical death. Feasting daily at the City of Zion, for the Holy Spirit feeds them through the Word daily. They wear special white garments with special armor that is almost impossible impenetrable. They know ELOHIM is on their side. They understand THE WAY OF HOLINESS; walking in the power of JESUS blood not through their meaningless works of kindness. Expecting miracles through the BLOOD OF JESUS to work supernaturally, these Believers' in the WAY see miracles in the natural world also. When they have tripped and fallen, they remember "totally forgiven". They stand

up and praise the LORD for forgiveness and start running again. Drawing closer to Jesus, they hear and see snares and traps better. Watching briefly the territories to where the **Children of Jesus' Light** was being sent to, Satan knew he needed to put something in their path to slow them down.

Then Satan saw some people wandering in the desert[3] wastelands. They were searching for someplace to sit and just rest. So busy about doing their good works, Satan noticed they were starving to death spiritually. They were being fed the dry moldy bread that had been taught since Moses. Barely living because of the famine in the wasteland, these believers produced little or no fruit. Were they searching for the **City of Peace** that held the **promise of rest**? Most were waiting for the promise of rest, after they die. They were hungry and thirsty for something new and fresh. The souls belonged to Jesus in salvation but they didn't believe His faithfulness of love. **Satan was thrilled these people didn't realize it wasn't their works that mattered but Jesus working through them**. They were busy providing for themselves, just as the Israelites who hardened their hearts with unbelief when they were in the wilderness. The "Black Maria" was able to torture these souls. These continually measured God's blessings on their lives by the material things of this world, which they worked so hard to obtain.

He sent out different demons of judgment to discourage **"Power in the WAY" Believers** from ministering to those that were willing to work in very little light. Enslaved daily, the weary traveler of salvation and self-works wore Satan's favorite strangulation chain made up of the Ten Commandments. Did they not have to stand on works, for faith without works is dead?[4] They were showing the world their faith by works. **Evidence of works following the "Victory Believer" left undeniable power that Jesus worked producing the supernatural change, which lasts.** Satan knew he could not afford to ease up on the suffocation that man's works mattered. Satan savored his favorite lie; **as long as mankind just loved 'God' and tried to live right, heaven awaited them.**

Satan continued searching the world that he controlled. He saw those that were sitting in darkness[5] saturated with deepest gloom.

They were his prisoners suffering in iron chains. These were his favorite for they had rebelled against the words of God. These refused to believe **the written Word was of God.** Satan smiled, for he had servants preaching from the pulpit the Bible isn't complete. Satan knew if everything written about Jesus was put in, the people still wouldn't read it. The book would be too long for all the **miracles of power over my destruction of lives.** I couldn't maintain the lies that I have subtly implanted through generations. The Jews are not God's chosen people. Jesus isn't the Messiah. Jesus and Satan were brothers. There are many paths to heaven. Jesus was an angel. Only 144,000 chosen, will be in heaven. Satan laughed at the stupidity and arrogance of humans. Vessels of clay believing they can become gods greater than or equal to creatures of the heavenliest? Even when he talked with Eve in the Garden of Eden he said, "they would be like the gods knowing good and evil. Blasphemy to the utmost, even to consider being equal to me.

Listening to the celebration from the world leaders, his attention was diverted. He watched as the ashes were gathered from the altar which burned the effigy of "Care." The ashes would be used in "religious" ceremonial rituals, throughout the world. The useless vessels that could contain power, they are so easily controlled, thought Satan. Satan felt shivers as he was reminded of **"Power in the WAY, Believers".** He had to find a way to convince the world, those leaders are useless. They are Useless in my plans for they refused to submit. I must rid the world of the useless leaders.

Using religion and politics, I have manipulated people's minds. Mormon, Islam and polluted Judeo-Christianity running against each for leadership leave the people confused and hopeless. In the people's eyes having to choose which man is better, all looked at their past track record. All of the men have hearts devoted to their 'religious' beliefs, and their works to mankind. Satan wanted to laugh for the commonalities were interesting to look at. One believes he can become a god equal to Jesus. One is against the Messiah Jesus and holds the truth on a wall, at the Mosque of Omar, correct. Their god doesn't need to correct a mistake. No son was born of their god. Let's not forget the polluted Christian faith. Yes, Jesus died but now, it's up to your works to receive blessings from God. The common thread was; all looking to their works and away from **Power of the blood of Jesus' finished work.** Satan knew the cross-denomination was working out marvelously.

Mankind is so willing to submit to the different eastern religions offering up many gods. The god within everything that has life taught by my 'Enlightened Ones', has done well. Written in stone by my direction, 'leave room for nature, leave room for nature'. The guide stones in Georgia are setting the path for the next generations. Patience was my forte. Convincing the world, mother earth is trying to heal her, people acccept the catastrophic events of nature. Worshipping creation instead of the Creator is now accepted by many.

He wanted to laugh at the group of self-awareness at the god within you. You are god. Satisfy your hearts desires. There is no sin, just good and bad. You have to experience both or you wouldn't know what good is. So enjoy life, you deserve it. Remember, it is all about you. If you don't love yourself, you won't know how to love others. Satan laughed uncontrollable. They don't realize they are willingly worshipping me, Beelzebub. I am the god within. Their ears were dull of hearing and their eyes were blind to the things going on around them. Their reality is all that matters to them. Satan laughed. Yes, this was his favorite group. These caught in the false religions, "Black Maria" controlled easily. The "Black Maria" will be overloaded soon with these, as they support the guide-stones. Stonehenge in Georgia is helping many of these to leave room for nature. Leaving room for nature isn't just the earth around them. It is looking to the cursed creation for direction. Satan laughed a sinister laugh. If they only knew the plans for demise, eliminating the useless vessels of clay that they are, many would realize they're in the last hour before the smoking gun. **Hearts would call out to Jesus, who doesn't consider them useless.**

His eyes continued to scan the vast territories. Satan spotted the ones that were total fools. [6] They were rebellious in all their ways. He had to smile at these. The mockers resented correction or direction of man, let alone a God they can't see. The mouth of the fool gushes forth ignorant comments considering it wise or humorous.

They suffer many afflictions for they choose their circumstances, loathing all food of the Heavens that can steer them from pain and suffering. The affliction through illness, misfortune and loss tried their patience and endurance. Instead of seeking God's advice, they became swallowed up by their calamity. They asked man's council. Oh, how many I would lose if they realized not to put their trust in man's direction. I will continue to instruct them, putting their confidence in the flesh. They search for other ways to correct the death and destruction that is certain. The "Black Maria" encourages the aimless folly of deception. Many of these draw near the gates of death.

Satan's eyes stopped, spotting Terri sitting at the grave of the nameless woman. He saw the emotion in Terri's face, while searching in the historical society's books. She was searching out the names that were on the tomb stones. She had paused for quite some time on the article about the "Black Maria". The women in Pottsville and other coal mining areas feared the message from the vehicle of sorrow. Satan saw the significance of the "Black Maria", being any vehicle that brings the humans to death and destruction. The jars of clay saw it as a literal object of dreadful sorrow. The black wagon carrying the wounded, dying or the dead of coal mining workers fit into his agenda. Antagonizing the women and children by instilling fear; would their husbands, brothers and sons come home? Satan looked down at the register of names of those who had died. The list of angry children had multiplied greatly after each death. Promises had been made by offspring, vengeance would be done.

The Spirit of Death rode beside the somber driver whose face was full of fear and sorrow. The demons rejoiced at the body count. As the alarm was sounding to let the earthly realm know of disaster, the demonic realm heeded the sound as a triumph. The seven deadly sins continued to bring the dead through the Seven Gates of Hell. Satan knew the gates; he had done them and experienced the casting out of the Almighty's presence. Opening the gates of Hades, where he now ruled and reigned, he lured the individual jars of clay toward the desires of their hearts. Promising death and destruction to God's creation, he was determined to see it through to the end using the seven sins God abhorred.

1. **Gate of Pride** - will be the ultimate downfall for man. The arrogance of superiority will be displayed in all aspects. The Illuminati, with the help of the Freemasons, are bringing into focus the wicked messianic leader that proclaims himself as god. These men are foolish for thinking they rule the world for it is not them. IT IS I, ABBADON that rules this world! All following the dictation will receive according to their devotion

    Religious pride has been the strongest weapon. Using the different religions, Spirits of the Air have manipulated circumstances so that soon, I will be exalted.

2. **Gate of Envy** - mistrust and hatred will constrain the flow of God's goodness, for jealousy toward the advantages or wealth of another, has bred resentment.

3. **Gate of Gluttony** - whether eating too much or craving the materialistic beyond man's needs will breed excessively the need to get more. I have made it so man is never satisfied. The rich will get richer and never find contentment.

4. **Gate of Anger** - breeds the desire for revenge. Due to unjust treatment throughout the miserable lives of mankind, hearts will continue to turn toward violence. Rage consuming their thoughts will drive man to kill one another.

5. **Gate of Greed** - will control their hearts and minds. The strong desire for wealth will consume, activating the other sins. Satan knew how to influence the vessels of clay for he exercised discontentment through every generation setting into motion many wars for land, wealth, and position desired.

6. **Gate of Lust** - for flesh has destroyed many marriages. The churches are full of the broken many, due to the unfaithfulness

of one. With the insatiable appetite, the desire for sex has culminated into what should not be. The hidden practice of homosexuality has been done in the most discreet way, until it was acceptable throughout the world. Satan grinned as he looked at the world leaders gathered at the Bohemian Grove. Women once considered possessions are now considered goddesses for they held the ability to entice not only man but also the sons of God.

7. **Gate of Sloth** - was the characteristic the slave owners of today had learned from those in the past. There were laborers and those who controlled the workers. Riches were obtained for the wealthy, by hard working servants who needed to feed their families. Satan knew the idleness of many would alter any nation that once stood strong. Concentration camps were now ready to be used by the Illuminati.

Satan considered the Seven Gates of Hell that he manipulated in the battlefields in Pottsville. The Irish, which was primarily Catholic, were fighting the Protestants in the town. The Illuminati had infiltrated the Catholics by using the Ancient Order of Hibernians and the Protestant Freemasons. Did either group realize the secret foundations had original roots in Babylonian worship? Esau proud of Jewish teachings was indoctrinated with Kabbalah and informed me the Freemasons were implemented in the building of Solomon's Temple. The Kabbalistic theological foundation (the Illuminati) was reinstated by three Jews in 1776, though it had been practiced for centuries through the Jesuit Order concealed as Catholic's. The political regime of Zionists Jews, leaders of the United World, controlled the banking and media. Through the false teaching Satan had worked hard to convince the Jews, the Messiah they were waiting for was going to rule the world setting up His Throne in Jerusalem.

Their Messiah couldn't come as a servant. The jars of clay were easily manipulated due to the ignorance. Satan smirked to think his blinding the eyes of the religious leaders, because of jealousy, was the smartest tactic. These jars of clay were easy to convince. Jesus' mistaken identity was cleverly disguised, for they still wanted to see the physical king. Their king had to rule and reign. They didn't want a humble servant. Religions today, still do not want the 'Servant-King' working for them.

Glancing back on Terri, Satan grinned. He had used the Protestants against the Catholics to start a Holy War that manipulated his master plan of the destruction. Each family came to America wanting to start fresh. America had freedom of religion. The traditions and beliefs brought a melting pot of religious resentment; Catholics against the Protestants. The hard hearts of the Protestants put up signs in the work place, "If Irish, need not apply". The undesirable Irish were worse than slaves.

The Spirit of Greed was given control. Owners of the coal mine and the business owners exhibited the controlling factors by raising prices on food, tools, and land to those of Irish descent. The land flowing with milk and honey was a land of blood, sweat and tears. The earth cried out about the blood spilt, as the caverns of hell continued to swallow up 'lost souls' upon death. Satan wasn't saddened because of the souls that went to Heaven. For no longer were they able to testify of God's Amazing Love. Was it not a 'win-win' situation for him, against the jars of clay? The Irish "slaves" had to buy their own tools in order to work in the mines. They toiled for gain, only after surveying all their labors it was meaningless. Barely able to feed their families because of marked up prices and tool required expenses, the circle of bitterness and resentment grew. The Irish fell back into the customs and traditions they had been taught being the "sons of Molly". The vengeance would be done by the wrath of the "Molly's". Every man did what was right in their own eyes.

The Irish worked within the legal organization of the Ancient Order of Hibernians. The Irish Mafia was powerful as it was led by the shadowy organization. Due to cave-ins, explosions and flooded mines something had to be done. The elevated prices for food and tools left only one recourse; fight for better conditions. The Irish Mafia destroyed property of the cruel owners. Man began to kill and destroy as the Irish lives were taken. The rule and reign of the Molly McGuire's left fear and intimidation following the different acts of violent vengeance. The Catholic Church severed its ties with the "Molly's" because they feared repercussions; people wouldn't trust any within the Catholic faith.

The revenge of the" Molly's" was so powerful, as the Irish mafia controlled those which once held power. Satan watched from the sidelines. The arena of hatred catered by the Spirits of Anger and Pride, the Irish began to seek justice. As lives of the workers were taken, the railways to the owners were destroyed. Fear of losing control of wealth, the protestants found someone to infiltrate the "Molly's".

The Pinkerton's found a man who was willing to be planted as a spy named James Parlan. With the appearance of having the same values and attitudes, he gathered enough incriminating evidence, of the killings of supervisors and owners, to bring the needed justice to those desiring to see the" Molly's" go down.

Of course, justice was perceived differently depending on the perception of all involved. The leaders of the town flourished, hiding secrets that some had met their death surrounded by a lie. Satan was so delighted Jesus was wrongfully accused, yet people wanted to believe the lie. With nothing new under the sun, people still choose to believe the lie. With secrets of the past brought forward, the modern day world saw that some of these men were wrongfully accused. At least the world doesn't understand I wanted all eliminated. People today saw them as martyred pioneers setting in motion the need for unions, to control hours and child labor laws. Man was still confused with the right and wrong of the situation, still leaving the Spirit of Justification in control. There was no black and white, it was more a dirty gray that was left for those living relatives.

Satan grimaced to think Terri met an Irish family in a totally different area of Pennsylvania. They changed their names out of fear, so they wouldn't be associated into the Irish Mafia or the "Molly's" in any way. Satan realized puzzle pieces of information holding the mysteries of his conspiracy to destroy mankind was coming to light. Their family carried the shame and the remorse in spite of their innocence. They saw the situation as fair due to the cruelty being shown to the Irish families. Oh foolish jars of clay. They are blinded to the fact, Jesus broke the generational curses. Would they ever understand the Royal blood line they could belong to?

Satan knew a hole had been punctured in the deep hidden vaults. The vapor was the secrets of the underworld. The phantoms, of the secret organizations, continued to surface of the Illuminati's intent using the Ancient Order of Hibernians and the Freemasons. In spite of the curse put on them, men talked to Terri about the organization they belonged to. Satan didn't care which group won for the Illuminati controlled both. He just couldn't afford to have 'Jesus' light' exposing the darkness, revealing the lies of the "Enlightened Ones" which mankind continued to listen to.

Satan said in his heart, "I will ascend to the heavens." [2] Satan was delighted with the ones he had chosen to carry the lies. The select few in the different secret societies, cults and religions on the quest for knowledge, were unaware the secrets were given by demons. They believe the message given. We are the true light beings of the solar system. We will be liberated from the entrapments of darkness that the false god put us in. The satanic web we designed has intermingled throughout the schools, churches, and the government. With occult ties, blood oaths were taken to keep what was learned silent. "They sacrificed their children to demons, clear to the 10th generation," Satan laughed as he rubbed his hands with delight. Leaving room for nature, the true (demons) light beings of the solar system would control the children of the future. They would worship him or die.

There was a sound of a trumpet being blown, the group saw the angel. The angel took a key [6] and opened the "Abyss". Billows of smoke rose from within the evil prison house. The demonic creatures that had been locked in the abyss for so long were now loosed on the world. All hell was to break forth on mere mortals. King Abaddon was leading the destroyers, who had been given power to torment. Some of the creatures were sent to where Kaylie and Xaiden lived.

*   *   *

The unique confrontations continuing to surface from the involvement of the underworld were constantly directing me to

YAHWEH NISSI. The LORD MY BANNER wanted me to slow down and really see what is around us. The unique creature from the abyss surfaced. Kaylie was outside watching her little boy army crawling toward adventure in the great outdoors. The strange looking locust flew right in front of her, placing itself in between her and Xaiden. Kaylie collects bugs and found the creature quite interesting. It would have been great to add to her collection. The black locust with a scorpion looking tail stared at Kaylie as she stared back at him. As the stare down progressed, a sinister eeriness came over her. Was this creature trying to convince the bug collector that he held power like no other? Fear never entered her thoughts as the stinger was shaking its powerful weapon of defense. Kaylie would try to move but the black locust would move following her direction. The black, scorpion locust leaving a curious fascination instead of fear flew away.

The conversation of the strange looking creature was brought up when the locust once again appeared. Entertaining Kaylie and me, the unique creature seemed to follow our every move. This creature was not normal. The large coal black eyes kept us in its vision even though one of us would try to distract its attention on the side of it. It seemed to see us both at all times. The intelligent flying creature would hop when needing to stop either of us from moving. It desired to control the situation. Waving aggressively the stinger on its tail, it was as if it was warning us of its foreboding venom. After the strange stare down the scorpion locust flew off.

Kaylie and I began talking about the end times. There was to be a locust looking creature that comes from the bottomless pit. We pulled out the Bible and opened the scripture to Revelation 9 and began reading. Having the face of a man, the creature would have hair like a woman's. The demonic being would have teeth like a lion. We laughed at the picture that popped in our heads, of something so grotesque. We stopped laughing when we read the locust creature would have a scorpion tail. The creature Kaylie had seen was it the same as what was prophesied? Had she seen a scout for the great body of creatures? The locust creature would be loosed to torment people. Not devouring the vegetation, they would attack those who did not have the seal of God on their foreheads. The suffering people would not die but would suffer from the attack of the sting. The evil creatures would be allowed five months of torture, people will want to die but death would elude them. Kaylie and I were not afraid of Abaddon, the destroyer. We both rejoiced the evil angel of the abyss had no power over us because of the blood of Jesus, the seal was on us.

That night Kaylie and Xaiden went to her neighbor's house. Kaylie visited with Tony as Xaiden played with his little girl. Kaylie hadn't been there long when there was a blood curdling scream pouring forth from her little son. She ran a grabbed him up when suddenly she got stung by the same black creature. There was extreme pain as she was stung and a strange heat shot down her arm. Immediately she felt like hot water shot from the top of her head down all over her body. Intense heat was pouring forth through the pores of Kaylie and Xaiden.

Automatically, her thoughts went to the creature that was not to harm those that belonged to the LORD. She ran down the stairs with her little one cradled and crying in her arms. When she entered the house Kaylie began telling me the sordid details of the incident that had happened. I looked for a stinger on both and couldn't find anything. The swelling was immediate. While treating the wound outwardly, I prayed in the spirit. My mind went to what Kaylie and I had studied earlier. Locust didn't normally bite people. Was this coincidental or was the creature from the underworld? They were not to harm God's children. Moments after the sting, Xaiden was up and crawling around again. Neither one had repercussions from the sting after prayer. I couldn't help but wonder what the creature was and why he attacked Children of God. Why were Kaylie and Xaiden allowed to experience something that was intended for the unsaved? Because of Jesus' mercy, we did not see the extent of suffering intended for mankind?

Pearl Drops of Wisdom

1. . . . And the house of Israel will possess the nations as menservants and maidservants in the Lord's land. They will make captives of their captors and rule over their oppressors.

    Isaiah 14:2 NIV

2. Some wandered in the desert wastelands, finding no way to a city where they could settle. They were hungry and thirsty and their lives ebbed away.

    Psalm 107:4-5 NIV

3. Some sat in darkness and the deepest gloom, prisoners suffering in iron chains, for they had rebelled against the words of God and despised the counsel of the Most High.

    Psalm 107:10-11

4. For as the body without the spirit is dead, so faith without works is dead also.

    James 2:26 KJV

5. Some became fools through their rebellious ways and suffered affliction because of their iniquities. They loathed all food and drew near the gates of death.

    Psalm 107:17-18 NIV

6.   You said in your heart, I will ascend to the heavens; I will raise
     my throne above the stars of God, I will sit enthroned on the
     mount of assembly, on the utmost heights of Mount Zaphon. I
     will ascend above the tops of the clouds; I will make myself like
     the Most High.

                                                    Isaiah 14:13-14 NIV

7.   . . . The star was given the key to the Abyss . . . . And out of the
     smoke locusts came down upon the earth and were given power
     like that of scorpions of the earth . . . They had tails and stings
     like scorpions . . . power to torment people . . . They had as king
     over them the angel of the Abyss, whose name in Hebrew is
     Abaddon.

                                               Revelation 9:1, 3, 10, 11

Chapter 28

No Room in Stone

In the heavens, the great crowd watched as Jesus talked with Terri. The tenderness in His voice brought tears to the Bride in the Heavens. They knew He was instructing and equipping her for the long awaited entrance in the house that had the reputation for being haunted. After three tries to see the house, the woman's voice said Terri could come at 4 o'clock. They heard her say to Jesus, "I don't know why you love me. Why do you choose to dwell inside a vessel that continues to have to be dumped out and refilled over and over? The groom spoke softly with tenderness in his eyes. "You will understand a little more here in a moment." The redeemed in the Heavens, knew Terri was entering the territory which welcomed the underworld dwelling in the house of man. The crowd heard Jesus say, "Come let's go together to the house. Be quiet and reserved. Be wise as a serpent but as harmless [1] as a dove."

*   *   *

I felt like I was to have someone go with me. Was the thought fear or wisdom? I couldn't say. I invited one of the ground keepers from the cemetery. He was from the area. Maybe the woman would be more comfortable with someone local visiting her, too. As I drove up, I realized there was a third person desiring to go into the house that held everyone's curiosity. Bob had brought his daughter Rebecca.

The three of us walked up to the door. I spoke into the intercom. The voice that answered was not as friendly as it was only hours before. "You're not alone. Why did you bring people with you? You're not coming in!" The voice exclaimed. "You will never see my house." I was a little surprised she knew, for the shutters were still closed. There was no peep hole through the door so I glanced around to see if there was a camera, but couldn't see an obvious one. I wasn't aware there were going to be three showing up but knew it wasn't smart going in alone.

Hearing the anger and frustration in the woman's voice left eeriness in the atmosphere amongst the three of us standing on the porch. The gentleness and kindness of the Spirit spoke through me and calmed the woman hidden behind the heavy doors. The woman finally opened the door. I briefly saw the interior of the house that held so many stories and fear. It held a regal beauty just in the entry way. I felt like my curiosity was being toyed with. I really wanted to see the rest of the beautiful mansion. With the coaxing of the Spirit in my voice, the woman came outside, shutting the door behind her. I felt a sorrow I couldn't explain. The first fifteen minutes was very strained, after walking out the door the woman exclaimed without any hesitation, "You should even be glad I'm talking to you." The awkwardness was broken by the Spirit within me. I had no clue whether the two people with me even knew the Lord. Genuine respect permeated from me, for the woman who was of another time period. Not only was she an elderly woman, but she was from another country and had "earned" her American citizenship. The way she said she earned it left me a little curious. She was a native born Ukrainian. Her husband's homeland was Germany. She informed us they both spoke their native language. I found the woman quite fascinating.

As the conversation progressed, I found an interesting fact that had surfaced. It wasn't what was said but how she said it. Her husband was an engineer that built on the 9/11 buildings. It sent shivers done my spine. I found it interesting she didn't say the twin towers. The way she said it left us with more questions, but she clammed up and wouldn't talk about it anymore. The steps and the porch being torn up were explained to the curious threesome instead. Information of what was eaten in their home was divulged. She even explained how she had won in a karaoke competition in Texas. The conversations that seemed to trigger something within Bob or me seemed to have the subject changed over and over. The woman was deliberately not divulging anything that could help fan the fire of curiosity.

The question of whether the house was haunted or not did come up eventually, her answer was a short and curt, "No"! As the conversation continued the woman seemed comfortable with Bob and me. After finding out that Bob had grown up in the territory, the woman relaxed a little more. The two chatted about general things they both knew in the territory. Slowly the question was asked again about the house. Ghosts in the territory had been brought up, revealing to her she wasn't the only one having spirits entertained in the home or business. She let it slip, "There is banging noises here. The window on the top floor has been broke several times with no explanation." Once again the woman clammed up. Had she seen the twinkle within my eyes or had something clammed her mouth shut?

I felt the presence of the Lord beside me. I heard His still quiet whisper, "Be still. Restrain from opening your mouth." Bob started talking about the encounters of the apparitions that he had experienced. Once again the lady seemed to relax enough to talk again about her home, "My children will not even stay with us. They are scared of this old mansion. Voices can be heard but there was never anyone there." The apparitions involved were never aggressive toward the elderly people but they never go upstairs anymore. Had the spirit realm claimed the territory that would be theirs and no human would be welcomed? It was sad to see the mansion which once held so much promise of comfort now slowly turning into a dark lonely deserted abode that was controlled by fear.

The woman shared how they had kept it exactly as it was when it was built. They had original cabinets to some of the original furniture. The house had been owned by a wealthy German businessman. This elderly couple was the second owners. The woman watched me as she laid out the marvelous description of the mansion. Bringing out all the unique characteristics, she made it sound magnificent. Her ability to be so descriptive antagonized the inquisitive group. She was tormenting our curiosity. To see the marble floors and the dark cherry wood stair case that took them to a ballroom on the second floor, would have been the icing of the cake. As the woman shared how the third floor had been used to train athletically, I wondered why she didn't know any details about those who had been trained there. I thought," Oh, if only the walls could talk." She let us know the view was remarkable, as the jail could be seen from the third floor. I thought it was quite an odd fact to be thrown out. Fascinating and twisted, the oldest prison in the United States was still being used today. It was the location where "Molly's" gang was hung. What happened to the owner of the mansion? He was German and a businessman. The woman said the house had stood empty for years after the man's death. Why and how did he die? Once again the subject was changed. After an hour and a half, the visitation was abruptly ended. She was done and quickly said her good-byes. The three intrigued ghost-hunters weren't finished with the house that held so many questions and no answers.

We went to a haunted school house and other areas that held ghostly experiences. With each story of haunting, the spirits never confronted the humans watching. The spirit realm seemed willing to oblige the physical realms curiosity, yet we didn't encounter any ghosts as we searched out the different spheres of supernatural influences. We found ourselves back at the house where we started at, only facing the back of the house. We parked the car and started walking toward the mansion that held so many secrets. Our intense conversation made it so we were not completely aware of what was going on as we walked past an adjacent wall to other old historical homes. Police had been called for the bricks from the wall fell with a clatter after we walked past. There was no explanation why it happened. No one was hurt, yet the curiosity was left in my thinking. What made the wall collapse that had withstood time and tragedies? Was it the supernatural? Was tearing down the physical wall intended to hit us in order to save the wicked fortress that the king of the underworld had built? Was man's dancing with the demons to be stopped?

What could I really do to tear down any of the spiritual walls that were built? The "living", [2] we praise you, Jesus. Give us courage as we go up against your enemy, Satan. Raise your right hand in battle, Lord as we sing forth your praise. We will continue to tell of your faithfulness as you take control of Your Kingdom here on earth as you did in heaven.

I considered all the facts that lay before the town. The Illuminati controlled both groups. It didn't matter whether the Freemasons or the Ancient Order of Hibernians won control of the town. The Illuminati led by the Kabbalah Jew and Zionists watched the issue of prejudices of the American races, knowing they controlled all. The strongest would survive and lead to their final destination, One World Order. With the Jesuit Order in the Roman Catholic Church and control of the Freemasons, it was a win-win situation. The poison of vipers set on their tongue, listening to lying spirits man's hope was in men and their organizations. Curses put on to the children's children up to the 10th generation were taught by treacherous people.

The running of the Underground Railroad for the African American's quest for freedom escalated an already gruesome sentence, plotted by men in leadership. Pottsville's tangled history held a dark shadow of slavery. With a few standing on the faith of Jesus, Grace is sufficient. [3] Man's pride, religion and race opened the door to Satan's leadership over the territory. Were the demons rejoicing over their wicked master's plan? Frequent ghostly appearances kept the town with a fear and respect, continually making their presence known. The demonic realm was not going to let the "dead" bury the dead. The gates of hell and darkness stand open welcoming the deceived in.

*　　*　　*

In the heavens, Jesus taught the redeemed a lesson from his heart. The analogy; Terri wanted to go in to the haunted house, so is the picture of the heart I desire to go into. The mansion that was beautiful and historical even though it was in shambles left her seeking entrance. In spite of wear and tear, the mansion could be awesome with its flaws which showed character. Unlike the second owners who chose not to change the house, I want to literally change ownership. I cast out every evil spirit and demonic controlled thought. The house cannot have two masters, [4] so Satan has to give up all rights to the soul. I paid an exorbitant price to acquire each broken life with My own. I want to open the storehouse of wealth from the Heavens and lavish My new dwelling with the best that can be given. Replacing every life that is broken and destroyed with peace and beauty of My righteousness, the Redeemed One shines for My face shines on them as I work through them.

Terri went to the house three times, hoping to be welcomed into the home. I stand at the hearts door knocking and waiting for the ALREADY forgiven one, to open the door. I knock [5] more than three times. I am persistent and patient. When the individual finally answers the voice, many have an excuse why I can't come into their lives. Some say what Terri heard, "You're not welcome here." It breaks my heart to hear I'm not welcome. Others open the door so I can see in, but won't allow me to step past the threshold. They will visit with Me on the porch. Many are embarrassed of the clutter that has been accumulated.

If you remember there was no room for Me when I came to your world the first day of putting on the flesh at the inn. Other things, even good things, can be more important than Me; there is no room for Me. I get pushed aside while My servants are so busy about their lives. Man's heart is like that old cold stone mansion. It is not inviting for man chooses not to let the Son-of-light in. When I'm allowed in, their hearts become soft, warm and tender. There is no handle on the side where I stand and wait. It is for the broken hearted to open the door for Me. When they open the door I will come in and eat with him and him with Me. I want them to choose a different life; one of victory not defeat. When I come in the first thing I want to do is change their thoughts about Me. I love them while they still see Me as their enemy. I am a God full of mercy, forgiveness and love. With changed thinking about Me, they don't desire to do evil. They may bring something undesirable in for a moment of time but soon realize it is not what they need or want. The abode shared by two won't feel peace if it is not good for both.

When I showed Terri her interior, she became like this woman, threatened. She was embarrassed to have the deepest thoughts and feelings exposed, causing shame and pain. The shame of the clutter of all the sin isolates the soul. Fame and fortune makes no difference, the cold heart thinks only of their own needs and feelings. Most do not want to see the areas in their lives that are cold, lonely and depressed. Irrational thinking continues to close the shutters and lock the doors of the heart, so no truth and light may enter. The haunting within the spirit chases people away, so that their presence is not revealed. That is why I continue prompting the heart. I woo them softly to Me so that man knows I love them and want to be friends. I want to share life with them. I work gently on the heart that has been broken and diseased.

Terri was willing to let Me help her clean out the dark, lonely room. Revealing what she had put on a pedestal and hid away, we talked about it and she decided to let Me fix up the add-on, My way. She said I could decorate it the way I deemed best. Taking John out of the high place, we put him in a place special, where his influence was still seen but as a help mate to growth in the Kingdom and a gift from Me. Pictures on the wall are of the two of us walking through life together. Tender moments of the beach and the mountains are some of My favorites. Pictures were hung, where we passed out shoes together. When she won two garbage bags full of popcorn, at the church we were visiting, pictures were taken then and the next day when we passed little bags of popcorn out together at the Daily Bread. The room is what I call Daily Wedding Momentous.

When I exposed my favorite room, it was Terri's favorite too. The warm inviting room with just the rocking chairs and fireplace is where the intimate things were shared between just the two of us. No one heard the most intimate details that meant something to her, good or bad. That is the room where the heart was softened and renewed daily. The trophy room was where the rejoicing heart handed out thanks and praise. I let her receive credit in the physical realm. When people thank her for things, then she turns it around and tells them, "Thank My Jesus. I am nothing without Him." It is a definite shared life. She prays, "My precious Ish, help me remember the position you put me in, Bride of Christ."

The weapons room was where she became strong, as she was trained for spiritual warfare. As the house had an exercise room, there is a determination to practice the things that are taught. The Holy Spirit uses that room moment by moment. From the private worship of Jesus as Lord of Lord's, self-awareness diminished as the mysteries of JESUS was revealed.

The banquet room that the woman wanted to use with her family, no longer was servicing what the heart intended. Unwelcome spirits often take over the feasting of one's soul. When the guests at your banquet table are unforgiveness, bitterness, resentment and anger it chases away other people who want to visit you, but don't desire to sit amongst your guests. You find your home stays empty. If I am invited to dine at a banquet in your home, your guests want to leave. They do not enjoy laughter, peace and forgiveness. I AM FORGIVENESS. I AM PEACE. Terri found I prepare the feast. Dining together, feasting on the Bread of Heaven, the Word is fresh daily.

Terri will return to the woman. It won't be to see the house but to see the discouraged and lonely woman. The house was calling out the sorrowful needs within. The Spirit directed her physical curiosity to the spiritual need. Cold and lonely the mansion of darkness is where the woman dwells. It will be exposed again to the light.[6] As Terri learns to listen more carefully with spiritual ears and having a sensitive heart to the woman's needs, the doors will continue to be opened. Sitting by the fireplace was where Terri and I met. Sitting on the porch for a moment in time can be the difference of a cold stone heart that melts into a warm and tender inviting heart.

Pearl Drops of Wisdom

1. Behold, I send you forth as sheep in the midst of wolves; be ye therefore wise as serpents, and harmless as doves.

Matthew 10:16 KJV

2. The living, the living—they praise you, as I am doing today; fathers tell their children about your faithfulness.

Isaiah 38:19 NIV

3. But he said to me, "My grace is sufficient for you, for my power is made perfect in weakness." Therefore I will boast all the more gladly about my weaknesses, so that Christ's power may rest on me.

II Corinthians 12:9 NIV

4. No one can serve two masters. Either he will hate the one and love the other, or he will be devoted to the one and despise the other. You cannot serve both God and Money.

Matthew 6:24 NIV

5. Behold, I stand at the door and knock: if any man hear my voice, and open the door, I will come in to him, and will sup with him, and he with me.

Revelation 3:20 KJV

6. For it is light that makes everything visible. That is why it is said: "Wake up, O sleeper, rise from the dead, and Christ will shine on you."

Ephesians 5:14 NIV

Chapter 29

Power Unleashed

The quiet time with the Lord was leading me to the next step of growth. He said, "Many are dwelling in the 'Field of the Woods'. Due to the fear of My presence working powerfully, the deception that was seen in the Field of Jaar [1] is being seen once again. A strategy is designed to trick My bride.

Displaying Jesus as the sacrifice, there are many saying, "See what we have done for God." The world is convinced these are right, for it is seen by their appearance. [2] To mankind they have the appearance of being clothed in garments of white, but they still are wearing the old sack cloth and worn out shoes. They show they have traveled a great distance to see God. But they can't see for all the trees in the woods. They continue to be woodcutters, cutting the things of the flesh. As water carriers they carry water that hold diseases to the soul and continue to hand out the dry moldy bread. The wineskins are old and cracked showing it's been mended. I hand out fresh bread daily and the wineskin is new. The old container is never seen again for I throw out the old. The wineskin contains not water but wine.

My people are listening to the speech presented, proclaiming to be servants announcing the power of God with His mighty hand. Instead of inquiring from Me whether they carry the truth, the whole truth and nothing but the truth, they follow empty advice like sheep being led to the slaughter. The crude appearance and stench has entered the Heavens. Be cautious they live under a curse. Learn from ME!"

*　　*　　*

Pork Chop and I rode to Murphy, North Carolina with a group of Christian bikers, to a place called Field in the Woods. It was amazing. On a hill, was a man's dream to tell the world in a huge way God's ordained plan! The Ten Commandments were created out of stones put together to form the words. Moses couldn't have been any more shocked when it was written with the finger of God. I stood humbled for the first commandment was still being broken today. Whether it was the enormous way it was displayed or the laws themselves, I felt the heavy weight of the load upon my shoulders due to the gravity of the message. Fighting tears, I heard, "Why do you want to feel the weight of the law? Walk with me, Terri," Jesus whispered softly.

There was a hill that one could climb or ride that took the soul searcher to the altar. Abraham was tested, as he walked three days to the place of sacrifice. I wondered about the Spirit of Judgment and Spirit of Doubt antagonizing his thoughts, "What kind of loving God would want to have you sacrifice your only son? Is that love? God promises you, you'll be the father of many nations and now he's asking you to kill the son that holds the promise.

Did the Spirit of Doubt whisper," Maybe this isn't the son that holds the promises God was talking about. If you sacrifice him, maybe you won't have any more children for you are old. Sarah isn't able to carry the promised seed for she is old. Isaac was a miracle." Then, he remembered how God told him to walk and be blameless. Abraham considered all the conversations with the angel of God. Yes, Isaac was a miracle. He had confidence the sacrifice would be provided. As he climbed, he looked for the lamb of sacrifice, standing on the promises that God had given him.

I put my hand on the altar that held so much importance to the Jew. My Jewish friends argued amongst themselves in Hebrew after I asked them, what was more important; the altar or the gift on the altar. They still couldn't decide which was more important. Torn between the Cabala Jew and one of the regular branches of Judaism, the one dedicated to Jehovah saw the sacrifice more critical. They did let me know the perfect sacrifice was what both had in common. They needed their temple to be built so they could build the altar in the presence of where the Holiest of Holies had been.

I wanted to cry for they missed the perfect sacrifice for Jesus was sacrificed on a tree. [2] I looked up to the heavens and whispered, "Thank you Jesus for the gift on the altar for me. The tree of the knowledge of good and evil was next to the tree that would bring life. Two trees created by God; one bringing death, the other bringing life. **'Perfection" (JESUS) took on the curse and died on the creation that was cursed. Jesus took all sin and died on the tree.**[3] **The POWER OF THE BLOOD LIFTED THE CURSE IN THE HEAVENS AND THE EARTH.** WE NO LONGER HAVE TO LIVE UNDER THE CURSE. WE ONLY HAVE TO **BELIEVE WE LIVE IN A RIGHTOUS BLESSING.** The more I understood His Goodness, Mercy and Love, the more I praised Him. I've found the more I praise Him for His Way of Righteousness the more I fall in love with Him.

I looked again at the altar. Abraham had peace ELOHIM would send his divine sacrifice. Isaac was young. He hadn't experienced the faith walk like his father. The fear in his eyes had to have crushed Abraham. Abraham praying, "Lord, provide your sacrifice." Looking into the eyes of his beloved son did Abraham say "Trust ELOHIM to provide, he said he would." ELOHIM did provide the lamb in his perfect timing. His son would carry the mantle of faith, not because of his preaching about God but because of **seeing the action of Abraham trusting his God.** The visitation of ELOHIM fulfilling his promise in such a powerful way set the course for the next generation to trust the faithfulness of God's word. Isaac had to learn to listen, and then obey. Without the written word, Abraham trusted God at his spoken word. He didn't seek advice or counsel to make sure he heard right. He knew the Lord's voice. Isaac would have to learn to hear the Lord's voice. Obedience in the big thing was given after he had learned about the faithfulness of his God.

I followed a trail going down the hill. On both sides of me, individual laws were written in stone that different churches had donated. Plaque after plaque exposed the sins, some I was still doing wrong. Even after all the years of loving the Lord, I still fell miserably short of the Glory of God. I knew with all the laws displayed, they had forgotten hundreds. If man had to follow the law, where were the others so man could know what else was sin? I was following a trail that was a walk of guilt and shame. Strange thing was, as I passed each of the written in stone laws, I heard, **"Forgiven"**. I knew there was forgiveness, but where was evidence that there was victory over the law for these coming to the Field in the Woods?

When I reached the bottom of the hill, I understood a greater picture of Mount Sinai. Three thousand people had died when the first Ten Commandments were given. Stop and consider the trail of sin, with each generation proclaiming new laws, there was no way any man could live without breaking one. Every generation claimed the ten but how many considered all the other ones that may be broken. One can't abide by the laws within the "today" realm let alone the past laws.

I stared at a smaller version of the Statue of Liberty sitting in a pond. The flame was not on the torch. A picture of why the woman carrying the torch had no light to be seen seemed to come alive from within. I stared at the old cold stone woman. As Eve enticed Adam to taste the fruit enslaving him to sin, so was the cold woman enticing freedom to all who come to America. Lifting a torch for freedom, the flame was missing, extinguished on the statue before me. The law only brought darkness. **Grace given through Christ is the only way a light of freedom could be lit.** A lit torch of Grace would stand in the darkness showing the real place of freedom. Staring at the statue made of stone. Many professing the faith were striving to live following the laws, the ten major ones. Those contained old, cold stones in the heart. The Spirit moved sending a rush from my head to my feet. I started laughing. I wasn't a cold statue with no flame.

Jesus took the old cold unattainable and broke it into pieces so I couldn't put the cold heart together again. He had replaced it with a heart that was alive because of the life He breathed into Me. I could move around and carry the torch for Jesus. Carrying the Word in one hand and holding Jesus' hand with the other. The light of Jesus in me would go before me and the power of the Holy Spirit would work through me, with goodness and mercy following behind me.[4]

I started climbing the hill toward the Wall of Praise with a little lighter spring in my footstep. Verses of praise to the Lord were written. Unlike the veterans wall in Washington D.C. there was joy. The verses proclaimed victory to those who put their trust in the Lord. As I read each verse out loud the Spirit leaped inside. I did a victory dance of praise, rejoicing in the God of Salvation. The washing of the Holy Spirit erased all the judgment and guilt I had felt just moments before. It was as if the promises that I was quoting were being reaffirmed by the Spirit of the GREAT I AM, who dwelt inside. The Holy Spirit was feasting off the manna of the Heavens.

Standing at the wall on a hill, I was standing on Mount Zion. To my left I could see the representation of the Hill of Golgotha. Humbled at the presence of Calvary, tears filled my eyes. All Jesus wanted was to ease the suffering that was intended for His creation from the beginning. The love was immeasurable and incomprehensible. **Love crucified rebellion, as Forgiveness hung on the cross of unforgiveness.**

A short distance away was the exhibit of the tomb, which the stone was rolled away. The tears Joseph of Arimathea [5]must have shed, as he wrapped Jesus' unrecognizable bloody body in clean linen. Knowing Jesus like he did; healing the sick, raising the dead and teaching a message of love and forgiveness, did his heart break as he antagonized over the loss of one so loving? Did he say it should have been me? The rich man, a follower of Jesus, gave his final gift of love to him by giving him his new tomb. I wondered if Joseph felt like a part of him died in the tomb with Jesus. The church leaders [6] went to the government in control to make sure the body wasn't moved. Where martyrdom is powerful, how many church leaders "today" are using the government to do their dirty work trying to stop the 'Truth'? The Chief priests and Pharisees (the religious dead white sepulchers) wanted the tomb sealed [7] with guards keeping watch to make sure no one would steal the body. How many of "today's" souls understood he wants to be in the dead tomb of their bodies so that he might raise them from the dead? The Pharisees and rulers of today still are trying to seal the tomb so Jesus can't be seen **raising the dead and giving life in abundance** in people's lives "today". I wanted to laugh when I considered the Pharisees and Rulers had no clue what was going on inside the burial vault. Imagine Jesus going into the depths of hell and opening the gates. Was jeering and the mockery coming from the demons and the wicked that were there? Only to be silenced then turning to wailing when they realized what He was doing? Tears turned to joy when Jesus rose. Joseph came alive as he testified of the miracle. He saw him dead, but JESUS, He's Alive!!!

Jesus whispered, "Rejoice! The curse of the woodcutter is lifted. Heavily wooded thoughts can be cut down. No longer do you have to build the altar of wood or stone for sacrifice. No longer do you have to strive on your works. The pieces you cut out of your life are not needed to turn the heat up to burn the sacrifice. **I took the full fiery wrath when My Father's sacrifice was accepted.** I will clear the dense parts in your thinking. You were slow to understand because of all the clutter. It isn't about you! It isn't about what you are giving up. Those chunks of wood are worthless so let's just throw them down to the caverns of hell. The curse of the water carriers is lifted also. The washing of water is not necessary for purifying yourself, so you may stand before the King. Remember, the thief beside Me on the cross was not baptized for salvation. **The blood and water that poured forth from My side washed you.**

*　*　*

In another lesson, I was taken to a Veteran's Memorial overlook. I was told to watch and listen. Car after car pulled into the scenic memorial view. Bikers had taken the winding road up just to enjoy the curves. It was a good place to stop and rest. Even the truckers would pull their rig over to the side of the road. All do the same thing. As the different individuals came and left, the Lord revealed what He saw and heard. Teaching tenderness and compassion, I admired the beauty of His love. Whether burden or free of care, each person seemed to take a deep breath of the fresh air as they enjoyed the majestic view of the great Smokey Mountains. Few said anything audibly. The valley captured their attention after a glimpse of the surrounding hills, standing with majesty, lured them into a grand view displaying peace.

I watched some who held so much sorrow in the face. The depressed soul's standing and pondering, "If there is a God out there, why doesn't He answer me? The broken sadness in their pleading had a melody that only Jesus took note to? Jesus tenderly spoke, "Let Me hold you while you hurt. You're disappointed because you can't see Me work. I knew you before you were thought of. I have plans designed from above. Look into My face at My love and Amazing Grace. Your burdens no longer will you have to carry, if you will only let Me bury. I will raise you up to heights unknown, as you let My Glory be shown. Trust My love at all cost then you will never be lost."

I took notice of the veterans who had served their country. Some carried the sorrow of the loss of their loved ones. Some took pictures of the memorial in honor of the veterans. The sign signified In Honor of Deceased Veterans. A Bible verse was written on the overlook sign "No greater love than this that a man lay down his life for a friend." Jesus began talking, "So much emphasis on freedom has been instilled in the American Dream. Freedom of eat, drink and be merry is seen even in the church today. You used to feel secure in your accomplishments of service till I showed you the trophy room inside your inner being. You also used to measure My goodness by the things you bought on credit, digging a hole deeper for a debt that could not be paid. Tell people I am the friend they seek that will stand closer than a brother. I will carry the weary one when they are too tired to walk. I gave My life not just for My friends, but also for those who see Me as their enemy."

The freedom of speech is no longer welcomed. If the believer takes stands against things not of God, they are ridiculed and judged. The majority of the world expects Christians to apologize for offending the public for exposing things I detest. The only thing that is freely accepted in America is the freedom to do what is right in man's eyes. They do not consider what is right in My eyes. They follow Lucifer. Christian families are hearing their children say," I want to experience life. I don't want your religion, so quit pushing it on me." Lucifer is trying hard to convince the world I take away their freedom? I offer freedom in no comparison and yet it is rejected. I want you to consider why? Many of those who claim the faith have built up the forefathers, the prophets, and the saints. They have built statues and monuments in honor of those powerful people in the faith and the generational churches.

Some modern day church leaders have tried to bring the church to life with louder "jamming" praise music. Praise doesn't come from the outward in but from the inside out. Praise comes from a Grace recognized heart. Many sing songs of praise but few have a heart recognizing Jesus' underserved kindness and love is for them. Grace isn't a subject, but Grace is Jesus. God's underserved kindness was Jesus to sinful and helpless man. The four Gospels, were four people's testimonies of good news concerning Me. They watched and told people miracles. The four faces you saw in your dream were four separate ways revealed that I serve.

1. I AM the Lion. I am your King and will go to conquer through every battle you face. When you are too tired or weary to fight, just sit and cheer me on. Praise Me for your Victory is won.

2. I AM the Ox. I was sacrificed for all your sin. It isn't, you were forgiven till you sinned. You were forgiven before you were born. When you fall, look to your sacrifice. Concentrate on My Blood. Remember you are forgiven. Praise Me for Forgiveness.

3. I AM the Man. Still a servant willing to heal. Concentrate on My blood. For by My stripes you are healed. Don't listen to anyone who says it is My will that there is illness on you. Would you want your children sick? I don't want My

children sick. By My stripes you are healed. Praise Me for your healing.

4. I AM the Eagle. When you are tired and weary be like the eagle and get away. Hide from all and listen to none. I renew the eagles wings, I will renew you My beloved child. If you need from the Heavens, ask. I descended from and ascended back to the heavens. Remember you are from a heavenly bloodline. Encourage Believers, reminding them of the benefits of being of Royal Blood. Praise Me for gifts from the Heavens. I give generously.

Most churches today have become living "deceased" veterans. People are running on the deceased veteran's faith. Where is the anointing on the message from the Holy Spirit through the power of the blood of Jesus? Preachers use sermons ordered from sources through their denomination and are no longer looking to Me to give them fresh bread from heaven which is full of power and life giving. If there is no victory or power in those in leadership the flock dies. Such as the one I sent you to. The flocks are following the walk and ways of the shepherds in their faith, [8] some have not the faith of a mustard seed. [9]

Jesus continued teaching, "I need those preaching, to let Me take the chains off their own leg like the seagull so they can fly like an eagle. As the squawking bird called to the other seagulls informing tiny morsels are being dished out, so has the preacher squawked leaving the multitude unfed and starving. Why would the youth today want Me, if I look dead?" I felt the sorrow and disappointment from deep within as the Lord spoke. Jesus said, "The powerful FAITH warriors all saw something grander. Turn and look at the mountain across the road."

The mountain was larger, than where all the people were looking. It was as if it was forgotten. The roughness in the climb was obvious. There was loose dirt so it would be hard to start the climb, without possibly starting a rock slide onto the road. There was jagged and broken rock, partially up the hill standing in dirt.

As the steep climb of the mountain went up there was trees that one could use to hang onto for the climb. After a moment where Jesus let me consider the mountain, He continued to speak. "People do not climb the mountain there. I want you to remember, Terri look closer." He reminded me of time a few years ago. It was if it was happening all over again.

There were two struggling to climb the mountain. One was a boy, 19 and the other a young girl, 17. I couldn't believe my eyes. It was Terrance and Kaylie. My son liked to push the limits in life. He was challenging his sister, with no knee caps, to climb the mountain. It was a miracle she was even walking, for doctors said she would never walk. Terrance had been used, powerfully, to help her learn to stand and walk. Now he was teaching her again. Challenging her to reach higher and climb a mountain with no gear. The slipping and sliding was sending dirt and rock down the hill. The two finally made it to the trees, after much effort. They continued climbing, and then hollered at me. The accomplishment was brought to a standstill when petrified, I hollered at them to come down. I had been looking out at the view, amazed at the beauty of the hills and the valleys in front. I did not notice the hill that could take me higher. Watching the two young adults struggle to get back to level ground, scared me.

I wondered why the Lord let me relive the moment. The Lord said softly, "You chewed them out for climbing where it wasn't safe. Did you even bother to ask what they saw and why they did it? I was somewhat embarrassed for I hadn't. Than without hesitation, I tried calling my two children. Neither one could be reached. The curiosity bothered my spirit. I had to know why and what? What seemed like an eternity to hear the answer, Kaylie said simply, "We wanted a grandeur view. The beauty had endless boundaries. There was no limit, for it was as far as the eye could see.

Elijah and Elisha's faith stories, of their powerful God made me desire to pass a powerful faith mantle to the Believers of this generation. I did not want to be accused of looking dead, "zombie churched" style or stamped on my forehead made in a Baptist Church. This Vessel of Praise wants to challenge Believers to leave the appearance of righteousness and step in **claiming only His**

Righteousness. Standing on the promises, they too would become **power walkers and mountain climbers** for the faint.

Take the climb up the mountain to watch your **HOLY RIGHTEOUS GOD FULL OF POWER AND MIGHT** work. No longer would there be living "deceased" veterans of the faith for Jesus has endless boundaries in what He can accomplish. After they see a bigger clearer unconstrained view of the **EL SHADDAI'S INFINITE MERCY, FORGIVENESS, PROTECTION, and LOVE AND POWER** within their life they would walk with **POWER UNLEASHED.**

Pearl Drops of Wisdom

1. Joshua 9—(Kirjayh-Jearim means town in the woods).

2. Having a form of godliness but denying its power. Have nothing to do with them.

   II Timothy 3:5 NIV

3. Who his own self bare our sins in his own body on the tree that we, being dead to sins, should live unto righteousness: by whose stripes ye were healed

   1Peter 2:24 KJV

4. For we are God's workmanship, created in Christ Jesus to do good works, which God prepared in advance for us to do.

   Ephesians 2:10 NIV

5. As evening approached, there came a rich man from Arimathea, named Joseph, who had himself become a disciple of Jesus . . . Joseph took the body, wrapped it in a clean linen cloth and placed it in his own new tomb that he had cut out of the rock. He rolled a big stone in front of the entrance to the tomb and went away.

   Matthew 27:57, 59-60 NIV

6. The next day, the one after Preparation Day, the chief priests and the Pharisees went to Pilate.

   Matthew 27:62 NIV

7. So they went and made the tomb secure by putting a seal on the stone and posting the guard.

Matthew 27:66 NIV

8. Remember your leaders, who spoke the word of God to you. Consider the outcome of their way of life and imitate their faith. Jesus Christ is the same yesterday and today and forever.

Hebrews 13:7-8 NIV

9. He replied. "Because you have so little faith. I tell you the truth, if you have the faith as small as a mustard seed, you can say to this mountain, "Move from here to there" and it will move. Nothing will be impossible for you.

Matthew 17:20 NIV

Chapter 30

Equipping for Battle

I was mortified. Michelle, a prayer warrior, strong in the faith, told me about a vision that God had given her about me. She saw me standing on a rock, with many people grabbing at me. They were all in a slimy tar pit trying, determinedly, to pull me in. She said I had to stand faithful, for it would be the last chance for some to hear the truth. Then she saw me pulled in and submerged. I stood aghast for what did it all mean? Audibly I exclaimed, "Lord if I don't stand, send someone else. I do not want to bring shame to your name."

I had been invited to a "Bible" college in South Carolina. Surely, there wasn't anything I should be concerned about or in danger there? Had the informers possibly set me up for destruction, literally, or was it a spiritual battle that I wasn't equipped for? The researchers for the book, had strange things happening to them, maybe it was tied in with that? If it was something in South Carolina, what kind of **Conquest for God's Glory Exercises** would be taught in order to teach me? Replacing faith in Jesus for something other than the life **changing AMAZING GRACE** sickened me. Only a week away, a lesson would be taught; fasting was called for! Michelle was to fast till God told her to stop. The soul searching fast would start at 6 a.m. the next morning.

God had a different time table, for at 5:30 in the morning, I was up heaving at the humble white throne. All the while, I heard, "**purge**" repeatedly. Feeling like my insides were being ripped out of

me, I went to the Bible. It opened up to Hebrews 9:14. I read, PURGE
¹ YOUR CONSIENCE. Forget everything you know. From now on I will
tell you of things; of hidden things unknown to you . . . You have
not heard of them before today. I will teach what you need to know.
Then I blacked out. All day the scenario was the same with different
verses of purge.

In one of my sleeping moments, God gave me a dream which left
me somewhat confused. I was in a court room. I was in the crowd.
I didn't see the defendant. Yet I was standing, defending someone.
Pleading for mercy, I shared the message of forgiveness to the judge
who had no face. Just the word 'man' was written across his forehead.
I was stripped down to almost nakedness when I was thrown out of
the courthouse doors. I stood up with boldness and walked down the
stairs. Raising my right hand to the heavens, I proclaimed, "Lord, let
them see I carry a message of truth. Show your power and might, they
don't want your mercy and love. Immediately the clouds gathered
and a whirlwind with a tail touched down on top of the courthouse
and the surrounding buildings. The whirlwind destroyed everything
that stood against the message of Grace.

Wow! What was about to happen? I was hungry to learn for
what I saw coming, needed MORE than what I had. The courage
alone had to be God given. Understanding and practicing the word
purge, determined the success in the next chapter of my life. I had
to know what Jesus meant, forget everything you know. The mini-
strokes had taken my memories, I had been taught by God at least
8 years. He talked to me, gave visions and dreams, what was I to
forget? Everything I knew was because He had refilled an empty
head, literally.

When I started studying, I realized there was more to the verse,
yet I only saw what God wanted me to see at that moment. The verse
says, "Purge your conscience from DEAD WORKS to serve the living
God. Looking up the definition of purge was quite fascinating. So I
was being told, not asked, to get rid of having a feeling or knowledge
of what he wanted to do through me. Rid myself of guilt-conscious
and self-conscious. I could no longer care what people thought of
me when God visited the situations, leaving His power and glory as

evidence. I could not take glory for anything when God worked. I was to be self-less.

He showed me four vessels. Some are used for a noble [2] purpose. Two of these vessels carry dishonorable character and purpose. I was told to purge (empty out) the vessel. Then I would be a vessel that would contain honor, set apart, for my Master's use and His life-changing works.

1. The dirt represents a fleshy vessel. Dirt is finely crushed rock.
2. Wood is a hard rebellious vessel.
3. A silver vessel is a lustrous precious metal that conducts heat.
4. A gold vessel is a soft precious metal worth value. It has a shiny brilliance which also conducts heat.

*   *   *

The gold and silver vessels were free-will [3] offering vessels. They were Christians who by choice wanted to be used for God's glory. The Lord wanted me to guard and protect those that were vessels for the kingdom. Their lives were conducting the fire of the Holy Spirit. Some of these vessels were carried away to the temple of the god in Babylonia.[4] They became ensnared in a trap. Worshipping [5] the Babylonian god made of gold, silver, bronze wood and stone.

Jesus spoke, "My power is within you." With the Lord's all surpassing power, lives would be changed and darkness would be exposed. This gift is a treasure that only the Almighty can give, and the Potter desired this out of this lump of clay. He brought me to the place where I was purged by Him. THE GREAT I AM desired an empty vessel willing to be used without any preconceived idea of what 'I know', so the flow of His Power changing in individual's lives was evident without boundaries. Raised up for this very purpose, [6] His name was to be proclaimed in all the earth, for at the name of Jesus, every knee shall bow, [7] including the "hidden" [8] underground kings.

The study was fascinating even though I really didn't have all the details or the whole picture. Understanding Christians were being sucked into false religion was all that was comprehended. The verses that continued to stand out was, "Do not listen to the prophets [9] who say, very soon now the articles from the LORD'S house will be brought back from Babylon. They are prophesying lies to you. DO NOT LISTEN TO THE THEM."

*   *   *

During the fast, I was told to go get water. Finding a well where the water is supposedly one of the purest water seen, I went. There is an interesting story behind the well that holds testimony of healing capabilities. A man was written off by physicians, dying from a diseased kidney. He even drew up the final wishes for his family. Not ready to leave the family he loved, he began to pray earnestly for God's divine intervention.

An angel appeared in a dream and told him to dig a well at this certain place down 252 feet. They found water at 100ft but the man insisted to continue to 252 ft. depth. They found water at 150 ft. The driller refused to go on. The driller took the 'dream believer' to court because the man wouldn't pay him for the job. The man of course said, "You didn't finish the job." It was settled, go finish what was agreed upon. They found an abundance of water at 252 ft. The water was shipped though out the United States during the drought and depression. Not asking advice whether he should drill the well, he obeyed and believed healing was to be received at that spot. Not stopping just because water was found in two different levels, he was determined to go the distance because healing would come at that exact 252 feet depth. He was told the answer to his prayer. Healing was received for him and others who believed in the God directed level of pure water. The government said they had to quit proclaiming healing properties in the sixties, yet people in the territory still testify the miracles that happen when they quit drinking city or bottled water. Something was different when consuming the purer water.

Then I considered the well, spiritually. Christians have been told to receive healing they must drink from the spring of "Living" water. Is it possible the spring has different levels for the thirsty to receive drink? How many people are willing to stop at 100 ft. in the walk with the Lord? Some say salvation is enough for me. The deeper the well, the harder it is to get through to water. Drill bits are broken as it bores a hole through rock to get to the next level. Water is running on the drill bit as it bores to reach the deeper healing spring of water.

The process is similar when the Holy Spirit bores through the heavy rock surrounding the Christian heart. The hardness takes a steadiness of two, the Holy Spirit, which is the driller and the student learning more Grace. The practice of repetition may hit a spot that is harder to get through breaking the power of the drill bit. When water is found at 150 ft., the believer is handing out cupfuls to those that are thirsty.

If not wise, the Believer listens to those around him and quits allowing the Holy Spirit to take him further. The Believer begins to pay close attention to the deceiving spirits who add "chemicals" to faith, slowly poisoning, somewhat like excessive amounts of fluoride, both which slow down man's thoughts, eventually killing the thoughts of Jesus working in and through him. Jesus circumcised out of the equation, man shows man God within. Is it still Jesus or is the god, man? How many religions lift up the works of man? All! What changes man's thinking of working for blessings to, **always receiving by the Love of One always giving?** The Spirit knows the depth that needs to be pierced in order to get to the spring of continual flowing fresh and unadulterated pure water. When the Christian finds that spring, they can't help but radiate the joy, for he is different. I had to admit I found the level to be sought after, of 252 ft., interesting. When you add up the numbers 2+5+2, what do you get? 9. The fruit [10] of the Spirit talked about in the Bible is 9. Coincidence? Jesus, the Groom knows His Bride is thirsty and offers a refreshing drink. When you drink out of the SPRING OF LIVING WATER, the HOLY SPIRIT IS refreshed. It took two of us to work through the solid hard rock of my heart. My part being willing to let the change be done and the Holy Spirit which did all the work. If I didn't drink the spiritual water, would He not be thirsty. If I drink polluted water, it could kill my spirit. Would it kill His working? Drinking from the Spring of Life, it refreshes my spirit and the Spirit that dwells within. When

He is refreshed, He can't help but come alive in me. The fruit of His working and refreshing is seen in me. The fruit is the evidence of the Holy Spirit in me. Jesus just wants to hear," Thank you for the cool drink and I love you." Jesus shines on and the Holy Spirit shines through the relationship built on faithfulness of love.

*   *   *

Hours after getting the water, a woman said to me, "I see you standing in water up to your neck. I knew than the lessons during the fast had penetrated into the depths of my soul. I was ready to face whatever I was to encounter for God's presence was seen on and in me.

Arriving in the territory that proclaimed they were "Christ centered", I realized the Messiah talked about was not the same Messiah. Christ means Messiah, so I assumed I was going to a place that recognized Christ Jesus, the Son of the Living God. I listened to a man that was in leadership of the college. He strived to have me join not in a position of leadership, but, one where I would learn to serve. I asked him what kind of service. Sometimes serving in soup kitchens, I was familiar with this. Next question brought me to a standstill. I asked, if the Lord asked me to lay hands on someone and pray over them, could I? No! You would have to ask the team leader. Over top what God tells me to do? I told him, I was already serving the Lord. I thanked him for considering me. He insisted over and over how they needed my experience, boldness and leadership qualities. I would be of great value to the school. Never once did the name of Jesus or even the generic name, God, enter the conversation. It was when he said, "We are cross-denomination. We intend to bring all into unity as we grow together. Learning to coexist with other religions; none holding power or control of another; peace could be established. The holy cleansing would eliminate the Spirit of Judgment.

Jesus being the Way, the Truth and the Life was bound from working at this place. Every Idolatrous abomination that religions brought to the table was held above any **One Way of Righteousness.** Christians are not to put anything before the God of our Salvation.

The mention of Islam set my thoughts in motion. Holding the two undeniable differences of the faith's of Islam and my **JESUS, WHO CARRY'S THE SCARS OF THE COVENANT OF GRACE.** The sword of truth is able to destroy the doctrine of demons. They pray to the god who has no son. **I pray to EL SHADDAI, who sent His Son.** Their god needs no companion. **My JESUS wants to be My Companion through my life.** Their god needs no helper to save him from dishonor. Christians, do you realize what they are saying? They are saying, the Almighty screwed up and Jesus is trying to cover The Almighty's mistake.

As I listened to the different religions presented, I realized there was **No Way Christians, BELIEVER'S IN JESUS' WAY OF RIGHTEOUSNESS, could ever even consider the other religions and teachings. The** Mormons teach Jesus and Satan were brothers. They believe they can become gods. We do not have to confess sins to priests. **JESUS is our HIGH PRIEST. He is our sacrifice for all sin. Not just our past sins. Remember, he died before we were thought of.** How could protestant churches agree to bring so much dishonor of the RISEN LORD to think the holy cleansing would be done in such an unholy way?

I did not flee the territory at that moment, for I knew Jesus had equipped me for the battle that only He could win. The battle field had to be exposed in its entirety. This left anticipation for I knew nothing of some of the things being revealed, yet my God would reveal all things done in secret.

The place was quite extraordinary. The man in leadership bought up condemned buildings and used the students to renovate the houses which they lived in. The students paid nothing for the education or their living in the dorms. All were required to attend classes and work. It was as yet, not an accredited college, so the people had degrees that were worthless if staying for four years. The town was not a big town and yet 80% of it was owned by one man. The rest of the town did not like what was there or what they stood for. The attitude of the people made me search deeper. Where the Lord sends he also exposes things of darkness. What was here?

I joined the work force for two days. Enjoying the great outdoors, trees and bushes were removed, clearing the path for more growth of buildings for the college, I met co-workers that were without a doubt "family". Others were sent there by court order to try to educate and show the criminal a purpose for their life. One was working on his mission statement. He showed me the plan for life; nothing was said about service to the LORD. Cutting the trees down and clearing the over grown bushes was done spiritually as well as physically. Many were confused about God but were eager to learn. I dropped kernels of Grace throughout the day.

The next day, I dug ditches. Some of the ground was easy to shovel, where some was hard and I really had to work at breaking the hard ground. Stopping at three, even though the others continued working till almost dark, I went to the library and tried searching out every book that had been donated. Everything there was a donation; furniture to books. The generosity of giving was amazing, leaving an antique lover in awe of the exquisite furniture. After checking out a few books, I went to the dorm to read. My roommate was a delightful woman who was there to learn English better. Radiating the joy of the Lord, I was elated the poor girl had been stuck with me. Waking up in the middle of the night, I heard her weeping softly. After visiting hours together, she let me know there was much evil in the house. I had sensed it, but let no fear reside.

Spending time with the woman of leadership of the dorm, I found it interesting she had only been there a couple of months. I knew she didn't really like me but couldn't understand why for I am friendly. In the middle of a conversation she stopped, then said, "I see you digging ditches and water following behind you." I was thrilled to know Jesus, the Spring of Living Water, was filling the ditches I dug spiritually while working with the guys. "I said, "The Spring of Living Water follows where God sends me to dig." She gave me a strange look. I thought she was talking God stuff! I asked her if she had the gift of interpretation. She said she did, so I proceeded to tell her my strange dream. When I hit the part of the whirlwinds tail touching down and destroying everything, she let out a deep gasp. The fear that was obvious in the sharp inhale of breath left me speechless. She was surprised, but mortified I didn't understand. She fled the room and I never saw her again until Sunday.

The next day my body ached from head to toe. God had told me long before; forget what you did in service yesterday. Today is a new day of service. I couldn't lift my arms, so how could I forget what I did for the last two days? I jokingly reminded Him, He was the only one that could help me forget my yesterday for I couldn't lift my arms. He would have to take the pain. I was sure, he laughed with me, for in minutes the pain was gone.

I went to the conference, the reason for the invite. Men with power and money sat in a room where I was nothing, but was shown much respect. They hoped with all my travel, I would become a TELLER for their dream. There were 35 different businesses, just in South Carolina, set up helping social needs from feeding the poor to housing the criminal of society. The goal was to have 500 across the United States by the end of 2012. There was no denying the need for help to the less fortunate. The selling of the "business" desiring to control all the burdens laid on the hearts was almost stifling. Even family members of the Kingdom of Heaven had joined with this man. Yet, what I saw and experienced was one of a little more sinister plan. Bart showed me around the school grounds sharing the service of ministering they did on Sundays to feeding the poor. The rest of the week they worked doing projects of service for the building of the school. With the comments put out, the concentration style work program made me question whether it was a cult or just heavily controlled?

I asked Bart if he wanted to go with me and I would show the way him the way I minister. We went to the "ruff" side of the very small town. The man was shocked, when I stopped the car in order to meet the people in the community. The ones we met were poor, but rich. The group of people standing outside, dressed in heavy coats standing around a burn barrel, had been set aside by the "Christian" college. Never had they ever gone to the poor in their own town. The Lord opened the eyes to the man, who was an intern in the ministry. He was unaware of the needs in his own backyard. The young intern found there was "family" outside his guarded circle.

Talking for some time, God was lifted up and praised. Two of the six people around the burn barrel did have weapons but they were never pulled out for the visitation was ordained by God. The Lord's righteous protection was over us. I watched the two that didn't trust us but wondered did they see more? For one mentally challenged woman, was announcing the angels she saw around me. About an hour later you can imagine our surprise! The leader of the group from the college drove up. He was angry at the intern, who's in his 30's. He hadn't asked permission to leave the grounds even though it was only a few blocks away from the school. The intern couldn't believe what he was hearing. What he did on his own time for the Lord was not their concern. He had noticed subtle messages that weren't doctrinally sound. The lessons were mixed with much confusion but focused on teaching the students the laws of obedience.[11] He had already taken stands against the occult several times when known witches were married at the school ground, but, this?

The challenges steadily surfaced. Sunday came and I was to speak at church. The challenge of the two different Gods would have a face-off with two believers against two who were against the Almighty. Seducing Spirits were in control of the college. The Spirit of the Lord was seen in a few but the few were scared to be bold, for they were always humiliated publically. The campus knew the day of confrontation was here even though I found out when the leader showed up and made the announcement, "he wanted this woman to make the decision whether I spoke or not. The woman had nothing to do with the church or the college of education. So why was her decision needed? The group of believers outside waited for the showdown to begin. I walked into the room and who is sitting there? The woman who had fled the room days before was sought for council instead of going to men in leadership at the college? She asked what my intentions were. I said my message was on Grace tied to my testimony. The woman was arrogant when she said;" You think you are the only one with truth?" I hadn't said, I carried the truth but the demon inside spewing it out knew I held the truth. The boldness of the two of us fighting, reminded me of the face off many different times in the Bible when messengers of Grace faced their opponent. The intern leader with smugness said, "How many followers do you have following you? That is the evidence, you carry the truth." I stood up and said, "I hope none are following me, but all that I encounter follow my **JESUS** that I represent. I am going to step out. You decide whether I speak or not. Come get me, when you've made your decision."

Walking out in confidence, I started praying in the Spirit. There were those at the college that were hungry for the Word. Had not the Lord showed me He had vessels of silver and gold that had been snared in the Babylonian Worship? The occult and voodoo was strong. Goddess worship was prevalent. How many of the fleshy vessels needed to hear? The hard rebellious hearts were strong but God had sent me to preach the truth. The demons knew, I carried the message of Jesus the Messiah. Michelle had said it would be the last chance for some to hear the truth. If the truth was to be preached, Jesus would open the door. It was as if the blind were trying to lead the blind.[12] The GRACE door was opened.

While waiting, a man named Mac, came up and told me his real name was Seifallah. No, he was not Muslim. He said his name was Aramaic; meaning sword of god. Belonging to a group called the Baufemet he laid out information that took my head for a tail spin. Giving me more information of the Illuminati, I was surprised that he held so much information. I asked him his age for he looked awful young. He came back with an answer, "I'm only an earthling with thousands of years of useless information. Stunned, once again what had I opened up? He revealed, through spiritual surgery many Christians had opened up the door to voodoo. Surgeries were done over the telephone; curses sent through the phone on an unsuspecting Christian. What?!?

He even divulged information exposing well known important 'religious leaders', professing to be a part of the body of Christ that were tied in with the Freemasons and Illuminati. Even after watching valuable Illuminati information from one who is now hiding from them, I still do not comprehend how they deceive and believe? I hoped my face didn't show it but the thought of Christians in leadership following a group that enjoyed burning the effigy of Care (Jesus) sickened me. Fighting back the wave of nausea, it was as if the Spirit within gave me a booster shot. For suddenly I was ready to fight for the amazing "Care", that cared for me. Once again I wondered was I talking to a demon possessed or a demon that was gloating at the ignorance and stupidity of Christians.

Satan's plan on hindering the "Word" to be spoken was stopped. I was able to speak but found once again, it was the Lord who was in control. Stepping out of the lions' den, where the intense shredding of my person and my inabilities to look credible, laid out the missing puzzle piece I needed to put everything together. The missing clues that had eluded me all summer revealed evil to the extreme that even the Royal Family of Heaven was being deceived. The Bride of Christ needed to be made aware of the shrewd manipulation of religion against them and their Groom.

Pearl Drops of Wisdom

1. How much more shall the blood of Christ, who through the eternal Spirit offered himself without spot to God, purge your conscience from dead works to serve the living God?

   Hebrews 9:14 KJV

2. Does the potter have the right to make out of the same lump of clay some pottery for noble purposes and some for common use?

   Romans 9: 21 NIV

3. I said to them, "You as well as these articles are consecrated to the LORD. The silver and gold are a freewill offering to the LORD, The God of your fathers. Guard them carefully . . .

   Ezra 8:28-29 NIV

4. . . . And he brought the vessels into the treasure house of his god.

   Daniel 1:2 KJV

5. They drank wine, and praised the gods of gold, and of silver, of brass, of iron, of wood, and of stone.

   Daniel 5:4 KJV

6. For the scripture saith unto Pharaoh," Even for this same purpose have I raised thee up, that I might shew my power in thee, and that my name might be declared throughout all the earth.

Romans 9:17 KJV

7. That at the name of Jesus every knee should bow, of things in heaven, and things in earth, and things under the earth.

Philippians 2:10 KJV

8. From now on I will tell you of new things, of hidden things unknown to you. They are created now, and not long ago; you have not heard of them before today. So you cannot say "Yes, I knew of them."

Isaiah 48: 6b-7 NIV

9. ... This is what the Lord says: Do not listen to the prophets who say," Very soon now the articles from the LORD's house will be brought back from Babylon. They are prophesying lies to you. Do not listen to them . . . .

Jeremiah 27:16-17 NIV

10. But the fruit of the Spirit is love, [1] joy, [2] peace,[3] longsuffering, [4] gentleness, [5] goodness,[6] faith,[7] meekness [8] and temperance [9]: against such there is no law. KJV But the fruit of the Spirit is love, [1] joy, [2] peace, [3] patience, [4]kindness, [5] goodness, [6] faithfulness, [7] gentleness [8] and self-control [9]. Against such things there is no law. NIV

Galatians 5:22-23

11. Know that a man is not justified by observing the law, but by faith in Christ Jesus . . . .

Galatians 2:16 NIV

12. If you are convinced that you are a guide for the blind, a light for those who are in the dark, an instructor of the foolish, a teacher of infants, because you have in the law the embodiment of knowledge and truth—you, then who teach others, do you not teach yourself? You who preach against stealing, do you steal? You who brag about the law, do you dishonor God by breaking the law? As it is written: "God's name is blasphemed among the Gentiles because of you."

Romans 2:1-21, 23-24 NIV

Chapter 31

The Bride Remembers Her Position

Still curious about the powerful dream given, it made me wonder. Is not every true believer standing and defending those he can't see and doesn't know? In this final hour, do we plead for mercy and forgiveness to be recognized before the judge "man" sitting on the throne of religion? Though we might be cast aside, ridiculed and shamed, maybe even cast out for the world to strip us and expose our nakedness for the world to see. Can we all stand up boldly and remember who we are standing in?

I was reminded of the tower I was standing in, which is Jesus. A Believer is surrounded by Strength, Protection and Righteousness. Hearing the power and glory of the Holy Spirit telling me not to go out of the tower, brought me to my knees. If I went out on my strength, I would get weary. If I chose to walk out of His Protection, I would open up myself to Satan's lies. If I walk out of His Righteousness, I would get discouraged for my righteousness could never match His. Jesus asked me, "What did you do yesterday to earn my blessings?" I sat contemplating my answer. Finally I answered, "Lord, I stood in your Righteousness over my own. More than that, I remembered my first love." Jesus asked," What was that?" I smiled timidly, "I love My Jesus' Love for me." We are not standing for a church or a religion. Do we have the courage it takes to let Jesus raise our empty vessel, before the one who desires to fill us with power so that His glory will be seen? The complete understanding would be revealed in order to present the hidden treasures [1] of God, in whom all wisdom and knowledge is shown.

Jesus began talking about the 10 bridesmaids. Ten have the cutting of the wicks but only five have oil [2] in the lamps. The cutting of the wick is cutting of the flesh. Many are looking to the outward appearances. It is the inner fleshy things in our hearts that must be cut. Should it not start with the cutting of pride? It is the Holy Spirit that bores down to the core and shows you pride, unforgiveness, bitterness, jealousy, anger, lust, greed and sloth. The seven gates of hell that Satan likes to use were the same ones that cast him out of his Heavenly Home. It wasn't coincidence that Satan used the same sins for gates to enter his domain. As the Holy Spirit exposes the wretchedness of the heart, than He fills you with His oil, in the lamp, so you shine with My Glory. As the Believer walks in My love, things happen without the knowledge of Me working through them. I remembered standing in the trophy room. It was not what I knew I did for God. Purging the awareness of what is going on is a humbling position to be in, yet the trophies were given when I didn't know what God was doing.

There was an antique store I wanted to check out. While there a man has a heart attack. I just went over without thinking laid my hand on him and prayed. When done he said, "Thank you." I told him it was nothing really, just wanted to take him to the "Great Physician". He said, "No you don't understand." He needed a triple by-pass done on his heart. With no insurance, it couldn't be done. He felt the rush of every chamber of his heart opened up when God opened the blockage. I knew nothing of what was going on behind the scenes, just as the guards guarding the stone in front of Jesus tomb, knew nothing of the 'Finishing of the Conquest of Glory' being done in the gates of hell.

I watched the "newly-weds", Terrance and Tiffany as they journeyed through their first years of marriage. The excitement and thrill of the passion of new love settled in. The real marriage began when they learned to live each day together. Ridding the single life and self-centered thoughts and behaviors, challenged the couple. Laying aside selfish-desires, even if it was "good" things, was necessary in order to achieve a more perfect relationship. Communication was one of the critical keys. Learning to share the hidden secrets of the heart that had developed the personalities of the other was necessary. Trusting each other in faithfulness was critical as the friendship of single life friends wanted to socialize with the couple. Friendships were severed when the one didn't trust or like the other one's friends. Battles of oneness while learning to share the money and time. Would their desire be to lay aside themselves and trust the love of the other? If both could understand love doesn't want to hurt the other, the road trusting love would be easier. Is that not somewhat like what God wants out of us? "Just trust My Love for you. I don't want you to worry, or hurt or be sick? Trust My Love for you!"

Terrance had to learn to not only take his needs and wants to the Lord for direction but, also his families. He needed to understand the position of being the Bride of Christ in order to learn how to love his bride as he loved himself. Asking God for help, Terrance was learning to submit his leadership to the One able to guide and direct. Trusting The LORD's leading, God was responsible for actions and decisions that would affect his family. The position was a frightful thought for the man. It was different than what he knew, for Terrance always trusted his thoughts and ways.

Tiffany thought of herself and her son. Her battle would be learning to submit to her husband's direction. Always making her decisions now required more of her husband's leadership, less of hers. Learning to trust a man for her and her son could only be done by the God who holds trust. Having to let go of the direction of her parents and friends was a must. The council that was needed on both sides could only be given when they were willing to listen to the Lord. Both needed to break the chains of control. Offended when the battles would heat up, words would be said that could never be taken back. Resentment and bitterness allowed in must be confronted in another moment. Forgiveness was required in order to maintain peace within the home.

*   *   *

The Bride in the spiritual realm really is no different than what is displayed in the physical realm. With reference to the picture of two different brides, one must look to the book of Esther. King Ahasuerus threw a banquet [3] for seven days where the least to the greatest were invited. Interesting we're in a "Grace" period where the least to the greater has been invited to celebrate with King Jesus. With vessels of gold, [3] all different, the king served wine to those invited. They could drink[3] as much as they wanted. Believers, all unique, are vessels of gold. Because of Him, we are gold. King Jesus has told the Holy Spirit to keep the 'wine' flowing as much as we want to consume. The drinking of the wine was done according to the law allowing all to consume as much as the individual so desired.[3] Notice, we are in control of the consumption.

The portrayal of the two different queens is quite fascinating when you look at the physical, but, it is just as interesting in the spiritual. In the physical realm, one forgot her position. The other was humbled, when chosen. Spiritually, the two women represent two different covenants: one standing with their idea of the king and her desire to do her own thing. Living under the Levitical law, Jehovah was recognized as a God of wrath to those who broke the laws. A God of mercy and love was seen when obedience was done. Esther is a picture of those who live under the law of Grace (underserved kindness).

Esther had wisdom and understanding. She was willing to listen to wise council. Listening to only those that desired to protect and lift up the king and his royal subjects. The loyalty and devotion of Mordecai and Hegai [4] gave only sound advice, taking no praise or credit to themselves. Hegai is a picture of the Holy Spirit telling us what we need when we go before the King. The favor [4] is poured out on the chosen Bride from Him. He wants to present her pure and beautiful [4]for the King by His purification process. Esther recognized the position she was in and remembered where she had come from. She was told to forget her heritage [4] and past. She was to live for the king's bidding. Her position required her to be ready for whenever the king called for her. A Believer in JESUS' WAY must not dwell on their physical heritage but on their new Royal bloodline. Concentrating on the past brings on sorrow, shame and bondage. When concentrating on ones Royal bloodline, thoughts are pure [5], loving and true.

Queen Vashti had her own banquet [6] inviting the women in the country. She brought disrespect [6] toward the king. Teaching disloyalty for the king to her friends, seeking her own thoughts and ways, she would not submit to anyone over her. Why should she present herself only when the king requested it? She was beautiful to behold and wanted to be noticed in her timing not the king's timing. The two different brides are represented today; the religious church that edifies itself and its works and the Bride of Christ which only edifies Christ's works.

I now understand why I was allowed to see the throne room. I was taught **REVERANCE BEFORE MY GOD.** He showed me how **Holy and Righteous He is.** Standing in **HIS PRESENCE,** humbled before **PURE RIGHTEOUSNESS,** I would never measure up in spite of all the things I did for Him. The beauty I beheld, left awe and amazement. I fell in love with the **AMAZING EYES FULL OF LOVE.** The Body of Christ needed to be told, the SOVEREIGN LORD, THE HOLY ONE says, **IN REPENTENCE[7] AND REST IS YOUR SALVATION, IN QUIETNESS AND TRUST IS YOUR STRENGTH.**

The woman sitting on the scarlet colored beast [8] is full of blasphemy. Churches have learned how to use Jesus' life, death and resurrection to manipulate a continual control. Jesus, the Holy One is the High Priest; confession doesn't have to be announced to a man with the appearance of holiness. Keeping the Bride on baby food, they are unable to feast on Jesus' righteous works instead of their works. Keeping the flock focused on sin keeps them from learning from the One who wants to redirect their focus to forgiven. As the woman of religion rides the beast, she has the appearance of truth, hoping to bring a demise to those who stand on the blood of Jesus requiring the blood of the saint if need be.

When Esther heard of threats to the king, She presented it showing loyalty to him.[9] Finding out a plan was devised to wipe out her people; she took heed to the warning. I have heard of a plan devised to wipe out Believers of the WAY. Just because Esther was royalty didn't mean she would be spared. Just because I am of the Royal Family doesn't mean I will be spared. Fasting and listening for God's voice and direction, presented to the king the plan set to wipe out her people. God directed my path and exposed the plan to rid the Believers. Though many including Mordecai were in sackcloth and ashes, Esther didn't for she was royalty. I do not wear sack cloth and ashes, instead my royal garments and the armor of God is worn. She pled for her people that had been sold for destruction and slaughter and annihilation. I plead as I warn the church, the Bride of Christ. There are wolves in sheep clothing hiding amongst us.

The Lord showed me the Religious Church was Queen Vashti, with disloyalty. Satan subtly planted seeds of confusion and unbelief in the church. The party of organized religion welcomes in celebration of praise and worship of man. Lifting up preachers, churches, and accomplished works. Notice Revelation 2: The church was recognized for their works, patience and hating evil. For His sake they had labored [10] and had not fainted. After all the wonderful things noticed there was one thing against them. They had lost their first Love. Had they forgotten the Love that took all their sin? Had they forgotten the Love that wanted healing for His children, for by His stripes we are healed? Had they forgotten Love that redeems life from destruction, because, He loves the one wanting to be redeemed? They don't lose salvation but the candlestick is removed. **The Light of Jesus isn't seen. The Power of the Holy Spirit is squelched.**

After reviewing the research and running into the things from the Synagogue of Satan, the resurrection from the burial vaults couldn't be, for the foundations were mixed with the lies of Lucifer. The wound from the sacred side of Jesus no longer matters, but boy your good works do? The direction of 'new' tolerance toward man's lifestyles and behaviors goes directly against what God abhors. As the Guide Stones in Georgia rule passion, faith, tradition and all things with tempered reason; **A BELIEVER IN JESUS' WAY** can't be tempered. **He walks in 'POWER OF THE HOLY GHOST'.**

Causing man and the "beast" to become one, their ultimate plan is to wipe out everyone that stands on **JESUS' AMAZING GRACE alone.** Concentration camps are open to try to convince the switch, as the purpose for man is to serve one another. The business of helping others is pushed more than the critical purpose. The WHOLE PURPOSE OF MAN IS TO WORSHIP EL SHADDAI, THROUGH THE BLOOD OF OUR RESURRECTED LORD, JESUS. LOVE THE LORD WITH ALL THINE HEART. With the other message, instead of bringing peace to the soul, love gives way to hate as people despise those that look lazy and worthless in their eyes. The age of 'REASONING', is redirecting people's lives without **JESUS' WAY OF LOVE.** It is directing them to 'what'? If we begin teaching, **No One can snatch them out of the Father's hand when put there,** would we see a revival in the land? Strength is drained out of the church when total love is taken out. Minds overflow as judgment and jealousy reign. The "Elite" ends up controlling the biggest money making business of all, compassion. Teaching from Guide Stones, the message to prize truth, beauty, and love, seeking harmony with the infinite is not Jesus. Love and worship of the created beings proclaiming all religions hold truth, one will be able to co-exist with harmony.

How ironic Satan uses compassion to re-veil what **JESUS THROUGH COMPASSION TORE DOWN.** The people have become slaves to the one who sits on a throne that will require them to sell their birth right for a bowl of porridge. Pride ruled Vashti's heart as does "dead white sepulcher's" rule the religious heart. When the King calls for the Bride, they won't show up. They joined the other side. Her loyalty is shown as she marches full speed ahead, being the water carriers and the tree cutters. Just as Queen Vashti was cast out of the kingdom so will those who don't Honor **the King in His Righteousness and abundance of life.**

Loving the Lord more than anything, automatically sets the heart different. You will care about the other people's lives around you. You help without considering what you may receive whether recognition or something of monetary value because you see through the Groom's eyes. The servant's heart no one can measure up to for the heart of the servant gave everything including his life. Satan didn't want to serve, he wanted to be served. Jesus wanted to serve and still wants to serve the Bride.

I was reminded of the elderly couple sitting across the table only able to hold fingers due to the table between them. The love that was seen between the lovers permeated the room. No one saw the journey of sorrow or pain as they both learned to listen, love and forgive one another. The quest for a glorious marriage was obvious as the tenderness was displayed in the helping the cherished bride put on her coat. The slow movements did not bother the groom for he loved his bride more today than the day they were wed.

Was Jesus pleased with the gift from the Father when He gave Him me? Did I look lovingly in my Groom's eyes, not questioning any longer His love for me? I saw his faithfulness in provision and strength toward me in spite of my unfaithfulness in depending on Him in every battle. HIS AMAZING GRACE **WAS SUFFICIENT**[11] **FOR ME.** His AMAZING Grace is sufficient for me. No longer did I worry whether Jesus abhorred His inheritance; I knew He didn't for **HIS FACE WAS SHINING ON ME.**

* * *

The study could go on but time was of the essence. The phone rang; the woman I visited in Georgia, was on the line. Her home was a place of refuge and a welcomed retreat for me. With fear and urgency in the voice, two black suburbans with black tinted windows had pulled around her house. The woman asked me if it was the Illuminati or the Freemasons. Who was following me? All I could say was "Thank you Lord, for PROTECTING me."

Researchers had strange things happening, such as packages showing up in the mail with an Egyptian head, and necklace with a beetle on it. Had the research of Seifallah, (Sword of God) with a name showing high ranking military status opened the door to ancient Babylonian worship? Why would a gift be sent from Egypt, from just searching on the web? I had sent my book to be proofread through the internet. Had it opened doors to those of higher rank? Did I have more information than what I knew I had? Is that why God allowed me to talk to a 32nd degree Mason? Or was it about the trucker carrying truckloads of Ritalin to Pennsylvania? The Mason told me it was something different. Had the Masons found out he gave me the name of the plague of destruction, stored in a vault under gun protection?

Then I considered the message I carried, the Gospel of Jesus. The attacks were orchestrated by the one who had no control over me, Satan. Believing God's Grace is sufficient for me, because of **HIS FULLNESS OF GRACE, I would continue to receive**[12] **HIS blessings.** Just as the king showed favor on Esther, so I would be shown favor from my Groom! I would continue the next leg of my journey, meeting the **Ones chosen from the beginning of time,** who are written in the **Book of Life**. With the Holy Spirit, (swiftly giving things needed for purification), an undivided heart, and the **Torch of Light** in my hand; JESUS' LIGHT would expose the hidden secrets[13] that Satan didn't want the **'Redeemed Elite'** to know.

Pearl Drops of Wisdom

1. My purpose is that they may be encouraged in heart and united in love, so that they may have the full riches of complete understanding, in order that they may know the mystery of God, namely Christ, in whom are hidden all the treasures of wisdom and knowledge.

   Colossians 2: 2-3 NIV

2. At midnight the cry ran out: "Here's the bridegroom. Come out and met him!" Then all the virgins woke up and trimmed their lamps. The foolish ones said to the wise, Give us some of your oil; our lamps are going out. "No," they replied," there may not be enough for both us and you. Instead go to those who sell oil and buy some for yourselves."

   Matthew 25: 6-9 NIV

3. . . . the king gave a banquet, lasting seven days . . . Wine was served in goblets of gold, each one different from the other and the royal wine was abundant . . . By the king's command each guest was allowed to drink in his own way, for the king instructed all the wine stewards to serve each man what he wished.

   Esther 1:5, 7-8 NIV

4. . . . Pleased him and won his favor . . . Esther had not revealed her nationality and family background . . . He sent back his answer: "Do not think that because you are in the king's house you alone

of all the Jews will escape." . . . "who knows but that you have come to a royal position for such a time as this?"

Esther 2:9-10, 4:13-14 NIV

5. Finally, brethren, whatsoever things are true, whatsoever things are honest, whatsoever things are pure, whatsoever things are lovely, whatsoever things are of good report; if there be any virtue, and if there be any praise, think on these things.

Philippians 4:8 KJV

6. Queen Vashti also gave a banquet for the women in the royal palace . . . refused to come . . . She has not obeyed . . . never to enter the presence of king.

Esther 1:9, 12, 15, 19 NIV

7. This is what the Sovereign LORD, the Holy One OF Israel says: "In repentance and rest is your salvation, in quietness and trust is your strength, but you would have none of it.

Isaiah 30:15 NIV

8. So he carried me away in the spirit into the wilderness; and I saw a woman sit upon a scarlet colored beast, full of names of blasphemy, having seven heads and ten horns.

Revelation 17:3 KJV

9. In those days, while Mordecai sat in the king's gate, two of the king's chamberlains, Bigthan and Teresh, of those which kept the door, were wroth, and sought to lay hands on the king Ahasuerus. But Mordecai found out about the plot and told Queen Esther, who in turn reported it to the king, giving credit to Mordecai.

Esther 2:21-22

10. I know thy works, and thy labor, and thy patience, and how thou canst not bear them which are evil: and thou . . . And hast borne, and hast patience and for my name's sake hast labored, and hast not fainted. Nevertheless I have somewhat against thee, because thou hast left thy first love.

Revelation2:2-4 KJV

11. But he said to me, "My grace is sufficient for you, for my power is made perfect in weakness."

II Corinthians 12: 9 NIV

12. From the fullness of his grace we have all received one blessing after another.

John 1:16 NIV

13. Now all has been heard; here is the conclusion of the matter: FEAR GOD . . . For God shall bring every deed into judgment, including every hidden thing, whether it is good or evil.

Ecclesiastes 12:13-14 NIV